A NEW OWNER'S
GUIDE TO
BRITTANYS

JG-158

Overleaf: A Brittany photographed by Isabelle Francais

Opposite page: Brittany photographed by Paulette Braun

The Publisher wishes to acknowledge the owners of the dogs in this book: including Mrs. L. Bennet, Mrs. K. Bride, Calypso Kennels, Robert Clark, Rob Dobey, Cindy Ford, Mrs. Geohegan, Indian Acres Kennels, Beverly Millette, Sequani's Kennels, Kathy Sweet, and Karen Wagner.

Photographers: Paulette Braun, Downey Photography, Isabelle Francais, Beverly Millette, Alice Pantfoeder, Vince Serbin, Robert Smith, Judith Strom, Karen Taylor, Missy Yuhl.

The author acknowledges the contribution of Judy Iby to the following chapters: Health Care, Sport of Purebred Dogs, Identification and Finding the Lost Dog, Traveling with Your Dog, and Behavior and Canine Communication.

Distributed in the UNITED STATES to the Pet Trade by T.F.H. Publications, Inc., One T.F.H. Plaza, Neptune City, NJ 07753; on the Internet at www.tfh.com; in CANADA Rolf C. Hagen Inc., 3225 Sartelon St. Laurent-Montreal Quebec H4R 1E8; Pet Trade by H & L Pet Supplies Inc., 27 Kingston Crescent, Kitchener, Ontario N2B 2T6; in ENGLAND by T.F.H. Publications, PO Box 15, Waterlooville PO7 6BQ; in AUSTRALIA AND THE SOUTH PACIFIC by T.F.H. (Australia), Pty. Ltd., Box 149, Brookvale 2100 N.S.W., Australia; in NEW ZEALAND by Brooklands Aquarium Ltd. 5 McGiven Drive, New Plymouth, RD1 New Zealand; in SOUTH AFRICA, Rolf C. Hagen S.A. (PTY.) LTD. P.O. Box 201199, Durban North 4016, South Africa; in Japan by T.F.H. Publications. Published by T.F.H. Publications, Inc.
MANUFACTURED IN THE
UNITED STATES OF AMERICA
BY T.F.H. PUBLICATIONS, INC.

A NEW OWNER'S GUIDE TO
BRITTANYS

BEVERLY MILLETTE

Contents

1999 Edition

The Brittany's loving and gentle disposition makes him the ideal family pet.

Brittanys are natural hunters and retrievers.

The Brittany has the alert, intelligent expression that is typical of a bird dog.

The Brittany is first and foremost a hunting dog and is happiest when allowed to use his talents in the field.

The athletic and agile Brittany excels in organized dog sports and activities.

ORIGIN and History of the Brittany

ANCIENT HISTORY

In the beginning, there were wolves and cave men. Centuries later, we have dogs of every size, shape, and color imaginable. Not only do they all look different, they act differently—they have such varied talents and purposes that it is hard to believe they are descendants of *Canis lupus*, the wolf! Everything dogs are and everything that they do was passed down to them from this common ancestor.

How did they get here from there? It wasn't easy, and it didn't happen overnight. It began during the Mesolithic period, which was roughly 12,000 BC. Man's earliest association with the wolf evolved because he needed all the help he could get just to survive. The wolf, having many social habits similar to those of man, was the most likely candidate to provide some of that necessary assistance.

In their enlightening study of the development of dog breeds, *The Natural History of Dogs*, authors Richard and Alice Feinnes classify most dogs as having descended from one of four major groups: the Dingo group, the Greyhound group, the Northern group, and the Mastiff group. Each of these groups can be traced back to separate and distinct branches of the wolf family.

The Dingo group traces its origin to the Asian wolf (*Canis lupus pallipes*). Two well-known examples of the Dingo group are the Basenji and, through the admixture of several European breeds, the Rhodesian Ridgeback.

The Greyhound group descends from a coursing-type relative of the Asian wolf. The group includes all dogs that hunt by sight and are capable of great speed. The Greyhound, the Afghan Hound, the Borzoi, and Irish Wolfhound are all examples of this group and are known as the coursing breeds. They are not true hounds in that they do not hunt by scent.

The Arctic or Nordic group of dogs is a direct descendant of the rugged northern wolf (*Canis lupus*). Included in the numerous breeds of this group are the Alaskan Malamute, Chow Chow, German Shepherd, and the much smaller Welsh Corgi and Spitz-type dog.

The fourth classification is the Mastiff group, which owes its primary heritage to the Tibetan wolf (*Canis lupus chanco* or *laniger*). The great diversity of the dogs included in this group indicates that they are not entirely of pure blood, in that they have undoubtedly been influenced by descendants of the other three groups.

The descendants of the Mastiff group are widely divergent, but are known to include many of the scenting breeds—breeds that find game by the use of their olfactory senses rather than by sight. These breeds include dogs we now classify as sporting or gun dogs and true hounds.

As man became more sophisticated and his lifestyle more complex, he found that he could produce dogs from these descendants of the wolf that could suit his specific needs. These needs were often based on the manner in which man hunted game and the terrain in which he was forced to do so.

The Brittany was bred throughout the ages to be an excellent hunter, retriever, and companion to man.

Important, also, was that man had taken control of mating the individual dogs because particular characteristics were prized, and inbreeding practices were employed in order to perpetuate those characteristics.

One type of hunting dog that man developed retained the wolf characteristic of pursuing prey until it was cornered, killed, chased up a tree, or until the dog gave up in exhaustion. This practice is more or less typical of the group of dogs known today as hounds. While the hound's tenacity was held in high regard, his willingness to continue the chase for miles if necessary became difficult and tiresome.

Thus was born a need for the hunting dog that would not follow through with the chase or attack. His job was not to do the hunting or killing, but rather to assist the human hunter by finding, flushing out, or retrieving game. These dogs worked quietly so they would not scare away the birds, and like any good assistant, they obeyed their master's commands without hesitation.

Developed to assist the hunter in finding, flushing out, and retrieving prey, the Brittany worked quietly and obeyed his master's commands without hesitation.

During the Middle Ages, before guns were invented, hunters used nets and trained hawks to capture their prey. Their other assistants were small dogs that originated in Spain. The Latin word for Spain is Hispania, and it is from Hispania that the name "spaniells" (later, spaniels) evolved. Once the game was located, the dogs would drop to the ground and remain motionless, waiting for the hunter to dash up and fling his net over the covey. These setting spaniels later developed into our modern-day Irish, English, and Gordon Setters.

Another group of spaniels was trained to find birds and drive them out of the underbrush so that they could be pursued by falcons. These dogs were called "springing spaniels" because of their talent for springing or flushing birds from their hiding places. Often tracking their prey through dense shrubs and tangled thickets, the dogs needed compact, small bodies and powerful legs to help them move through the difficult terrain

8

All eight spaniel breeds that are recognized today share the same collective ancestry and heritage as a working dog and hunting companion.

that stopped other breeds cold. They had long silky coats to protect them and to easily shed thistles and brambles, docked tails to prevent them from being caught in the brush and brambles, and higher, rounded foreheads to shield their eyes from branches. Their long, lobular ears gathered scent molecules and channeled them to their large, ultrasensitive noses.

THE FRENCH DEVELOP THE BRITTANY

The Brittany or Brittany Spaniel, as he is known in all parts of the world except the United States, was developed in France around the 1850s by crossing the early land spaniels with setters in the Bretagne region of France. (It is important to note, however, that the English Setter of that period is most

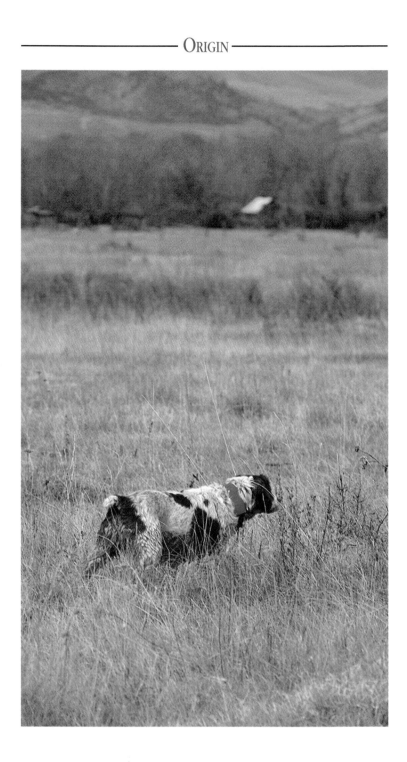

probably not the dog as we know him today.) The Brittany, therefore, derived his name from the area of France in which he was developed.

Just after the turn of the century, Major P. Gran-Chavin, a cavalry officer and veterinarian assigned to the Bretagne region of France, wrote about the small spaniels he saw there. The dogs, he said, had short tails or no tails at all and rather short ears for the spaniel breeds. He describes their coats as being colored white-orange, white-liver, or white-black, and some tricolor as well. He also made special note of their distinctive, "short-gaited" movement.

First known as the "Dog of Brittany," and later as the Brittany Spaniel, we find the first mention of the "Chien de Bretagne" appearing in 1910 when M. Le Comte Le Conteux de Canteleu drew up his chart of the French breeds.

Much speculation exists regarding which specific spaniel and setter form the basis for the breed. In truth, it is a moot point because in England littermates were often considered different breeds, depending upon how large they grew or what they looked like at maturity. To further complicate matters, the French bred their setters with some of the spaniels to enhance scenting ability and improve staunchness.

There is a clear indication that there was a tendency toward the dog having a short tail or no tail in the resulting cross and that the color of the coat was often white-orange or white-liver. The short tail and supple spaniel skin were preferred as they lessened the likelihood of the dog getting torn up by the region's dense cover.

THE BRITTANY IN NORTH AMERICA

The first Brittanys were brought to North America by Senor Juan Pagibet of Villa Obregon near Vera Cruz, Mexico, in 1928. The next individual of note is Louis A. Thebaud, who imported Brittany Spaniels into the United States in 1933. Upon Mr. Thebaud's request, the French Kennel Club sent him the "Standard of Perfection" for the breed in July 1934.

The premier retriever of France, the Brittany derived his name from the Bretagne region in which he was developed.

The American Kennel Club (AKC) recognized the breed in August of that same year, but did not approve the standard until March 1935, after an acceptable translation of the standard had been completed. The first litter known to have been born in the US was that of Gilda de Causses, a bitch that was mated to Douglas de l'Odet. The puppies were born in June 1935. The Brittany Spaniel Club of North America was founded in 1936 and it received official membership in the AKC in September 1936. There were 11 Brittanys registered with the AKC in that year.

In April of 1935, Franche du Cosquerou achieved the distinction of placing third in the Jockey Hollow Shooting Dog Stake—the first official placing of a Brittany in field trials held in the United States.

World War II was ruinous for the Brittany Spaniel Club of North America, scattering its membership around the globe. Frequent wartime transfers made finding or contacting the officers and members of the organization extremely difficult, and at times impossible.

Eventually, it became necessary for a second organization to be founded. This group was called the American Brittany Club. However, it was and

The American Kennel Club recognized the Brittany in 1934, and the breed's popularity quickly rose with American sportsmen.

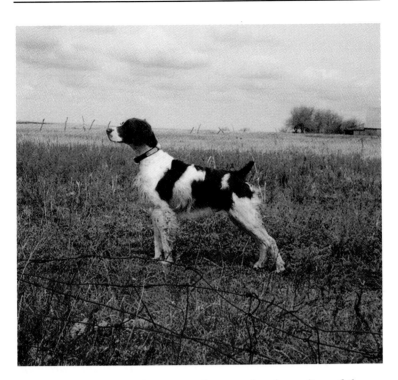

One of the breed's high achievers in both the show ring and the field, Ch. Millette's Downtown Brown stands at attention.

continues to be the policy of the AKC to recognize only one organization as the official breed club. It was not until July 1944, after the two clubs had merged under the name, The American Brittany Club, that the AKC declared it as the official parent club.

EUROPE RECOVERS

Needless to say, the war did a great deal of damage to the Brittany Spaniel in Europe, depleting the breed's gene pool to an alarmingly low level. Brittany fanciers in America rallied to the cause and sent stock to France to help get the breed re-established.

In order to assist the effort, the previously barred black color was readmitted in France. Meanwhile, back in the US, the gene pool was sufficiently rich, so it was felt that there was no need to change the standard to allow black coloration.

A large number of Brittany Spaniels have been imported from France and other parts of Europe since the end of the war. Extensive interbreeding has occurred between the European and American dogs, which makes it impossible to clearly determine a Brittany's actual origin today. However, black coloration does remain a disqualification in the AKC standard.

Brittany devotees have always been adamant about protecting the breed's ability to work in the field. Yet, understandably, they also want the breed to receive equal consideration as a conformation dog, particularly when Brittanys compete with the other breeds in the Sporting group. The first Brittany to be given that consideration was the female, Ch. Queen of Paradise, owned by Walter S. Oberlin. Queen of Paradise won the Sporting Group at Ravenna, Ohio, in September 1946 under William L. Kendrick. Kendrick was known for his courage and readiness to give the lesser known breeds their due consideration in Group and Best in Show levels.

The 1950s were good years for the Brittany, as more and more quality specimens of the breed followed Queen of Paradise to recognition in Sporting Group competition. In 1957, what seemed to have been a Best in Show barrier was hurdled by Ch. Havre Des Bopis Henri. He achieved that distinction at the Livonia Kennel Club under judge Selwyn Harris. Henri was bred, owned, and shown by Paul R. Vollmar.

Henri remained unique in his achievement until 1971, when Ch. Beelflower Dirty Dan became the breed's second Best in Show winner at Salinas, California, under judge Maxwell Riddle in August of that year. He was owned and shown by Paul and Linda Mooney.

From the breed's earliest days in America, many wanted the spaniel association removed from the Brittany name. Their reasons were that the Brittany is, in actuality, a small setter and that he points his game rather than flushing it like other spaniels. This argument was waged for many years, but it was not until April 1982, at a meeting of the AKC Board of Directors, that the name change was approved. The Brittany Spaniel officially became, simply, the Brittany in September of 1982.

This brings us to a unique situation currently involving the breed. Any French bred and registered "Brittany Spaniel" can be imported into the United States and registered by the AKC as a Brittany. The dog can be shown and hunted in any AKC event and can compete in obedience trials. However, if the Brittany has black in his coat he will be disqualified from the conformation ring.

At the close of 1998, 9,252 Brittanys had been registered with the AKC in that year alone. This placed the breed in 32nd position among the 145 breeds registered by the American Kennel Club.

Brittany fanciers have always been concerned with protecting the breed's ability to work in the field. Am. Bda. Ch. Sequani's Dana Macduff was an all-around top winner in the 1970s.

Without a doubt, the dedication of breeders has kept the Brittany a triple-threat dog that excels in the field, in the conformation ring, and as a treasured family companion. The Brittany's accomplishments on many more levels make the breed worthy of consideration by the most demanding dog lover.

CHARACTERISTICS of the Brittany

There is probably nothing quite as captivating as the comical Brittany puppy with his mischievous expression. If you haven't fully decided whether or not to add a Brittany puppy to your life, a visit to a breeder's home or kennel to see a litter of puppies is probably not the best idea in the world. Anyone even thinking of dog ownership is going to be hard pressed to resist these little charmers.

For this very reason, anyone who anticipates owning a Brittany should give serious thought to a final decision. All puppies are cute— Brittany puppies are certainly no exception. There is nothing more adorable than a litter of Brittany puppies at play or nestled together sound asleep, one on top of the other. In addition to being cute, however, Brittany puppies are living, breathing, and very adventurous creatures that are totally dependent upon their human owner for all of their needs once they have left their mother and littermates.

It is hard to resist an adorable Brittany puppy, but make sure that the decision to take one home has been carefully considered.

Buying a dog, especially a puppy, before being absolutely sure you want to make that commitment can be a serious mistake. The prospective dog owner must clearly understand the amount of time and work involved in caring for a pet. Failure to understand the extent of commitment that dog ownership requires is one of the primary reasons there are so many unwanted canines ending their lives in animal shelters or rescues.

Before contemplating the purchase of a dog, there are some very basic situations to consider. One of the first significant questions that must be answered is whether or not the person who will ultimately be responsible for the pet's care and well-being actually wants a dog.

Often, the mother is the member of the household who must take on the responsibility of the dog's day-to-day care. Although the children in the family, and perhaps even the father, may be wildly enthusiastic about having a dog, it must be remembered

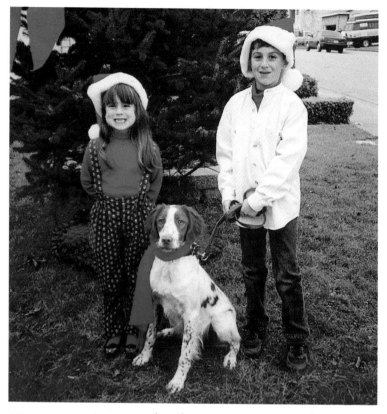

The Brittany's loving disposition and eagerness to please make him a welcomed addition to most families. that they are away most of the day at school or work. It is often Mom who will be taking on yet another responsibility as primary caregiver for the family pet. Somehow this seems to be the case even when Mom works outside the household. In addition to her work away from home, there are all those chores it appears only a Mom can handle. Does she, in fact, share the enthusiasm for what could easily become another responsibility on her unending list?

Owning a pet is a wonderful way to teach children responsibility, but the enthusiasm that inspires children to promise anything in order to have a new puppy may quickly wane. Who will take care of the puppy once the novelty wears off? Does that person want a dog?

Desire to own a dog aside, does the lifestyle of the family actually allow for responsible dog ownership? If the entire family is away from early morning to late at night, who will provide for the puppy's needs? Feeding, abundant exercise, outdoor access, and the like cannot be provided if no one is home.

Another important factor to consider is whether or not the breed of dog you choose is suitable for the person or the family with which he will be living. A full-grown Brittany can handle the rough and tumble play of young children. However, a very young Brittany puppy should only be allowed playtime with young children when adults are present to supervise them.

A little puppy is a big responsibility. Make sure everyone in your household has the time and inclination to provide a puppy with everything he needs.

The upkeep of an adult Brittany doesn't require as much time and patience as the luxuriously coated breeds do, but that does not mean the breed does not need grooming—on the contrary!

As great as the claims are for a Brittany's adaptability and intelligence, there is not a dog, regardless of breed, that doesn't need to be taught the household rules. Some dogs catch on more quickly than others, and puppies are just as inclined to forget or disregard lessons as young children do.

CASE FOR THE PUREBRED DOG

As mentioned, all puppies are cute, with their little pink tongues and zest for life. However, not all puppies grow up to be particularly attractive adults. Yet, beauty is indeed in the eye of the beholder—what is considered beauty by one person is not necessarily seen as attractive by another.

It is almost impossible to determine what a mixed-breed puppy will look like as an adult. Nor will it be possible to determine if the mixed-breed puppy's temperament is suitable for the person or family who wishes to own him. If the puppy grows up to be too big, too hairy, or too active for the owner, what then will happen to him?

Size and temperament can vary to a degree, even with purebred dogs. That being the case, selective breeding over many generations has produced dogs that can give the would-be owner a reasonable assurance of what the purebred puppy will look like and how he will act as an adult. Aesthetics completely aside, this predictability is more important than one might think.

Purebred puppies will grow up to look like their adult relatives and essentially, will behave very much like the rest of their family. Any dog, mixed breed or not, has the potential to be a loving companion. However, the predictability of a purebred dog offers some insurance that he will not only suit the person's aesthetic demands, but also the owner's lifestyle as well.

Size, appearance, and temperament will be passed down through each generation in purebred dogs. Your Brittany puppy should look and act like his ancestors.

Before bringing a Brittany puppy into your household, visit breeders and spend as much time as you can with both puppies and adults. Be sure that the adult Brittany is a dog that appeals to you aesthetically and temperamentally.

CHARACTER

The Brittany is a gentle, devoted companion, but this doesn't mean he's a couch potato. On the contrary, he is the gymnast of the canine world—a Mary Lou Retton with personality and energy to burn! The Brittany can turn on the charm in a flash, especially when he wants to get his way.

The breed is essentially a family dog. A Brittany can be found in the kitchen helping Mom with the cooking (and begging a

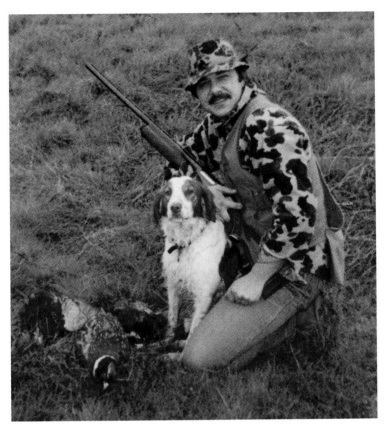

Although the Brittany makes a wonderful pet, he should always be able to retain and exercise his hunting instincts.

tidbit or two), in the playroom with the kids (enticing them into one game after another), with Dad out in the garden helping him plant (or dig up!) the spring flowers, or with the elderly folks in the family room watching TV. All this, and the Brittany is ready for a day's hunt with split-second notice. When Dad gets out the gun and hunting clothes, it's all business.

Speaking of hunting, it must be clearly understood that the Brittany is a hunting dog. I have been asked many times if Brittanys are bred "just as pets." The answer is a resounding *no*! Certainly not by anyone who truly loves the breed. The desire and ability to hunt is what makes the Brittany unique. There are in excess of 400 Dual Champions (bench and field) in this breed, far more than any other AKC breed. Most Brittany show dogs are dad's "hunting buddy" on Saturday and the family's show dog on Sunday. People who love the Brittany wouldn't have it any other way.

With its high degree of intelligence (Brittanys are listed among the top 20 breeds in intelligence), the breed can become bored easily. As a rule, Brittanys cannot be left on their own continuously or kept outdoors alone. Their long-standing history of working at man's side in the field has made the Brittany very much a "people dog." Denied the opportunity to be with those they love, Brittanys can demand attention by becoming barkers. One of the breed's finest qualities is its desire to bond with and please its master. Not being allowed to do so can make even the best Brittany difficult to live with.

The Brittany is an ideal family dog in that he is able to share his devotion with every member of the family and has an innate ability to adjust his own mood to that of the family member he is with. He will sound the alarm to alert the family to an approaching stranger, but will be delighted to greet that same stranger if given assurance that all is well.

First and foremost, the Brittany has been bred to be a hunting dog. However, there are few limits to what the breed can do if properly trained.

The intelligence, athleticism, and trainability of the Brittany have helped him retain his popularity throughout the years as a fine field dog and loyal family member.

TRAINABILITY

There are few limits to what the breed can be trained to do. The modern Brittany is a crackerjack obedience dog and loves the agility trials that have become so popular. But it is the breed's natural hunting ability that sells him to the hunter, beginner or fully experienced, because the Brittany always seems to know just that much more than the hunter himself.

Once trained, the Brittany does not forget. He may occasionally invent new (and often better!) ways to do things, but you can rely on him to get the job done. A Brittany's nose is exceptional, which guarantees that he will pass up few birds. Normally, he works in a way similar to a pointer, but without the same great range. However, if greater range and speed are desired, a Brittany pup can be purchased from a line that is from field trial stock versus hunting/show stock.

The Brittany points and holds his game. He retrieves on both land and water, although he must be protected after water retrieval in freezing weather—Brittanys do not have the double, oil-coated coat or fat layer of retrievers. Although Brittanys are used primarily on upland game in the US, the breed is used for both fur and feather in France.

OFFICIAL Standard for the Brittany

The AKC standard for the Brittany is well written in a straightforward manner that can be read and understood by even the beginning fancier. The ability to interpret all of its nuances, however, may take many years of experience and observation. Also, each country's standards is different.Reading as much as possible about the breed helps a great deal, but nothing benefits the novice more than putting himself in the hands of a dedicated and experienced breeder.

AKC STANDARD FOR THE BRITTANY

General Appearance— A compact, closely knit dog of medium size, a leggy dog having the appearance, as well as the agility, of a great ground coverer. Strong, vigorous, energetic, and quick of movement. Ruggedness, without clumsiness, is a characteristic of the breed. He can be tailless or has a tail docked to approximately four inches.

Ch. Jen-Mar's Carosel Jolly Jester, owned by Calypso Kennels.

Size, Proportion, Substance—*Height—* 17 1/2 to 20 1/2 inches, measured from the ground to the highest point of the shoulders. Any Brittany measuring under 17 1/2 inches or over 20 1/2 inches shall be disqualified from dog show competition. Weight—Should weigh between 30 and 40 pounds.

Proportion— So leggy is he that his height at the shoulders is the same as the length of his body.

Body Length— Approximately the same as the height when measured at the shoulders. Body length is measured from the point of the forechest to the rear of the rump. A long body should be heavily penalized.

Substance— Not too light in bone, yet never heavy-boned and cumbersome.

Head—*Expression—* Alert and eager, but with the soft expression of a bird dog.

Eyes— Well set in head. Well protected from briars by a heavy, expressive eyebrow. A prominent, full or popeye should be heavily penalized. It is a serious fault in a dog

that must face briars. Skull well chiseled under the eyes, so that the lower lid is not pulled back to form a pocket or haw that would catch seeds, dirt, and weed dust. Preference should be for the darker colored eyes, though lighter shades of amber should not be penalized. Light and mean-looking eyes should be heavily penalized.

Ears—Set high, above the level of the eyes. Short and triangular, rather than pendulous, reaching about half the length of the muzzle. Should lie flat and close to the head, with the tip rounded very slightly. Ears well covered with dense, but relatively short hair, and with little fringe.

Skull—Medium length, rounded, very slightly wedge-shaped, but evenly made. Width, not quite as wide as the length and never so broad as to appear coarse, or so narrow as to appear racy. Well defined, but gently sloping stop. Median line rather indistinct. The occiput only apparent to the touch. Lateral walls well rounded. The Brittany should never be "apple-headed" and he should never have an indented stop.

Muzzle—Medium length, about two-thirds the length of the skull, measuring the muzzle from the tip to the stop, and the skull from the occiput to the stop. Muzzle should taper gradually in both the horizontal and vertical dimensions as it approaches the nostrils. Neither a Roman nose nor a dish-face is desirable. Never broad, heavy, or snipy.

Nose—Nostrils well open to permit deep breathing of air and adequate scenting. Tight nostrils should be penalized. Never shiny. Color: fawn, tan, shades of brown or deep pink. A black nose is a disqualification. A two-tone or butterfly nose should be penalized.

Lips—Tight, the upper lip overlapping the lower jaw just to cover the lower lip. Lips dry, so that feathers will not stick. Drooling to be heavily penalized. Flews to be penalized.

Bite—A true scissors bite. Overshot or undershot jaw to be heavily penalized.

Neck, Topline, Body—*Neck*—Medium length. Free from throatiness, though not a serious fault unless accompanied by dewlaps, strong without giving the impression of being overmuscled. Well set into sloping shoulders. Never concave or ewe-necked.

26

Topline—Slight slope from the highest point of the shoulders to the root of the tail.

Chest—Deep, reaching the level of the elbow. Neither so wide nor so rounded as to disturb the placement of the shoulders and elbows. Ribs well sprung. Adequate heart room provided by depth as well as width. Narrow or slab-sided chests are a fault.

Back—Short and straight. Never hollow, saddle, sway, or roach backed. Slight drop from the hips to the root of the tail.

Flanks—Rounded. Fairly full. Not extremely tucked up, or flabby and falling. Loins short and strong. Distance from last rib to upper thigh short, about three to four finger widths. Narrow and weak loins are a fault. In motion, the loin should not sway sideways, giving a zig-zag motion to the back, wasting energy.

A compact, rugged dog, the Brittany should give the appearance of agility, speed, and energy.

Tail—Tailless to approximately four inches, natural or docked. The tail not to be so long as to affect the overall balance of the dog. Set on high, actually an extension of the spine at about the same level. Any tail substantially more than four inches shall be severely penalized.

Forequarters–*Shoulders*–Shoulder blades should not protrude too much, not too wide apart, with perhaps two thumbs' width between. Sloping and muscular. Blade and upper arm should form nearly a ninety degree angle. Straight shoulders are a fault. At the shoulders the Brittany is slightly higher than at the rump.

***Front Legs*–**Viewed from the front, perpendicular, but not set too wide. Elbows and feet turning neither in nor out. Pasterns slightly sloped. Down in pasterns is a serious fault. Leg bones, clean, graceful, but not too fine. Extremely heavy bone is as much a fault as spindly legs. One must look for substance and suppleness. Height at elbows should approximately equal distance from elbows to withers.

***Feet*–**Should be strong, proportionately smaller than the

The Brittany's coat should be dense and flat, helping to make the dog ideal for field hunting.

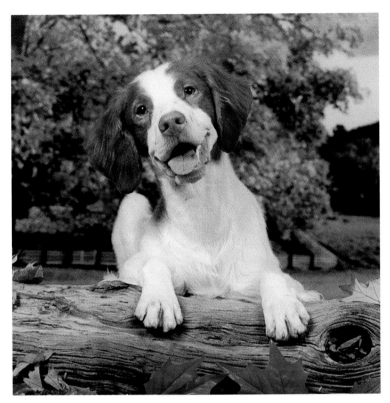

The Brittany possesses the alert, eager, and friendly expression that is typical of a bird dog.

spaniel's, with close fitting, well arched toes and thick pads. The Brittany is not "up on his toes." Toes not heavily feathered. Flat feet, splayed feet, paper feet, etc., are to be heavily penalized. An ideal foot is halfway between the hare and the cat foot. Dewclaws may be removed.

Hindquarters—Broad, strong, and muscular, with powerful thighs and well bent stifles, giving the angulation necessary for powerful drive.

Hind Legs—Stifles well bent. The stifle should not be so angulated as to place the hock joint far out behind the dog. A Brittany should not be condemned for straight stifle until the judge has checked the dog in motion from the side. The stifle joint should not turn out making a cowhock. Thighs well feathered but not profusely,

FIRST PLACE
FIELD TRIAL CLASS
AMERICAN
BRITTANY CLUB
1990
PHOTO BY DOWNEY

halfway to the hock. Hocks, that is, the back pasterns, should be moderately short, pointing neither in nor out, perpendicular when viewed from the side. They should be firm when shaken by the judge.

Feet—Same as front feet.

Coat—Dense, flat, or wavy, never curly. Texture neither wiry nor silky. Ears should carry little fringe. The front and hind legs should have some feathering, but too little is definitely preferable to too much. Dogs with long or profuse feathering or furnishings shall be so severely penalized as to effectively eliminate them from competition.

Skin—Fine and fairly loose. A loose skin rolls with briars and sticks, thus diminishing punctures or tearing. A skin so loose as to form pouches is undesirable.

Color—Orange and white or liver and white in either clear or roan patterns. Some ticking is desirable. The orange or liver is found in the standard parti-color or piebald patterns. Washed out colors are not desirable. Tri-colors are allowed but not preferred. A tri-color is a liver and white dog with classic orange markings on eyebrows, muzzle, and cheeks, inside the ears and under the tail; freckles on the lower legs are orange. Anything exceeding the limits of these markings shall be severely penalized. Black is a disqualification.

Gait—When at a trot, the Brittany's hind foot should step into or beyond the print left by the front foot. Clean movement, coming and going, is very important, but most important is side gait, which is smooth, efficient, and ground covering.

Temperament—A happy, alert dog, neither mean nor shy.

Ch. Millette's Downtown Brown, pictured with trainer Lyle Johnson and co-owned by author Beverly Millette, is a perfect example of a liver-and-white Brittany.

DISQUALIFICATIONS

Any Brittany measuring under 17 ¹/₂ inches or over 20 ¹/₂ inches.

A black nose.

Black in the coat.

Approved April 10, 1990
Effective May 31, 1990

SELECTING the Right Brittany for You

WHAT TO LOOK FOR IN A BREEDER

Once the prospective Brittany owner satisfactorily answers all of the questions relating to responsible pet ownership, he or she will undoubtedly want to rush out and purchase a puppy on the spot. Take care not to act in haste. It is extremely important for the buyer of any dog to do his homework, because it is not possible to ask a breeder the right questions if you know nothing about the breed. Read as much as you can. There are many breed-specific and general care books available at local libraries and bookstores.

The purchase of any dog is an important step, because the animal will live with you for many years. In the case of a Brittany, this could easily be 12 or 13 years. You will undoubtedly want the experience

To ensure against genetic disease and preserve the quality of their programs, reputable breeders will screen all Brittanys before breeding them.

Breeding should only be done by people who have the ability to care for the mother and all the resulting offspring. These pups will soon need good homes.

of living with and caring for your dog to be one you enjoy.

It is extremely important that your Brittany be purchased from a breeder who has earned a reputation for consistently producing dogs that are mentally and physically sound. There are always those who are ready to exploit a breed for financial gain, with no thought given to its health, welfare, or to the homes in which the dogs will live.

The only way a breeder can earn a reputation for quality is by having a well-thought-out breeding program in which rigid selectivity is imposed. Selective breeding is aimed at maintaining the virtues of a breed and eliminating genetic weaknesses. This process is time-consuming and costly. Therefore, responsible Brittany breeders protect their investment by providing the utmost in prenatal care for their brood matrons and maximum care and nutrition for the resulting offspring.

Once the puppies arrive, the knowledgeable breeder initiates a thorough socialization process. This process is not one to be overlooked—it is what produces a mentally sound dog that will be able to live with people in harmony. Brittany puppies need human contact right from the beginning, so it is important that the breeder spends a lot of time with each puppy individually in order to establish the human-canine relationship.

A prospective owner should ask the breeder what the number one characteristic he breeds for is. Deal only with breeders that respond by saying, "good temperament." The responsible Brittany breeder puts compatibility far ahead of any other characteristic.

Before you purchase a puppy, be sure that you have done your homework and that the Brittany is the right dog for your family and home.

The buyer should also ask what activities the breeder engages in with his or her Brittanys. This will give some insight to the characteristics that a breeder wishes to propagate. Does the breeder hunt his dogs or compete in field trials? Are the dogs shown in conformation competition or in obedience? If the Brittanys are bred only for sale, go elsewhere for your dog.

The healthiest and happiest puppies are born and raised in close proximity to their human family. Puppies kept close to their owner are imprinted with the scents and sounds of humans; puppies born in a barn or garage and given few opportunities to be with humans seldom achieve their full potential as companions.

The buyer should look for cleanliness in both the dogs and the areas in which they are kept. Cleanliness is the first clue to knowing how much the breeder cares about the dogs he owns.

The governing kennel clubs in different countries of the world maintain lists of local and national Brittany clubs that can direct you to responsible breeders of quality stock. If you are

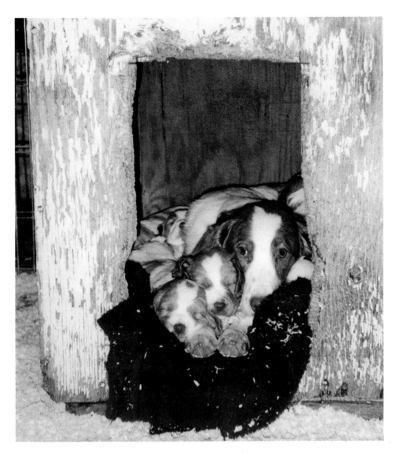

Your pup will have a great start in life if his parents are healthy and well adjusted. Try to see the dam and sire of the pup you are considering.

not sure where to contact a respected breeder in your area, contact the American Brittany Club, the Kennel Club in your country, or your local kennel club for recommendations.

There is every possibility that a reputable breeder residing in your area will not only be able to provide the right Brittany for you, but will often have both of the puppy's parents on the premises as well. At times, however, particularly in the case of hobby breeders, the males may not be available as they are not always kept on the premises and the female may have been sent a good distance away to be bred.

Seeing the parent or parents of your Brittany gives you an opportunity to examine the background of the puppy you are considering firsthand. Good breeders are not only willing to have you see their dogs, but will also allow you to inspect the facility in which the dogs are raised. These breeders will be able to discuss problems that exist in the breed and how they are dealt with.

Do not be surprised if a concerned breeder asks many questions about you and the environment in which his Brittany will be raised. Good breeders are just as concerned with the quality of the homes their dogs are going to live in as you, the buyer, are in obtaining a sound and healthy dog.

Energetic puppies make great playmates for children and caring for a dog teaches a child responsibility.

Do not think a good Brittany puppy can only come from a large kennel. Today, many of the best breeders raise their dogs at home as a hobby. It is important, however, that you do not allow yourself to fall into the hands of an irresponsible "backyard breeder." Backyard breeders differ significantly from small hobby breeders in that they lack the responsibility to bring their breeding stock to its full potential. A hobby breeder's dogs will find their way out into the field, the show, and obedience rings, and will participate in the numerous activities in which the Brittany excels. A backyard breeder, on the other hand, is an individual who simply breeds dogs to sell.

If there aren't any local breeders in your area, you can locate legitimate and reliable breeders throughout the country on American Brittany Club or local breed club lists. These established breeders are accustomed to safely shipping puppies to different states, even different countries.

Always check the references of these breeders and do not hesitate to ask for documentation. The breeder will undoubtedly have as many questions for you as you will have for him. When you call a breeder, phone at a reasonable hour and expect to have a lengthy conversation. The amount of money you invest in a satisfying telephone discussion may save you huge veterinary costs and a great deal of unhappiness.

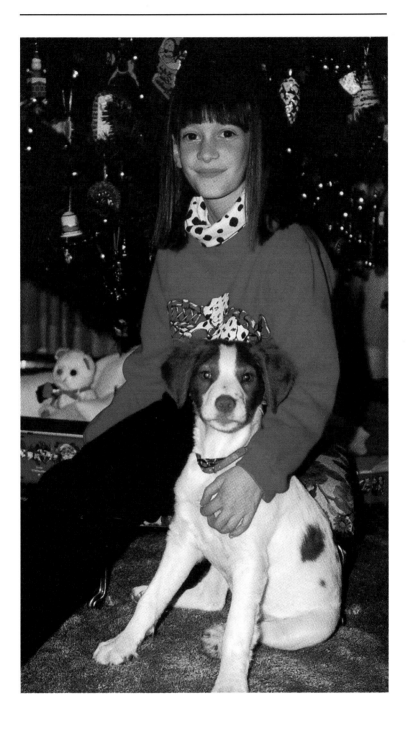

Health Concerns

People who qualify as good Brittany owners are indeed fortunate. The breed is relatively free of serious diseases and conditions. If breeders watch for any health concern closely, it would be hip dysplasia, a problem that seems to plague practically all breeds.

Hip dysplasia is a condition in which the ball and socket arrangement of the hip and upper femur is so poorly developed that the femur rotates within the socket. Depending upon the severity of the condition, hip dysplasia can cause stiffness, limping, and possibly total paralysis of the rear quarters.

Corrective surgery has been perfected, but needless to say, because the Brittany is an active, versatile dog, it makes sense to seek out a breeder who screens his stock and does his best to avoid using affected animals in his breeding programs.

Some cases of epilepsy have been reported in the breed. Here again, however, discussing the problem with your breeder will relieve you of the concern regarding the frequency of this disorder, if any, in the breeder's line.

The responsible breeder does everything possible to match the right puppy with the right home. Households with boisterous children will generally require a puppy with a different temperament than one appropriate for a sedate, single adult. The time you spend in making the right selection ensures you of getting the right Brittany for your lifestyle.

Recognizing a Healthy Puppy

Most breeders will not consider releasing their puppies until they have been given their "puppy shots." Normally, this occurs at about eight weeks of age. At this age, the puppies are entirely weaned and will bond extremely well with their new owners.

Nursing puppies receive some temporary immunization from their mother. Once weaned, however, a puppy is highly susceptible to many infectious diseases that can be transmitted via the hands and clothing of people. Therefore, make sure your puppy is fully inoculated before he leaves his former home environment and ask when any additional inoculations should be given.

Above all, the Brittany puppy you buy should be a happy, bouncy extrovert, although what the puppy is selectively bred for has a good deal to do with determining which one will be best for you.

If you are not going to hunt your Brittany and want to keep him strictly as a pet, you may not want to select the litter's most extroverted pup, as he will undoubtedly demand a lot more exercise and attention to keep him calm. You may be happier with his more tractable littermate.

The worst thing you could possibly do is buy a shy, shrinking-violet puppy or one that appears to be sick and listless because you feel sorry for him. Doing this will undoubtedly lead to heartache and difficulty, to say nothing of the veterinary costs that you may incur in getting the puppy well.

The puppy you choose should be bright-eyed, healthy-looking, and interested in the world around him.

Ask the breeder if it is possible to take the puppy you are interested in away from his littermates and into a different room or another part of the kennel. The smells will remain the same for the puppy, so he should still feel secure and maintain his outgoing personality. Doing this gives you an opportunity to inspect the puppy more closely.

A healthy Brittany puppy will be strong and sturdy to the touch, never bony, obese, or bloated. His coat will be soft and lustrous, with no sign of dry or flaky skin. The inside of the puppy's ears should be pink and clean. Dark discharge or a bad odor could indicate ear mites, a sure sign of poor maintenance. The healthy Brittany puppy's breath smells sweet. His teeth should be clean and white, and there should never be any malformation of the mouth or jaw. The puppy's eyes should be

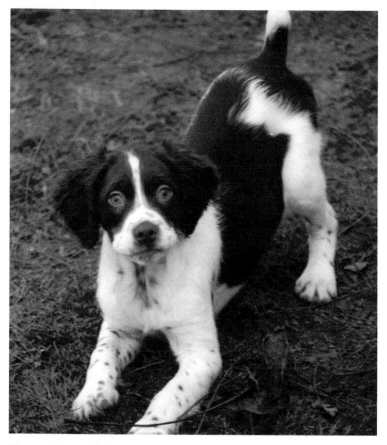

Try to play with the puppy you are considering away from his littermates. He should be outgoing and eager to be in your company.

clear and bright. Eyes that appear runny and irritated indicate serious problems. There should be no sign of discharge from the nose, nor should it ever be crusted or runny. Coughing or diarrhea is a danger signal, as are any eruptions on the skin.

The Brittany's front legs should be as straight as little posts and his movement light, bouncy, and free. There should never be a limp in the puppy's gait. Of course, there is always a chubby, clumsy puppy or two in a litter, but do not mistake this for unsoundness. If you have any doubts or questions, discuss them with the breeder.

Remember, your pet will be living with you for a long time. Make sure the puppy reacts well to you. Run your fingers along the ground and see if he is willing to play. If the puppy has no interest in you and the only thing he seems to want to do is get back to his littermates, definitely choose another puppy.

MALE OR FEMALE?

If you have decided on the sex you want your puppy to be, stand by your decision and do not let someone change your mind because your choice is not available and this is "all that is left." Other than size and a minor difference in the amount of coat, the Brittany is one breed that doesn't have many sex-related differences.

Whether male or female, sexually altering your Brittany pup is often the best option for your pet's health and well-being.

Females do have semiannual heat cycles once they reach nine or ten months of age. During these 21-day cycles, the female must be confined in order to avoid soiling her surroundings with the bloody discharge that accompanies estrus. She must also be carefully watched to prevent males from gaining access to her or she will become pregnant.

Although owners of other breeds find training the male not to lift his leg to mark his territory indoors troublesome, most Brittanys are not difficult to correct in this respect. Brittany males can get "wanderlust" if not kept active and interested at home, particularly if the female Dachshund or Cocker Spaniel up the hill is in heat.

Most sexually related problems can be avoided by having your pet "altered." Spaying the female or neutering the male saves the pet owner the headaches associated with these problems without changing the character of the breed. If there is any change at all in the altered Brittany, it is in making the dog an even more amiable companion. Above all, altering your pet precludes the possibility of his adding to the serious pet overpopulation problem that exists worldwide.

SELECTING A SHOW-PROSPECT PUPPY

Anyone interested in showing a puppy should go to dog shows and decide which line or look is the most appealing. Needless to say, a puppy with show potential is going to cost more than one that will be kept strictly as a companion. However, my father once advised, "The cheapest dog you can own is the most expensive one you can afford to buy." Food and veterinary bills are the same for a pet as they are for a show dog.

In determining the show potential of a particular puppy, the most any breeder can offer is an opinion. A promising eight-week-old puppy can grow up to be a mediocre adult. Testicles may not descend on a male or a bite may not stay correct. Although these are not normally problems in the breed, a breeder has no control over these changes.

Any predictions a breeder makes about a puppy's future are based on his experience with past litters that have produced winning show dogs. It is obvious that the more successful a breeder has been in producing winners over the years, the broader his basis for comparison will be.

A puppy's potential as a show dog is determined by how closely he adheres to the demands of the standard for the breed. Most breeders concur there is no such thing as "a sure thing" when it comes to predicting winners. However, they are also quick to agree that the older a puppy is, the better your chances are of making any predictions at all.

It makes little difference to the owner of a pet if his dog grows to be a bit too large (or too small) or if the alignment of the teeth is a bit off. Nor would it make a difference if a male pup has only one testicle. These faults do not interfere with a Brittany becoming a healthy, loving companion. However, these flaws in the standard for the breed would keep that individual from a winning show career.

While it certainly behooves the prospective owner of a show-prospect puppy to be as familiar with the standard of the breed as possible, it is even more important for the buyer to put himself in the hands of a successful and respected breeder of winning Brittanys. The experienced breeder knows that there are certain age-related shortcomings in young Brittanys that maturity will take care of and other faults that will completely eliminate him from consideration as a show prospect. Furthermore, most breeders are delighted to find the right homes for their show-prospect puppies and will be particularly helpful in this respect when they know you plan to show one of their dogs.

An important thing to remember in choosing your first show prospect is that "cuteness" may not be consistent with quality. An extroverted puppy in the litter might decide he belongs to you. If you are simply looking for a pet, this is the puppy you should take. However, if you are genuinely interested in showing and breeding your Brittany, you must keep your head, and without disregarding good temperament, give serious

This looks like a pup with potential! If you are looking for a show Brittany, he must have a certain "star" quality and overall balance and soundness.

consideration to both what the breed standard says a show-type Brittany must look like and to what the breeder's recommendations are.

The complete standard of the breed is presented in the book and meeting its requirements is, in the end, what determines the show potential of a puppy. When we are selecting a show-quality puppy, all of the previous information regarding soundness and health will apply. A point to keep in mind, however, is that spaying and castration are not reversible procedures, and, once done, will eliminate the possibility of future breeding or of showing your Brittany in conformation shows. Altered dogs can, however, compete in field and obedience trials and many other competitive events.

Even if the Brittany you choose is not of show quality, he will still make a devoted and loyal pet.

There are a good number of additional characteristics to be considered for the potential show dog. When we are selecting a show-quality puppy, we are looking for overall balance and that "look-at-me attitude" that is so important in the show ring. A show dog endures much more stress than a companion dog that spends his days at home, and he must be able to hold up under the pressure that will be created by frequent travel.

Even in an eight-week-old puppy, we expect to see good movement and soundness, which are also of paramount importance when judging this working breed. The dogs must be sturdy but moderate in bone, and above all, agile in order to perform as stock dogs. Although not a great number of show Brittanys double as stock dogs, there is no reason they should be any less sound and agile than their working relatives.

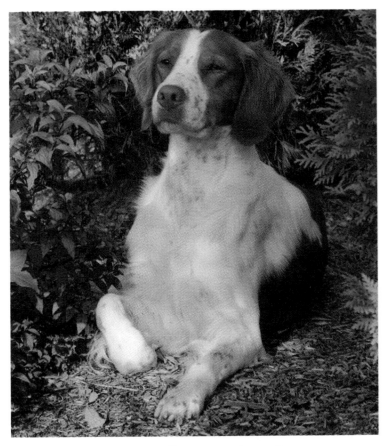

If you do not have the time to spend training and housebreaking a young puppy, an adult Brittany may be the right choice for you.

PUPPY OR ADULT?

You can rear a puppy and train him in any way you wish, but an adult dog may have characteristics that you might find undesirable. Until the adult Brittany has decided that you and your family are his "one and only," he may look to see if the grass is greener on the other side of your fence. And, once he is determined to scale your fence, you may have a devil of a time convincing him that this is unacceptable. Also, if an adult Brittany has never been around young children, he may find these noisy, "miniature people" very intimidating. It usually works out just fine, but supervision of both the dog and the children is extremely important during this initial period of adjustment.

In some cases, an adult dog or older puppy may be just the answer. It certainly eliminates the trials and tribulations of housebreaking, chewing, and the myriad of other problems associated with raising a very young puppy. Inoculations are a once-a-year event instead of frequent visits to the vet for puppy shots. Very often, an adult Brittany will already be spayed or neutered.

Although we may like to think otherwise, Brittanys adapt easily to a new home. They love people, and as long as their home is a place where attention, fun activities, and love abound, most adult Brittanys will adjust well. Arrange to bring an adult Brittany into your home on a trial basis. That way you won't be obligated if you discover that you are incompatible.

IMPORTANT PAPERS

The purchase of any purebred dog entitles you to three very important documents: a health record containing an inoculation list, a copy of the dog's pedigree, and the registration certificate.

Health Record

Most Brittany breeders have initiated the necessary inoculation series for their puppies by the time they are eight weeks of age. These shots protect puppies against hepatitis, leptospirosis, distemper, and canine parvovirus. In most cases, rabies inoculations are not given until a puppy is four months of age or older.

There is a series of inoculations specifically developed to combat these infectious diseases, and it is extremely important that you obtain a record of the shots your puppy has been given and the dates that they were administered. In this way, the veterinarian you choose will be able to continue with the appropriate inoculation series.

Pedigree

The pedigree is your dog's "family tree." The breeder must supply you with a copy of a document authenticating your puppy's ancestry as far back as the third generation. All purebred dogs have a pedigree, which, however, does not imply that a dog is of show quality. It is simply a chronological list of ancestors.

Registration Certificate

The registration certificate is the canine world's "birth certificate." This document is issued by a country's governing kennel club. When you transfer the ownership of your Brittany from the breeder's name to your own name, the transaction is entered on this certificate and mailed to the kennel club. It is then permanently recorded in their computerized files. Keep all of these documents in a safe place, because you will need them when you visit your veterinarian or if you ever decide to breed or show your Brittany.

A happy healthy puppy is a reflection of his breeder's good care. You must continue to care for your Brittany's needs once you take him home.

DIET SHEET

Happy, healthy Brittany puppies are that way because the breeder has been carefully feeding and caring for them. Every breeder has his own particular regimen. Most breeders give the new owner a written record that details the amount and kind of food a puppy has been receiving. Follow these recommendations to the letter, at least for the first month or two after the puppy comes to live with you.

The diet sheet should indicate the number of times a day your puppy is fed and the kind of vitamin supplementation, if any, he receives. Following the prescribed procedure will reduce the chance of upset stomach and loose stools.

Socialization with littermates will help your Brittany get along with other dogs when he is older.

Usually, a breeder's diet sheet projects the increase and change in food that will be required as your puppy grows from week to week. If the sheet does not include this information, ask the breeder for suggestions regarding increases and the eventual change to adult food.

Introduce your Brittany to as many people as possible, especially children. The more people he meets, the better adjusted he will become.

In the unlikely event that you are not supplied with a diet sheet by the breeder and are unable to get one, your veterinarian will be able to advise you. There are countless foods now being expressly manufactured to meet the nutritional needs of puppies and growing dogs. A trip down the pet aisle at your supermarket or pet supply store will prove just how many choices you have. Two important tips to consider: Read labels carefully for content, and choose established, reliable manufacturers because you are more likely to get what you pay for. Feeding and nutrition are discussed in greater detail in this book.

HEALTH GUARANTEE

Any reputable breeder is more than willing to supply a written agreement that the sale of your Brittany is contingent upon several factors. Although all are equally important, the

49

Take your Brittany pup everywhere with you. Different experiences and situations will help to socialize him and build his confidence.

puppy must first be able to pass a veterinarian's examination. Furthermore, the breeder should guarantee against the development of any hereditary problems. Last, but not least, the temperament of the dog you purchase should be vouched for. There is always a period of adjustment that a puppy experiences when he first arrives at a new home, but it should be relatively short.

Ideally, you should be able to arrange an appointment with your chosen veterinarian right after you have picked up your puppy from the breeder and before you take him home. If this is not possible, you should not delay this procedure much longer than 24 hours from the time you take your puppy home. Give the results of any tests that the breeder may have completed on your puppy, such as eye examinations or hearing examinations, to your veterinarian.

TEMPERAMENT AND SOCIALIZATION

Temperament is both hereditary and learned. Inherited good temperament can be ruined by poor treatment or lack of proper socialization. A Brittany puppy that has inherited a bad temperament is a poor risk as a companion, show dog, or hunting dog and should certainly never be bred. Therefore, it is critical that you obtain a happy puppy from a breeder who is determined to produce dogs with good temperaments and has taken all the necessary steps to provide the early socialization necessary.

It is important to remember a Brittany puppy may be as happy as a lark living at home with you and your family, but if the socialization begun by the breeder is not continued, that sunny disposition may not extend outside of your front door. From the day the young Brittany arrives at your home, you must be committed to accompanying him on an unending pilgrimage to meet and like all human beings and animals.

Your Brittany may go through an awkward phase while growing up, but eventually he should end up looking very much like his parents.

If you are fortunate enough to have children well past the toddler stage in the household or living nearby, your socialization task will be assisted considerably. Brittanys raised with children seem to have a distinct advantage in socialization. The two seem to understand each other, and in some way known only to the puppies and children themselves, they give each other the confidence to face the trying ordeal of growing up.

The children in your own household are not the only children your puppy should spend time with. It is a case of the more the merrier! Every child (and adult for that matter) that enters your household should be asked to pet your puppy.

51

Your puppy should go everywhere with you: the post office, the market, the shopping mall, wherever. Little Brittany puppies create a stir wherever they go, and dog lovers will want to stop and pet the puppy. There is nothing in the world better for the puppy. They are social dogs by nature.

If your Brittany has a show career in his future, there are things in addition to being handled that will have to be taught. All show dogs must learn to have their mouths opened and teeth inspected by the judge. Males must become accustomed to having their testicles touched so that the show judge can determine that the male is "complete," which means there are two normal-sized testicles in the scrotum. These inspections must begin in puppyhood and be done on a regular and continuing basis.

All Brittanys must learn to get along with other dogs as well as with humans. If you are fortunate enough to have a "puppy preschool" or dog training class nearby, attend with as frequently as you possibly can. A young Brittany that has been regularly exposed to other dogs from puppyhood will learn to adapt and accept other dogs and other breeds much more readily than one that seldom sees strange dogs.

THE ADOLESCENT BRITTANY

You will find it amazing how quickly the "no more than a handful" you first brought home develops into a full-grown Brittany. Some lines shoot up to full size very rapidly, while others mature more slowly. Some Brittanys pass through adolescence quite gracefully, but most become lanky and ungainly, growing in and out of proportion from one day to the next.

Food needs increase during this growth period. Some Brittanys act as though they can never get enough to eat, while others experience a very finicky stage and appear to eat only enough to keep from starving. Think of Brittany puppies as being as individualistic as children and act accordingly.

The amount of food you give your Brittany should be adjusted to how much he will readily consume at each meal. If the entire meal is eaten quickly, add a small amount to the next feeding and continue to do so as the need increases. This method will ensure that you give your puppy enough food, but you must also pay close attention to the dog's appearance and condition, because you do not want a Brittany of any age to become overweight or obese.

At eight weeks of age, most Brittany puppies are accustomed to eating four meals a day. By the time the puppy is four months old, he can do well on two meals a day, fed morning and evening, with perhaps a snack in the middle of the day. If your puppy does not eat the food offered, he is either not hungry or not well. Your dog will eat when he is hungry. If you suspect the dog is not well, a trip to the veterinarian is in order.

As an adolescent, your Brittany may start to challenge your authority. Discipline, training, and guidance will ensure that he knows that you are the boss.

After a Brittany is a year old, he can be fed once a day or the meal can be split into morning and night portions. The evening meal should be given just after your own dinner time. In this way, a trip outdoors just before bedtime will usually ensure the dog will spend an accident-free night.

Many dog owners feel their pets need to be fed far more food than what they actually require. Overfeeding is very harmful. It puts stress on their kidneys and heart. Overeating can also make them very lazy, which, in turn, will cause them to gain even more weight from lack of exercise.

The adolescent period is a particularly important and sometimes difficult one. Hormones are developing and can have an effect on the temperament of the dog. Males may begin to test their ability to dominate. Females can get giddy and act foolishly.

This is also the time your Brittany must learn the household and social rules that he will live by for the rest of his life. Your patience and commitment during this difficult time will not only produce a respected canine good citizen, but will forge a bond between the two of you that will grow into a wonderful relationship.

CARING for Your Brittany

FEEDING AND NUTRITION

The best way to make sure your Brittany puppy is obtaining the correct amount and type of food for his age is to follow the diet sheet provided by his breeder. Do your best not to change the puppy's diet and in so doing you will be less likely to run into digestive problems and diarrhea. Diarrhea is very serious in young puppies; they can dehydrate very rapidly, causing severe problems and even death.

If it is necessary to change your puppy's diet for any reason, it should never be done abruptly. Begin by adding a tablespoon or two of the new food, gradually increasing the amount until the meal consists entirely of the new product. A rule of thumb is this: You should be able to feel the puppy's ribs and backbone, with just a slight layer of fat and muscle over them.

As mentioned, overfeeding is very harmful to the Brittany. It puts stress on the kidneys and heart and can make your dog very lazy and disinterested in the exercise he needs to stay in shape.

By the time your Brittany puppy is 12 months old, you can reduce feedings to once a day. This meal can be given either in the morning or evening. It is really a matter of choice on your part. There are two important things to remember: Feed the main meal at the same time every day and make sure it is nutritionally complete.

If you wish, the single meal can be cut in half and fed twice a day. A morning or nighttime snack of hard dog biscuits made especially for large dogs can also be given. These biscuits not only become highly anticipated treats, but they are also genuinely helpful in maintaining healthy gums and teeth.

Balanced Diets

In order for a canine diet to qualify as "complete and balanced" in the United States, it must meet standards set by the Subcommittee on Canine Nutrition of the National Research Council of the National Academy of Sciences. Most commercial foods manufactured for dogs meet these standards and prove this by listing the ingredients contained in the food on every package and can. The ingredients are listed in descending order, with the main ingredient listed first.

Fed with any regularity at all, refined sugars can cause your Brittany to become obese and will definitely create tooth decay. Refined sugars are not part of the canine's natural food acquisition, and a dog's teeth are not genetically disposed to handling sugars. Do not feed your Brittany products that contain sugar to any high degree.

Fresh water and a properly prepared, balanced diet that contains the essential nutrients in correct proportions are all a healthy Brittany needs to be offered. Dog foods come canned, dry, semi-moist, "scientifically fortified," and "all-natural." A visit to your local supermarket or pet store will reveal the vast array of available products.

Be sure to choose the dog food that is most beneficial to your Brittany's stage of life. Puppies need a growth formula.

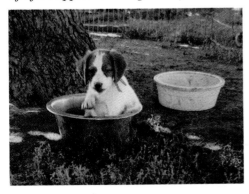

The important thing to remember is that all dogs, whether they are Brittanys, Chihuahuas, or Great Danes, are carnivorous (meat-eating) animals. While the vegetable content of your dog's diet should not be overlooked, his physiology and anatomy are based on carnivorous food acquisition. Animal protein and fats are essential to the well-being of your Brittany. However, a diet too high in proteins can lead to problems as well. Not all dry foods contain the proper amount of protein to keep a healthy Brittany in top condition. It is best to discuss this with your breeder or veterinarian.

In the wild, carnivores eat practically the whole beast they capture and kill. These kills consist almost entirely of herbivores (plant-eating animals). Invariably, the carnivore begins his meal with the contents of the herbivore's stomach, which provides the carbohydrates, minerals, and nutrients present in vegetables.

Through centuries of domestication, we have made our dogs totally dependent upon us for their well-being. Therefore, we, as owners, are completely responsible for duplicating the food balance that wild dog finds in nature. The domesticated dog's diet must include protein, carbohydrates, fats, roughage, and small amounts of essential minerals and vitamins.

Finding commercially prepared diets that contain all of the necessary nutrients will not present a problem. Because these prepared foods do contain all of the nutrients your Brittany needs, it is unnecessary to add vitamin supplements to your dog's diet, except in special circumstances prescribed by your veterinarian. These "special" periods in a Brittany's life may include the time of rapid growth the breed experiences in puppyhood, or throughout the female's pregnancy and the nursing of her puppies.

Proper nutrition is imperative to your dog's health. Veterinarians recommend elevated feeders to help reduce stress on your dog's neck and back muscles. The raised platform also provides better digestion while reducing bloating and gas. Photo courtesy of Pet Zone Products, Ltd.

Even when supplements are required in these special circumstances, it is never a case of "if a little is good, more is better." Oversupplementation and forced growth are now looked upon by some breeders as major

Reputable breeders will start their puppies on the road to good nutrition, so stick to this original diet when you first get your new Brittany home.

contributors to many skeletal abnormalities found in the purebred dogs of the day.

Oversupplementation

A great deal of controversy exists today regarding the orthopedic problems that afflict some Brittanys and many other breeds. Some experts claim that these problems and a wide variety of chronic skin disorders are caused entirely by hereditary conditions, but many others feel that they can be exacerbated by diet and overuse of mineral and vitamin supplements for puppies.

When giving vitamin supplementation, you should never exceed the prescribed amount. Some breeders insist that all recommended dosages be halved before including them in a dog's diet because of the highly fortified commercial foods being fed. Yet, other breeders feel supplementation should not be given at all, believing a balanced diet that includes abundant milk products and a small amount of bone meal to provide calcium is all that is necessary and beneficial.

If the owner of a Brittany eats healthy, nutritious food, there is no reason his dog cannot be given table scraps. Table scraps, however, should only be given as part of the dog's meal and never from the table. A Brittany that becomes accustomed to being hand-fed from the table can quickly become a pest at mealtime. Also, dinner guests may find the pleading stare of your Brittany less than appealing when dinner is being served.

Dogs do not care if food looks like a hot dog or wedge of cheese. Truly nutritious dog foods are seldom manufactured to look like food that appeals to humans. Dogs only care about how food smells and tastes. It is highly doubtful that you will be eating your dog's food, so do not waste your money on these "looks-just-like" products. Along these lines, most of the moist or canned foods that have the look of "delicious red beef" look that way because they contain large amounts of preservatives, sugars, and dyes. These additives are no better for your dog than they are for you.

Special Diets

There are now a number of commercially prepared diets for dogs with special dietary needs. The overweight, underweight, or geriatric dog can have his nutritional needs met, as can puppies and growing dogs. The calorie content of these foods is adjusted accordingly. With the correct amount of the right foods and the proper amount of exercise, your Brittany should stay in top shape. As always, common sense must prevail. What works for humans, works for dogs as well—increasing calories will increase weight; stepping up exercise and reducing calories will bring weight down.

Occasionally, a young Brittany going through the teething period will become a finicky eater. The concerned owner's first response is to tempt the dog by hand-feeding him special treats and foods that the problem eater seems to prefer. This practice only serves to compound the problem. Once the dog learns to play the waiting game, he will turn up his nose at anything other than his favorite food, knowing full well that what he wants to eat will eventually arrive. Give your Brittany the proper food to eat. He may well turn up his nose a day or two and refuse to eat anything. However, you can rest assured that when your dog is really hungry, he will eat.

Unlike humans, dogs do not have suicidal tendencies. A healthy dog will not starve himself to death. He may not eat enough to keep himself in the shape we find ideal and attractive, but he will definitely eat enough to maintain himself. If your Brittany is not eating properly and appears to be too thin, it is probably best to consult your veterinarian.

GROOMING

The Brittany is a breed that is naturally well groomed and requires minimal clipping or trimming. Anything that has to be done can be done with a pair of straight shears, thinning shears, and a brush. Regular, thorough brushing and a bath when needed are an important part of keeping your dog clean, healthy, and a pleasant companion.

It is not necessary to give your Brittany a bath unless he begins to smell foul. You can freshen up the coat by sprinkling a little baby powder on it, working it in well, and then brushing it out. This, of course, also helps to make the dog smell very good. It is important to note that excessive bathing can lead to dry skin problems. Dry skin creates a need to scratch, which can lead to severe

The Brittany is a breed that requires minimal grooming to look his best.

scratching and "hot spots," moist sore areas in which the coat is entirely scratched away.

The easiest way to groom a Brittany is by placing him on a grooming table, which can be built or purchased at your local pet shop. Make sure that the table is a comfortable height to work at, either sitting or standing. Adjustable-height grooming tables are available at most pet outlets.

Although you will buy the grooming table when your puppy first arrives, anticipate your dog's full-grown size when making your purchase and select or build a table that will accommodate an adult Brittany. It is best to use a grooming table that has an "arm" and a "noose." The noose slips around the dog's neck when he is standing and keeps him from fidgeting about or deciding he has had enough grooming.

Any attempt to groom your puppy on the floor may result in spending a good part of your time chasing him around the room. Sitting on the floor for long stretches of time is not the most comfortable position in the world for the average adult either.

You will need to invest in a good, natural-bristle brush that has some nylon bristles inserted in it. You will also need a steel comb to remove any debris that collects in the longer furnishings. A comb that has teeth divided between fine and coarse is ideal. Considering the fact that you will be using this equipment for many years, it is recommended that you buy the best of these items that you can afford.

When brushing, proceed vigorously from behind the head to the tail. Brush the entire body and be especially careful to attend to the hard-to-reach areas between the legs, behind the ears, and under the belly. While the groomed Brittany coat seldom mats or tangles, this could occur during the time the dog is shedding his puppy coat or when an adult catches burrs or sticky substances in his longer furnishings. If you encounter a mat that does not brush out easily, use your fingers and the steel comb to separate the hairs as much as possible. Do not cut or pull out the matted hair. Apply baby powder or one of the specially prepared grooming powders directly to the mat and brush completely from the skin out.

A grooming table is a useful piece of equipment to have when taking care of your Brittany's coat.

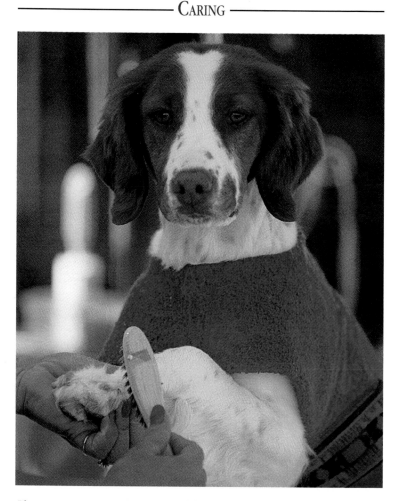

If you accustom your Brittany to grooming procedures like nail trimming while young, he will soon get used to it.

Nail Trimming

This is a good time to accustom your Brittany to having his nails trimmed and his feet inspected. Always check your dog's feet for cracked pads, splinters, and thorns between the toes, and pay particular attention to any swollen or tender areas.

Attending to your dog's nails at least every three or four weeks is recommended. Long nails spread and weaken the foot. The nails of any Brittany that isn't exercising outdoors on rough terrain will grow long very quickly. Do not allow them to become overgrown and then expect to cut them back easily. Each nail has a blood vessel running through the center called the "quick," which grows close to the end of the nail and contains very sensitive nerve endings. If the nail is allowed to grow too long, it will be impossible to cut it back to a proper length without cutting into the quick. This causes the dog severe pain and can also result in a great deal of bleeding that can be difficult to stop.

Nails can be trimmed with canine nail clippers or an electric nail grinder (also called a drummel). We prefer using the fine grinding disk because it allows you to trim back the nail a little bit at a time, which practically eliminates any bleeding from occurring. Regardless of the device you use, proceed with caution and remove only a small portion of the nail at a time.

Trimming your Brittany before taking him out in the field will save you lots of work when the hunt is over.

If the quick is nipped during the trimming process, there are a number of blood-clotting products available at pet shops that will almost immediately stem the flow of blood. It is wise to have one of these products on hand in case your dog breaks a nail in some way.

The Hunting or Utility Clip

Trimming a Brittany for hunting ahead of time will save you work when the hunt is over. Also, the type of terrain you and your dog cover when you go out in the field will determine how much hair will be appropriate. The grooming method can be modified to accommodate the situation.

Begin by lifting the ear and taking out all of the excess hair on the upper cheek and under the ear. This is one of the worst places for picking up and holding burrs, stickers, and other debris. Use thinning shears or an electric clipper with a #10 blade to do this.

Next, hold the ear out and away from the head, and cut off all hair that is longer than the ear leather. Use straight shears for this. If the hair on the top of the ear becomes too thick, it can be stripped using a stripping knife or thinning shears.

The hair in the armpits, where the legs join the body, should also be cut away to protect against collecting burrs. Do not shave the underline of the Brittany because removing all hair exposes the belly to being scratched and becoming sore. The hair in these areas should be trimmed to about an inch in length to provide protection.

Feet should be groomed by removing all excess hair between the toes and trimming any excess around the foot. This helps to keep foxtails and other field debris from catching between the toes, as well as making it easier to inspect them when coming out of the field.

If you can eliminate the tugging and tearing of your dog's coat in the detangling process, your dog will appreciate it, and his coat is less likely to be split or torn. Photo courtesy of Wahl, USA.

The Brittany will grow a "flag" on his tail. Some owners like this flag, most do not. Shape this hair neatly using thinning sheers.

BATHING

Consistent brushing will keep the Brittany's coat surprisingly clean, but there are occasions where a full bath may be required. When your Brittany requires a wet bath, you will need to gather the necessary equipment ahead of time. A rubber mat should be placed at the bottom of the tub to stop

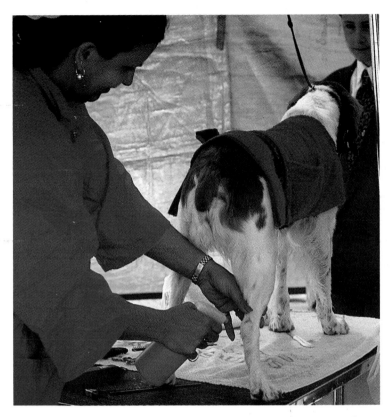

Following a regular grooming regimen is an excellent way to detect any health or coat problems, as well as a great way to spend quality time with your dog.

your dog from slipping and becoming frightened. A rubber spray hose is absolutely necessary to remove all shampoo residue.

A small cotton ball placed inside each ear will stop water from running down into the ear canal. Be very careful when washing around the eyes as soaps and shampoos can be extremely irritating. Putting a tiny dab of petroleum jelly or a drop of mineral oil in each eye will help prevent irritation.

When bathing, start behind the ears and work back. Use a washcloth to soap and rinse around the head and face. Once you have shampooed your dog, you must rinse the coat thoroughly until you feel quite certain that all shampoo residue has been removed. Then, rinse once more.

Shampoo residue in the coat is sure to dry the hair and cause skin irritation.

After completing the bath, use heavy towels to remove as much of the excess water as possible. Your Brittany will undoubtedly assist you in the process by shaking a great deal of the water out of his coat on his own.

Brush drying the coat with the assistance of a hair dryer (human or a special canine blower) will reduce drying time significantly. When using a hair dryer of any kind, always keep the setting on "medium." Anything warmer can dry the coat and, in extreme cases, can actually burn the skin. Do not blow directly into the coat but over it, and use your brush to fluff out the hair and assist the drying process.

EXERCISE

Sufficient exercise not only makes good sense, it is a bottom-line must for the Brittany. Remember the breed's heritage—the Brittany was bred to work a full day, every day, in the field. Needless to say, puppies should never be forced to exercise. Normally, they are little dynamos of energy and keep themselves busy all day long, interspersing play with frequent naps.

Mature Brittanys are not only capable of jogging, they are delighted to be running companions. It is important, however, to use good judgment with any exercise program. Begin slowly and gradually increase the distance covered over an extended period of time. Use special precautions in hot weather. High temperatures and forced exercise are a dangerous combination.

The best exercise for a Brittany is one that he acquires in the pursuit of the many organized activities for which the breed is particularly well suited. Hunting, agility, flyball, and obedience activities exercise the Brittany's mind and his body. There is no better way to ensure your Brittany of a happy, healthy existence.

SOCIALIZATION

A young dog that has never been exposed to strangers, traffic noise, or boisterous children could become confused and frightened. It is important that a Brittany owner give his or her dog the opportunity to experience all of these situations

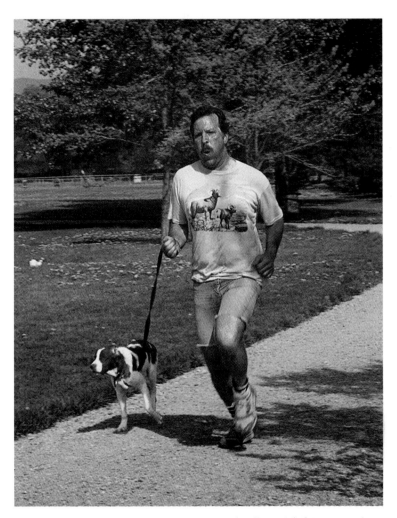

Because the Brittany was bred to be a working dog, he needs an ample amount of exercise to keep fit. Most Brittanys make excellent and enthusiastic jogging companions.

gradually, with his trusted owner present for support. Brittanys are good-natured and happy dogs and are very pleasant to be around. They are social by nature, but any dog that is never given the opportunity to experience new and different things will grow quite hesitant about life in general. Help your Brittany to develop the wonderful, loving personality that is his heritage.

HOUSEBREAKING and Training Your Brittany

There is no breed of dog that cannot be trained. It does appear that some breeds are more difficult to get the desired response from than others. In many cases, however, this has more to do with the trainer and his training methods than the dog's inability to learn. With the proper approach, any dog that is not mentally deficient can be taught to be a good canine citizen. Many dog owners do not understand how a dog learns or that they should be breed-specific in their approach to training.

Brittanys are extremely sensitive animals. Whereas it may be necessary to employ stern measures to get the attention of some breeds, a Brittany will be shattered by a scolding. The

Young Brittanys are very intelligent and have an amazing capacity to learn whatever you wish to teach them.

Do not let your puppy do something that you do not want him to continue to do as an adult. Four-month-old Millette's Try Tri Again looks pretty comfortable on the furniture.

breed lives to please; all an owner needs to do is let the mischievous Brittany know he has misbehaved and he will have a dejected little fellow on his hands.

Young Brittany puppies have an amazing capacity to learn that is greater than most humans realize. It is important to remember, though, that these young puppies also forget quickly unless they are reminded of what they have learned by continual reinforcement.

As Brittany puppies leave the litter, they begin searching for two things: a pack leader and the rules set down by that leader. Many owners fail miserably in supplying these very basic needs. Instead, they immediately respond to the demands of the puppy, and this can lead to a very confused and demanding youngster.

For example, a Brittany puppy quickly discovers that he will be allowed into the house because he is whining, instead of learning that he can only enter the house when he is not whining. Instead of learning that the only way he will be fed is to follow a set procedure (i.e., sitting or lying down on command), the poorly educated Brittany puppy learns that leaping about the kitchen, barking up a storm, or creating a stir is what gets results.

The key to successful training lies in establishing the proper relationship between dog and owner. The owner, or owning family, must be the pack leader and must provide the rules by which the dog abides. Once this is established, a Brittany will live to be praised by his pack leader.

The Brittany is easily trained to do almost any task. It is important to remember, however, that the breed does not comprehend violent treatment. A Brittany's spirit can be broken very quickly and easily by heavy-handed treatment. Patient, positive reinforcement is the key to successful training. Always show your dog the right thing to do and be consistent in having him behave that way.

Puppies will have to eliminate after eating, drinking, sleeping, and playing. Make sure that your Brittany has ample time outside to tend to his needs.

Housebreaking and training are easy with a Brittany. (My daughter is convinced that if our Brittanys could only reach the pedals, they would be driving us to dog shows!) A recommended method of housebreaking is to avoid accidents before they happen. Take a puppy outdoors to relieve himself after every meal, every nap, and after every 15 or 20 minutes of playtime. Carry the puppy outdoors to avoid the possibility of an accident occurring on the way.

CRATE TRAINING

Housebreaking your Brittany becomes a much easier task with the use of a crate. Most breeders use the fiberglass crates approved by the airlines for shipping live animals. They are

Provide your Brittany with a crate that he can use as his den. Line it with a blanket and give him some toys to make him more comfortable.

easy to clean and can be used throughout the dog's lifetime.

Some first-time dog owners may see the crate method of housebreaking as cruel. What they do not understand is that all dogs need a place of their own to retreat to. A puppy will soon come to think of his crate as his own private den.

Use of a crate reduces housetraining time to an absolute minimum and avoids keeping a puppy under constant stress by incessantly correcting him for making mistakes in the house. The anticrate advocates who consider it cruel to confine a

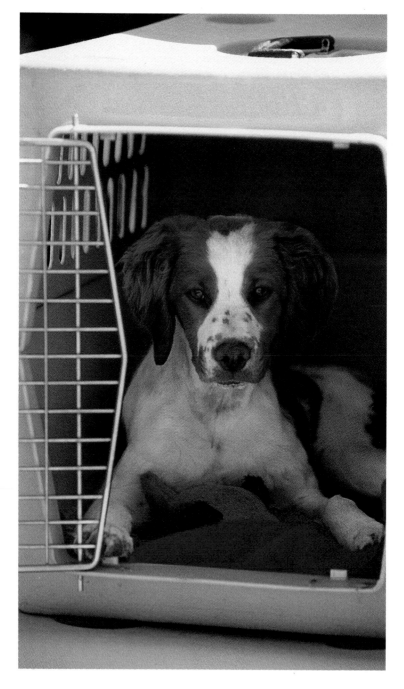

puppy for any length of time do not seem to have a problem with constantly harassing and punishing the puppy because he has wet on the carpet or relieved himself behind the sofa.

Begin training by using the crate when you feed your Brittany puppy his meals. Place him in the crate and keep the door closed and latched while the puppy is eating. When the meal is finished, open the crate and carry the puppy outdoors to the spot where you want him to learn to eliminate. In the event that you do not have outdoor access or will be away from home for long periods of time, begin housebreaking by placing newspapers in an out-of-the-way corner that the puppy can easily get to. If you consistently take your puppy to that same spot, you will reinforce the habit of going there for that purpose.

As your Brittany puppy grows, you will undoubtedly want to train him to eliminate outdoors and, in many cases, the dog will prefer to do so. This can be accomplished very simply by getting the paper-trained puppy outdoors immediately after eating. Lavishing praise after the puppy has eliminated often gets the message across.

It is important that you do not let the puppy loose after eating. Young puppies will eliminate almost immediately after eating or drinking. They will also be ready to relieve themselves when they first wake up and after playing. If you keep a watchful eye on your puppy, you will quickly learn when this is about to take place. A puppy usually circles and sniffs the floor just before he relieves himself. Do not give him any opportunity to learn that he can eliminate in the house or away from his designated spot. Your housetraining chores will be reduced considerably if you avoid bad habits from being learned in the first place.

If you are unable to watch your puppy every minute, he should be in his crate, with the door securely latched. Each time you put your puppy in the crate, give him a small treat of some kind. Throw the treat to the back of the crate and encourage the puppy to walk in on his own. When he does so, praise him and perhaps hand him another piece of the treat through the wires of the crate door.

Crate training is the fastest and easiest way to housebreak your Brittany.

Understand that an 8- to 12-week-old Brittany puppy will not be able to

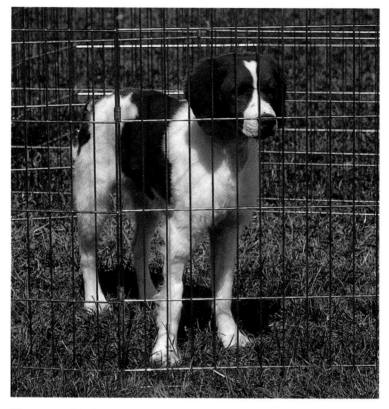

If you need to leave your Brittany unattended, put him in a safe enclosure to keep him out of mischief.

contain himself for long periods of time. Puppies that age must relieve themselves often, except during the night. Your schedule must be adjusted accordingly.

Also, make sure that your puppy has relieved himself just before the last member of the family retires for the evening.

Your first priority in the morning is to get the puppy outdoors. How early this will take place will depend much more on your puppy than on you. If your Brittany is like most other puppies, there will be no doubt in your mind when he needs to be let out. You will also quickly learn to tell the difference between the puppy's "emergency" signals and just unhappy grumbling. Do not test the young puppy's ability to contain himself. His vocal demand to be let out is confirmation that the housebreaking lesson is being learned.

Naturally, if you find it necessary to be away from home all day, you will not be able to leave your puppy in a crate. However, do not make the mistake of allowing him to roam the house, or even a large room, at will. Confine the puppy to a small room or partitioned-off area and cover the floor with newspaper. Make this area large enough so that the puppy does not have to relieve himself next to his bed, food, or water bowls. You will soon find that the puppy will be inclined to use one particular spot to perform his bowel and bladder functions. When you are home, take the puppy to this exact spot to eliminate at the appropriate time.

Basic obedience training is necessary if you want your Brittany to go on to more advanced training.

BASIC TRAINING

It is important for Brittany owners to remember that the breed thrives on learning. The Brittany has a great capacity to learn and the best training tip offered the new owner is to proceed with lots of patience and much repetition. If your dog is learning easily and suddenly won't do anything for you, go back one step in the training process and retrain before going forward.

Training should never take place when you are irritated, distressed, or preoccupied. Nor should you begin basic training in crowded or noisy areas that will interfere with your dog's concentration. Once the commands are understood and learned, you can begin testing your dog in public places. First, the two of you should work in an environment where you can concentrate fully upon each other.

The No Command

There is no doubt whatsoever that one of the most important commands your Brittany puppy will ever learn is the meaning of the word, "no." It is critical that your puppy learns this command as soon as possible. One important piece of advice in using this and all other commands—never give a command you are not prepared and able to enforce! The only way a puppy learns to obey commands is to realize that once issued, commands must be complied with. Learning the no command should begin the first day of the puppy's arrival at your home.

Leash or Lead Training

It is never too early to accustom your puppy to his leash and collar, which are a fail-safe way of keeping your dog under control. It may not be necessary for the puppy or adult Brittany to wear his collar and identification tags within the confines of your home, but no dog should ever leave the house without wearing a collar and without the attached leash held securely in your hand. Some countries require dogs to be leashed at all times in public places.

Teaching your dog to walk on a leash will not only keep him safe; it will also make your outings much more enjoyable.

Begin training by putting a soft collar around your puppy's neck for a few minutes at a time, gradually extending

Retractable leashes provide dogs with freedom while allowing the owner complete control. Leashes are available in a wide variety of lengths for all breeds of dog. Photo courtesy of Flexi-USA, Inc.

the time you leave it on. Most Brittany puppies become accustomed to their collar very quickly and, after a few scratches to remove it, forget they are even wearing one.

While you are playing with the puppy, attach a lightweight leash to the collar. Do not try to guide the puppy yet. The point here is to accustom the puppy to the feeling of having something attached to the collar.

Encourage your puppy to follow you as you move away. If the puppy is reluctant to cooperate, coax him with a treat of some kind. Hold the treat in front of the puppy's nose to encourage him to follow you. As the puppy takes a few steps toward you, praise him enthusiastically, and continue to do so as you move along.

Make the initial sessions short and fun. Continue the lessons in your home or yard until the puppy is completely unconcerned about the fact that he is on a leash. With a treat in one hand and the leash in the other, you can begin to guide the puppy in the direction you wish to go. Begin your first

walks in front of the house and eventually extend them down
the street and around the block.

The Come Command

Another very important lesson for the any puppy to learn is
to come when called. Therefore, it is vital that the puppy
learns his name as soon as possible. Constantly repeating the
dog's name is what does the trick. Use the puppy's name every
time you speak to him. "Want to go outside, Lad?" "Come, Lad,
come!"

Learning to come on command could save your Brittany's
life when the two of you venture out into the world. A dog
needs to understand that he must obey the come command
without question, but he should not associate the command
with fear. Your dog's response to his name and the word
"come" should always be connected with a pleasant
experience, such as receiving great praise, being pet, or
getting a food treat.

All too often novice trainers get very angry at their dogs for
not responding immediately to the come command. If the
owner scolds the dog for not obeying, when the dog finally
does come or after he's chased he will begin to associate the
word "come" with an unpleasant result.

It is much easier to avoid learning bad habits than it is to
correct them once set. At all costs, avoid giving the come
command unless you are sure your puppy will come to you.
Also, the very young puppy is far more inclined to respond to
learning the come command than an older dog that will be less
dependent on you.

Initially, use the command when the puppy is already on his
way to you, or give the command while walking or running
away from him. Clap your hands and sound very excited about
having him join in on this "game."

The very young Brittany will normally want to stay as close
to his owner as possible, especially in strange surroundings.
When your puppy sees you moving away, his natural
inclination will be to get close to you. This is a perfect time to
use the come command.

Later, as a puppy grows more self-confident and
independent, you may want to attach a long leash or rope to
his collar to ensure the correct response. Again, do not chase

or punish your dog for not obeying the come command. Doing so in the initial stages of training makes him associate the command with something to fear, which will result in avoidance rather than the immediate positive response you desire. It is imperative that you praise your puppy and give him a treat when he does come to you, even if he voluntarily delays responding for several minutes.

The Sit and Stay Commands

Learning the sit and stay commands is as important to your Brittany's safety (and your sanity!) as the no command and learning to come when called. Even very young puppies can learn the sit command quickly, especially if it appears to be a game and a food treat is involved.

Obedience classes will help you train your Brittany and will allow him time to socialize with other dogs.

Your puppy should always be on a collar and leash for his lessons. Young pups are not beyond getting up and walking away when they have decided you and your lessons are boring.

Give the sit command immediately before gently pushing down on your puppy's hindquarters or scooping his hind legs from under him to mold him into a sitting position. Praise him lavishly when he does sit, even though it is you who made the action take place. Again, a food treat always seems to get the lesson across to a learning youngster.

Continue holding the dog's rump down as you repeat the sit command several times. If your dog makes an attempt to get up, repeat the command again, while exerting light pressure on the rear end until the correct position is assumed. Make your Brittany stay in this position for increasing lengths of time with each training session. Begin with a few seconds and increase the amount of time as lessons progress over the following weeks.

If your young student attempts to get up or to lie down, correct him by simply saying, "sit!" in a firm voice. The command should be accompanied by returning the dog to the desired position. Your dog should get up only when you decide he should be allowed to do so.

When you decide that your puppy can get up, call his name, and say, "OK." Make a big fuss over him. Praise and a food treat are in order every time your puppy responds correctly.

Do not test a young puppy's patience to the limits. Remember that you are dealing with a baby. The attention span of any youngster, canine or human, is relatively short.

The Brittany's natural love of the outdoors and great desire to please make him an enthusiastic and instinctual hunter.

Once your puppy has mastered the sit lesson, you may begin teaching the stay command. With your dog on leash and facing you, command him to sit and then take a step or two backward. If your dog attempts to get up to follow, firmly say, "Sit, stay!" While you are saying this, raise your hand, palm toward the dog, and again command, "Stay!"

Any attempt on your dog's part to get up must be corrected at once by returning him to the sit position and repeating the command, "Stay!" Once your Brittany begins to understand what you want, you can gradually increase the distance you step back. With a long leash attached to your dog's collar (even a clothesline will do), start with a few steps and gradually increase the distance to several yards. Your Brittany must eventually learn that the sit/stay command must be obeyed regardless of how far away you are. Later on, with advanced

The sit command is the foundation for all the other commands because it teaches your Brittany self-control.

training, your dog will learn that the command must be obeyed, even when you move entirely out of sight.

As your Brittany masters this lesson and is able to remain in the sit position for as long as you dictate, avoid calling him to you at first. This will make the dog overly anxious to get up and run to you. Instead, walk back to your dog and say, "OK," which will be a signal that the sit/stay command is over. Later, when your Brittany becomes more reliable in this lesson, it will be acceptable to begin calling him to you.

Teaching the sit/stay lesson can take considerable time and patience, especially with the puppy whose attention span will be very short. It is best to keep the stay command part of the lesson to a minimum until the puppy is at least five or six months old. Everything about a young Brittany's makeup urges him to stay close to you wherever you go. Forcing a young puppy to operate against his natural instincts can be bewildering.

The Down Command

Once your Brittany has mastered the sit and stay commands, you may begin work on the down command. This is the single-word command for lie down. Use the down command only when you want the dog to lie down. If you want your dog to get off your sofa or to stop jumping up on people, use the off command. Do not interchange these two commands. Doing so will only confuse your dog, after which evoking the right response will become next to impossible.

The down position is especially useful when you want your Brittany to remain in a particular place for a long period of time. A dog is usually far more inclined to stay put when he is lying down than when he is sitting.

Teaching your Brittany this command may require more time and patience than the previous lessons. Some animal behaviorists believe that assuming the down position somehow represents submissiveness to the dog.

Every experience, whether good or bad, will affect your dog's attitude toward training. If he has positive experiences in the field, your Brittany will be eager to hunt with you.

With your dog seated facing you, hold a treat in your right hand and the excess part of the leash in your left hand. Hold the treat under the dog's nose and slowly bring your hand down to the ground. Your dog will follow the treat with his head and neck. As he does, give the down command and exert light pressure on the dog's shoulders with your left hand. If your dog resists the pressure on his shoulders, do not continue pushing down; doing so will only create more resistance.

An alternative method of getting your Brittany into the down position is to move around to the dog's right side and, as you draw his attention downward with your right hand, slide your left hand or arm under the dog's front legs, gently sliding them forward. In the case of a very young Brittany puppy, you will undoubtedly have to be on your knees in order to do this.

As your dog's forelegs begin to slide out in front of him, keep moving the treat along the floor until the dog's whole body is lying on the ground, while continually repeating the word, "down." Once your Brittany has assumed the position you desire, give him the treat and a lot of praise. Continue assisting your dog into the down position until he does it on

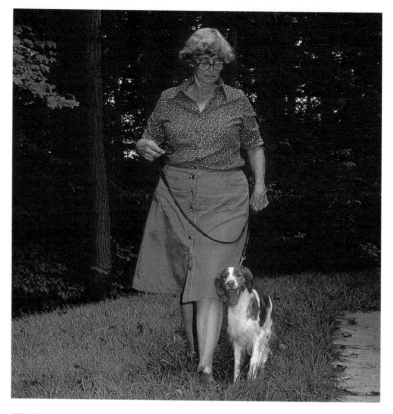

The heel command will help your Brittany learn to walk by your side without pulling or tugging.

his own. Be firm and patient, and be prepared for those occasional "I have no idea what you mean" looks your Brittany student may give you.

The Heel Command

In learning to heel, your dog should walk on your left side, with his shoulder next to your leg, no matter which direction you might go or how quickly you turn. Teaching your Brittany to heel will not only make your daily walks far more enjoyable, it will make your dog a far more tractable companion when the two of you are in crowded or confusing situations.

A lightweight, link-chain training collar is very useful for the heel lesson. It provides both quick pressure around the neck and a snapping sound, both of which get the dog's attention.

Erroneously referred to as a "choke collar," the link-chain, when properly used, does not choke the dog. The pet shop where you purchase the training collar will be able to show you the proper way to put it on your dog. Do not leave this collar on your puppy when training sessions are finished. Puppies are ingenious at getting their lower jaw or legs caught in the training chain. Changing to the link-chain collar at training time also signals your Brittany that he must get down to the business at hand.

When you begin training your puppy to walk on the leash, teach him to walk on your left side. The leash should cross your body from the dog's collar to your right hand. The excess portion of the leash will be folded into your right hand, and you will use your left hand on the leash to make corrections.

Treats can be a great motivational tool to use when training your Brittany.

A quick, short jerk on the leash with your left hand will keep your dog from lunging from side to side, pulling ahead, or lagging behind. As you make a correction, give the heel command. Keep the leash slack when your dog maintains the proper position at your side.

If your Brittany begins to drift away, give the leash a sharp jerk and guide him back to the correct position as you give the heel command. Do not pull on the leash with steady pressure. What is needed is a sharp but gentle jerking motion to get your dog's attention.

TRAINING CLASSES

There are few limits to what a patient, consistent Brittany owner can teach his dog. For advanced obedience work beyond the basics, however, it is wise for the inexperienced owner to consider local professional assistance. Professional trainers have had long standing experience avoiding the pitfalls of obedience training and can help you to avoid these mistakes as well.

This training assistance can be obtained in many ways. Group classes are particularly good for your Brittany's socialization and attentiveness skills. The dog will learn that he must obey, even when other dogs and people are around providing the temptation to run off and play. You can find free-of-charge classes at many parks and recreational facilities, as well as very formal, and sometimes very expensive, individual lessons with private trainers.

Some obedience schools will train your Brittany for you. However, unless your schedule does not provide any time to train your own dog, having someone else train the dog for you would be last on our list of recommendations. The rapport that develops between the dog and owner who has trained his Brittany to be a pleasant companion and good canine citizen is very special—well worth the time and patience it requires.

Accustoming your Brittany to the scents of the game and the field will make him more receptive to training exercises.

Versatility

The Brittany's intelligence, energy, stamina, and desire to please have led him to a variety of highly specialized roles.

Field Work

As we have repeatedly said, the Brittany is a natural-born hunter. Whether this ability is used to put dinner on the owner's table or purely for recreational purposes is entirely up to the owner. It would, however, be unfortunate to deny the dog his birthright or to deny the owner of the thrilling prospect of seeing his dog perform in the capacity for which the breed was created.

The Brittany has been a longtime worker, guardian, and companion to man. Ch. Millette's Regal Sherry owned by the author.

Hearing and Sight Dogs

The Brittany trained as a hearing or sight dog can be used in the home to help the hearing impaired by alerting the person that the doorbell or telephone has rung. Sight assistance dogs can be trained to locate objects or help their restricted-vision owners to avoid falls.

Therapy Dogs

Brittanys love people and are extremely successful in providing retirement home residents and hospital patients with the feeling that someone really cares about them. Brittanys, of course, love children, and when the dogs make appearances at children's hospitals, the youngsters are absolutely delighted.

Throughout the ages, the Brittany has been a worker, a guard, and a companion to mankind. Through the efforts of dedicated breeders and guardians of the breed, the Brittany has remained consistently popular. This is a breed eager and willing to please, and one that never needs a rough hand to develop its intelligence and versatility. Those are qualities that are a part of the Brittany's heritage and are given freely to the families they love.

SPORT of Purebred Dogs

elcome to the exciting and sometimes frustrating sport of dogs. No doubt you are trying to learn more about dogs or you wouldn't be deep into this book. This section covers the basics that may entice you, further your knowledge and help you to understand the dog world.

Dog showing has been a very popular sport for a long time and has been taken quite seriously by some. Others only enjoy it as a hobby.

The Kennel Club in England was formed in 1859, the American Kennel Club was established in 1884 and the Canadian Kennel Club was formed in 1888. The purpose of these clubs was to register purebred dogs and maintain their Stud Books. In the beginning, the concept of registering dogs was not readily accepted. More than 36 million dogs have been enrolled in the AKC Stud Book since its inception in 1888. Presently the kennel clubs not only register dogs but adopt and enforce rules and regulations governing dog shows, obedience trials and field trials. Over the years they have fostered and encouraged interest in the health and welfare of the purebred dog. They routinely donate funds to veterinary research for study on genetic disorders.

Below are the addresses of the kennel clubs in the United States, Great Britain, and Canada.

The American Kennel Club
51 Madison Avenue
New York, NY 10010
(Their registry is located at: 5580 Centerview Drive, STE 200, Raleigh, NC 27606-3390)

The Kennel Club
1 Clarges Street
Piccadilly, London, WIY 8AB, England

The Canadian Kennel Club
100-89 Skyway Avenue
Etobicoke, Ontario
Canada M9W6R4

Today there are numerous activities that are enjoyable for both the dog and the handler. Some of the activities include conformation showing, obedience competition, tracking, agility, the Canine Good Citizen Certificate, and a wide range of instinct tests that vary from breed to breed. Where you start depends upon your goals which early on may not be readily apparent.

PUPPY KINDERGARTEN

Every puppy will benefit from this class. PKT is the foundation for all future dog activities from conformation to "couch potatoes." Pet owners should make an effort to attend even if they never expect to show their dog. The class is designed for puppies about three months of age with graduation at approximately five months of age. All the puppies will be in the same age group and, even though some may be a little unruly, there should not be any real problem. This class will teach the puppy some beginning obedience. As in all obedience classes the owner learns how to train his own dog. The PKT class gives the puppy the opportunity to interact with other puppies in the same age group and exposes him to strangers, which is very important. Some dogs grow up with

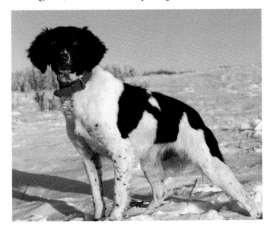

The robust and powerful Brittany is happiest when at work. Razmataz Bailiff, MH owned by Rod Dobey, was the youngest Brittany to earn his Master Hunter title.

Whether working in the field or playing at home, every puppy can benefit from obedience training.

behavior problems, one of them being fear of strangers. As you can see, there can be much to gain from this class.

There are some basic obedience exercises that every dog should learn. Some of these can be started with puppy kindergarten.

CONFORMATION

Conformation showing is our oldest dog show sport. This type of showing is based on the dog's appearance—that is his structure, movement and attitude. When considering this type of showing, you need to be aware of your breed's standard and be able to evaluate your dog compared to that standard. The breeder of your puppy or other experienced breeders would be good sources for such an evaluation. Puppies can go through lots of changes over a period of time. Many puppies start out as promising hopefuls and then after maturing may be disappointing as show candidates. Even so this should not deter them from being excellent pets.

Usually conformation training classes are offered by the local kennel or obedience clubs. These are excellent places for training puppies. The puppy should be able to walk on a lead before entering such a class. Proper ring procedure and technique for posing (stacking) the dog will be demonstrated as well as gaiting the dog. Usually certain patterns are used in the ring such as the triangle or the "L." Conformation class, like the PKT class, will give your youngster the opportunity to socialize with different breeds of dogs and humans too.

In conformation, your dog will be judged on how closely he conforms to the standard of the breed.

It takes some time to learn the routine of conformation showing. Usually one starts at the puppy matches that may be AKC Sanctioned or Fun Matches. These matches are generally for puppies from two or three months to a year old, and there may be classes for the adult over the age of 12 months. Similar to point shows, the classes are divided by sex and after completion of the classes in that breed or variety, the class winners compete for Best of Breed or Variety. The winner goes on to compete in the Group and the Group winners compete for Best in Match. No championship points are awarded for match wins.

A few matches can be great training for puppies even though there is no intention to go on showing. Matches enable the puppy to meet new people and be handled by a stranger—the judge. It is also a change of environment, which broadens the horizon for both dog and handler. Matches and other dog activities boost the confidence of the handler and especially the younger handlers.

Earning an AKC championship is built on a point system, which is different from Great Britain. To become an AKC Champion of Record the dog must earn 15 points. The number of points earned each time depends upon the number of dogs in competition. The number of points available at each show depends upon the breed, its sex and the location of the show. The United States is divided into ten AKC zones. Each zone has its own set of points. The purpose of the zones is to try to equalize the points available from breed to breed and area to area. The AKC adjusts the point scale annually.

Junior showmanship is a wonderful way to build a child's confidence and start a strong foundation in the world of dog sports.

The number of points that can be won at a show are between one and five. Three-, four- and five-point wins are considered majors. Not only does the dog need 15 points won under three different judges, but those points must include two majors under two different judges. Canada also works on a point system but majors are not required.

Dogs always show before bitches. The classes available to those seeking points are: Puppy (which may be divided into 6 to 9 months and 9 to 12 months); 12 to 18 months; Novice; Bred-by-Exhibitor; American-bred; and Open. The class winners of the same sex of each breed or variety compete against each other for Winners Dog and Winners Bitch. A Reserve Winners Dog and Reserve Winners Bitch are also awarded but do not carry any points unless the Winners win is disallowed by AKC. The Winners Dog and Bitch compete with the specials (those dogs that have attained championship) for Best of Breed or Variety, Best of Winners and Best of Opposite Sex. It is possible to pick up an extra point or even a major if the points are higher for the defeated winner than those of Best of Winners. The latter would get the higher total from the defeated winner.

At an all-breed show, each Best of Breed or Variety winner will go on to his respective Group and then the Group winners will compete against each other for Best in Show. There are seven Groups: Sporting, Hounds, Working, Terriers, Toys, Non-Sporting and Herding. Obviously there are no Groups at

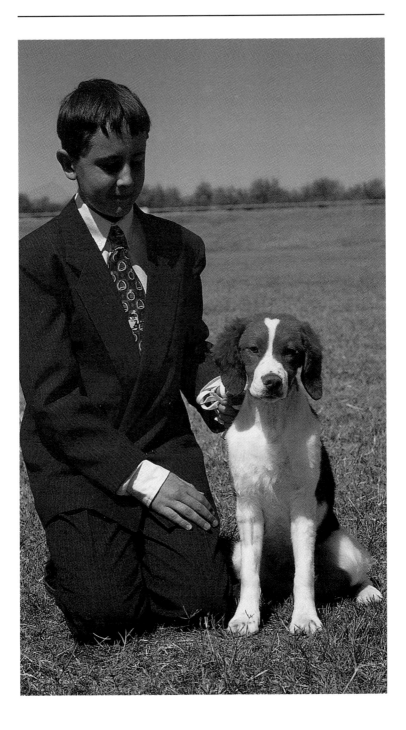

speciality shows (those shows that have only one breed or a show such as the American Spaniel Club's Flushing Spaniel Show, which is for all flushing spaniel breeds).

Earning a championship in England is somewhat different since they do not have a point system. Challenge Certificates are awarded if the judge feels the dog is deserving regardless of the number of dogs in competition. A dog must earn three Challenge Certificates under three different judges, with at least one of these Certificates being won after the age of 12 months. Competition is very strong and entries may be higher than they are in the US. The Kennel Club's Challenge Certificates are only available at Championship Shows.

In England, The Kennel Club regulations require that certain dogs, Border Collies and Gundog breeds, qualify in a working capacity (i.e., obedience or field trials) before becoming a full Champion. If they do not qualify in the working aspect, then they are designated a Show Champion, which is equivalent to the AKC's Champion of Record. A Gundog may be granted the title of Field Trial Champion (FT Ch.) if it passes all the tests in the field but would also have to qualify in conformation before becoming a full Champion. A Border Collie that earns the title of Obedience Champion (Ob Ch.) must also qualify in the conformation ring before becoming a Champion.

The US doesn't have a designation full Champion but does award for Dual and Triple Champions. The Dual Champion must be a Champion of Record, and either Champion Tracker, Herding Champion, Obedience Trial Champion or Field Champion. Any dog that has been awarded the titles of Champion of Record, and any two of the following: Champion Tracker, Herding Champion, Obedience Trial Champion or Field Champion, may be designated as a Triple Champion.

The shows in England seem to put more emphasis on breeder judges than those in the US. There is much competition within the breeds. Therefore the quality of the individual breeds should be very good. In the United States we tend to have more "all around judges" (those that judge multiple breeds) and use the breeder judges at the specialty shows. Breeder judges are more familiar with their own breed since they are actively breeding that breed or did so at one time. Americans emphasize Group and Best in Show wins and promote them accordingly.

The shows in England can be very large and extend over several days, with the Groups being scheduled on different days. Though multi-day shows are not common in the US, there are cluster shows, where several different clubs will use the same show site over consecutive days.

Westminster Kennel Club is our most prestigious show although the entry is limited to 2500. In recent years, entry has been limited to Champions. This show is more formal than the majority of the shows with the judges wearing formal attire and the handlers fashionably dressed. In most instances the quality of the dogs is superb. After all, it is a show of Champions. It is a good show to study the AKC registered breeds and is by far the most exciting—especially since it

A dog that competes in conformation will need to be perfectly groomed. Luckily for Brittany owners, it's a fairly easy job to keep your dog looking good.

is televised! WKC is one of the few shows in this country that is still benched. This means the dog must be in his benched area during the show hours except when he is being groomed, in the ring, or being exercised.

Typically, the handlers are very particular about their appearances. They are careful not to wear something that will detract from their dog but will perhaps enhance it. American ring procedure is quite formal compared to that of other countries. There is a certain etiquette expected between the judge and exhibitor and among the other exhibitors. Of course it is not always the case but the judge is supposed to be polite, not engaging in small talk or acknowledging how well he knows the handler. There is a more informal and relaxed atmosphere at the shows in other countries. For instance, the dress code is more casual. I can see where this might be more fun for the exhibitor and especially for the novice. The U.S. is very handler-oriented in many of the breeds. It is true, in most instances, that the experienced professional handler can present the dog better and will have a feel for what a judge likes.

In England, Crufts is The Kennel Club's own show and is most assuredly the largest dog show in the world. They've been known to have an entry of nearly 20,000, and the show lasts four days. Entry is only gained by qualifying through winning in specified classes at another Championship Show. Westminster is strictly conformation, but Crufts exhibitors and spectators enjoy not only conformation but obedience, agility and a multitude of exhibitions as well. Obedience was admitted in 1957 and agility in 1983.

If you are handling your own dog, please give some consideration to your apparel. For sure the dress code at matches is more informal than the point shows. However, you should wear something a little more appropriate than beach attire or ragged jeans and bare feet. If you check out the handlers and see what is presently fashionable, you'll catch on. Men usually dress with a shirt and tie and a nice sports coat. Whether you are male or female, you will want to wear comfortable clothes and shoes. You need to be able to run with your dog and you certainly don't want to take a chance of falling and hurting yourself. Heaven forbid, if nothing else, you'll upset your dog. Women usually wear a dress or two-piece outfit, preferably with pockets to carry bait, comb, brush, etc. In this case men are the lucky ones with all their pockets. Ladies, think about where your dress will be if you need to kneel on the floor and also think about running. Does it allow freedom to do so?

You need to take along dog; crate; ex pen (if you use one); extra newspaper; water pail and water; all required grooming equipment, including hair dryer and extension cord; table; chair for you; bait for dog and lunch for you and friends; and, last but not least, clean up materials, such as plastic bags, paper towels, and perhaps a bath towel and some shampoo— just in case. Don't forget your entry confirmation and directions to the show.

If you are showing in obedience, then you will want to wear pants. Many of our top obedience handlers wear pants that are color-coordinated with their dogs. The philosophy is that imperfections in the black dog will be less obvious next to your black pants.

Whether you are showing in conformation, Junior Showmanship or obedience, you need to watch the clock and be sure you are not late. It is customary to pick up your conformation armband a few minutes before the start of the class. They will not wait for you and if you are on the show grounds and not in the ring, you will upset everyone. It's a little more complicated picking up your obedience armband if you show later in the class. If you have not picked up your armband and they get to your number, you may not be allowed to show. It's best to pick up your armband early, but then you may show earlier than expected if other handlers don't pick up. Customarily all conflicts should be discussed with the judge prior to the start of the class.

Retrieving skills are inherent in the Brittany, which is why they are so popular and successful in field trials.

Junior Showmanship

The Junior Showmanship Class is

a wonderful way to build self-confidence even if there are no aspirations of staying with the dog-show game later in life. Frequently, Junior Showmanship becomes the background of those who become successful exhibitors/handlers in the future. In some instances it is taken very seriously, and success is measured in terms of wins. The Junior Handler is judged solely on his ability and skill in presenting his dog. The dog's conformation is not to be considered by the judge. Even so the condition and grooming of the dog may be a reflection upon the handler.

Usually the matches and point shows include different classes. The Junior Handler's dog may be entered in a breed or obedience class and even shown by another person in that class. Junior Showmanship classes are usually divided by age and perhaps sex. The age is determined by the handler's age on the day of the show.

There are certain pieces of equipment that are very useful to bring to a dog show. An exercise pen can help keep your Brittanys confined in a safe area.

CANINE GOOD CITIZEN

The AKC sponsors a program to encourage dog owners to train their dogs. Local clubs perform the pass/fail tests, and dogs who pass are awarded a Canine Good Citizen Certificate. Proof of vaccination is required at the time of participation. The test includes:

1. Accepting a friendly stranger.
2. Sitting politely for petting.
3. Appearance and grooming.
4. Walking on a loose leash.
5. Walking through a crowd.
6. Sit and down on command/staying in place.
7. Come when called.
8. Reaction to another dog.

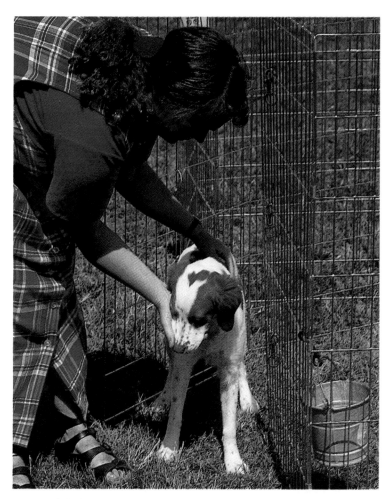

Successful showing requires preparation and dedication, but most of all it should be enjoyable for both the dogs and their handlers.

9. Reactions to distractions.
10. Supervised separation.

If more effort was made by pet owners to accomplish these exercises, fewer dogs would be cast off to the humane shelter.

OBEDIENCE

Obedience is necessary, without a doubt, but it can also become a wonderful hobby or even an obsession. Obedience classes and competition can provide wonderful companionship, not only with your dog but with your classmates or fellow competitors. It is always gratifying to discuss your dog's problems with others who have had similar experiences. The AKC acknowledged Obedience around 1936, and it has changed tremendously even though many of the exercises are basically the same. Today, obedience competition is just that—very competitive. Even so, it is possible for every obedience exhibitor to come home a winner (by earning qualifying scores) even though he/she may not earn a placement in the class.

Most of the obedience titles are awarded after earning three qualifying scores (legs) in the appropriate class under three different judges. These classes offer a perfect score of 200, which is extremely rare. Each of the class exercises has its own point value. A leg is earned after receiving a score of at least 170 and at least 50 percent of the points available in each exercise. The titles are:

Companion Dog—CD
Companion Dog Excellent—CDX
Utility Dog—UD

After achieving the UD title, you may feel inclined to go after the UDX and/or OTCh. The UDX (Utility Dog Excellent) title went into effect in January 1994. It is not easily attained. The title requires qualifying simultaneously ten times in Open B and Utility B but not necessarily at consecutive shows.

The OTCh (Obedience Trial Champion) is awarded after the dog has earned his UD and then goes on to earn 100 championship points, a first place in Utility, a first place in Open and another first place in either class. The placements must be won under three different judges at all-breed obedience trials. The points are determined by the number of dogs competing in the Open B and Utility B classes. The OTCh title precedes the dog's name.

Obedience matches (AKC Sanctioned, Fun, and Show and Go) are usually available. Usually they are sponsored by the local obedience clubs. When preparing an obedience dog for a title, you will find matches very helpful. Fun Matches and Show and Go Matches are more lenient in allowing you to make corrections in the ring. This type of training is usually very necessary for the Open and Utility Classes. AKC Sanctioned Obedience Matches do not allow corrections in the ring since they must abide by the AKC Obedience Regulations. If you are interested in showing in obedience, then you should contact the AKC for a copy of the Obedience Regulations.

TRACKING

Tracking is officially classified obedience. There are three tracking titles available: Tracking Dog (TD), Tracking Dog Excellent (TDX), Variable Surface Tracking (VST). If all three tracking titles are obtained, then the dog officially becomes a CT (Champion Tracker). The CT will go in front of the dog's name.

A TD may be earned anytime and does not have to follow the other obedience titles. There are many exhibitors that prefer tracking to obedience, and there are others who do both.

Hunting tests measure a Brittany's skill in the field to determine if he is a suitable and competent hunting companion.

AGILITY

Agility was first introduced by John Varley in England at the

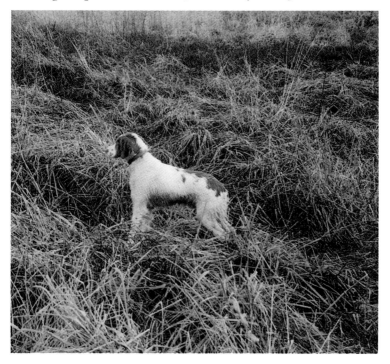

Crufts Dog Show, February 1978, but Peter Meanwell, competitor and judge, actually developed the idea. It was officially recognized in the early '80s. Agility is extremely popular in England and Canada and growing in popularity in the U.S. The AKC acknowledged agility in August 1994. Dogs must be at least 12 months of age to be entered. It is a fascinating sport that the dog, handler and spectators enjoy to the utmost. Agility is a spectator sport! The dog performs off lead. The handler either runs with his dog or positions himself on the course and directs his dog with verbal and hand signals over a timed course over or through a variety of obstacles including a time out or pause. One of the main drawbacks to agility is finding a place to train. The obstacles take up a lot of space and it is very time consuming to put up and take down courses.

The titles earned at AKC agility trials are Novice Agility Dog (NAD), Open Agility Dog (OAD), Agility Dog Excellent (ADX), and Master Agility Excellent (MAX). In order to acquire

Agility obstacles, like the bar jump, allow your Brittany to apply his natural abilities to the show ring.

Agility is just one of the many activities in which Brittanys can compete that shows off their athletic prowess.

an agility title, a dog must earn a qualifying score in its respective class on three separate occasions under two different judges. The MAX will be awarded after earning ten qualifying scores in the Agility Excellent Class.

PERFORMANCE TESTS

During the last decade the American Kennel Club has promoted performance tests–those events that test the different breeds' natural abilities. This type of event encourages a handler to devote even more time to his dog and retain the natural instincts of his breed heritage. It is an important part of the wonderful world of dogs.

For retrievers, pointing breeds and spaniels. Titles offered are Junior Hunter (JH), Senior Hunter (SH), and Master Hunter (MH).

Flushing Spaniels: Their primary purpose is to hunt, find, flush and return birds to hand as quickly as possible in a

Your Brittany must be able to find, flush out, and retrieve all types of game in order to receive his hunting title.

pleasing and obedient manner. The entrant must be at least six months of age and dogs with limited registration (ILP) are eligible. Game used are pigeons, pheasants, and quail.

Retrievers: Limited registration (ILP) retrievers are not eligible to compete in Hunting Tests. The purpose of a Hunting Test for retrievers is to test the merits of and evaluate the abilities of retrievers in the field in order to determine their suitability and ability as hunting companions. They are expected to retrieve any type of game bird, pheasants, ducks, pigeons, guinea hens and quail.

Pointing Breeds: Are eligible at six months of age, and dogs with limited registration (ILP) are permitted. They must show a keen desire to hunt; be bold and independent; have a fast, yet attractive, manner of hunting; and demonstrate intelligence not only in seeking objectives but also in the ability to find game. They must establish point, and in the more advanced tests they need to be steady to wing and must remain in position until the bird is shot or they are released.

A Senior Hunter must retrieve. A Master Hunter must honor. The judges and the marshal are permitted to ride horseback during the test, but all handling must be done on foot.

GENERAL INFORMATION

Obedience, tracking and agility allow the purebred dog with an Indefinite Listing Privilege (ILP) number or a limited registration to be exhibited and earn titles. Application must be made to the AKC for an ILP number.

The American Kennel Club publishes a monthly *Events* magazine that is part of the *Gazette*, their official journal for the sport of purebred dogs. The *Events* section lists upcoming shows and the secretary or superintendent for them. The majority of the conformation shows in the U.S. are overseen by licensed superintendents. Generally the entry closing date is approximately two-and-a-half weeks before the actual show. Point shows are fairly expensive, while the match shows cost about one third of the point show entry fee. Match shows usually take entries the day of the show but some are pre-entry. The best way to find match show information is through your local kennel club.

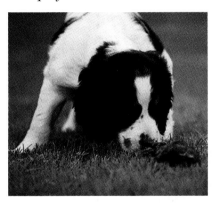

Hunting tests allow your Brittany to display his inherent talents.

Upon asking, the AKC can provide you with a list of superintendents, and you can write and ask to be put on their mailing lists.

Obedience trial and tracking test information is available through the AKC. Frequently these events are not superintended, but put on by the host club. Therefore you would make the entry with the event's secretary.

As you have read, there are numerous activities you can share with your dog. Regardless what you do, it does take teamwork. Your dog can only benefit from your attention and training. We hope this chapter has enlightened you and hope, if nothing else, you will attend a show here and there. Perhaps you will start with a puppy kindergarten class, and who knows where it may lead!

HEALTH CARE

Veterinary medicine has become far more sophisticated than what was available to our ancestors. This can be attributed to the increase in household pets and consequently the demand for better care for them. Also human medicine has become far more complex. Today diagnostic testing in veterinary medicine parallels human diagnostics. Because of better technology we can expect our pets to live healthier lives thereby increasing their life spans.

THE FIRST CHECKUP

You will want to take your new puppy/dog in for its first checkup within 48 to 72 hours after acquiring it. Many breeders strongly recommend this checkup and so do the humane shelters. A puppy/dog can appear healthy but it may have a serious problem that is not apparent to the layman. Most pets have some type of a minor flaw that may never cause a real problem.

Puppies are very vulnerable to certain diseases. You should take your new puppy to the veterinarian within 72 hours of acquiring him.

Unfortunately if he/she should have a serious problem, you will want to consider the consequences of keeping the pet and the attachments that will be formed, which may be broken prematurely. Keep in mind there are many healthy dogs looking for good homes.

This first check up is a good time to establish yourself with the veterinarian and learn the office policy regarding their hours and how they handle emergencies. Usually the breeder or another conscientious pet owner is a good reference for

By breeding only the best quality dogs, good health and temperament is passed down to each generation.

locating a capable veterinarian. You should be aware that not all veterinarians give the same quality of service. Please do not make your selection on the least expensive clinic, as they may be short changing your pet. There is the possibility that eventually it will cost you more due to improper diagnosis, treatment, etc. If you are selecting a new veterinarian, feel free to ask for a tour of the clinic. You should inquire about making an appointment for a tour since all clinics are working clinics, and therefore may not be available all day for sightseers. You may worry less if you see where your pet will be spending the day if he ever needs to be hospitalized.

THE PHYSICAL EXAM

Your veterinarian will check your pet's overall condition, which includes listening to the heart; checking the respiration; feeling the abdomen, muscles and joints; checking the mouth, which includes the gum color and signs of gum disease along with plaque buildup; checking the ears for signs of an infection or ear mites; examining the eyes; and, last but not least, checking the condition of the skin and coat.

He should ask you questions regarding your pet's eating and elimination habits and invite you to relay your questions. It is a good idea to prepare a list so as not to forget anything. He should discuss the proper diet and the quantity to be fed. If this should differ from your breeder's recommendation, then you should convey to him the breeder's choice and see if he approves. If he recommends changing the diet, then this should be done over a few days so as not to cause a gastrointestinal upset. It is customary to take in a fresh stool sample (just a small amount) for a test for intestinal parasites. It must be fresh, preferably within 12 hours, since the eggs hatch quickly and after hatching will not be observed under the microscope. If your pet isn't obliging then, usually the technician can take one in the clinic.

IMMUNIZATIONS

It is important that you take your puppy/dog's vaccination record with you on your first visit. In case of a puppy, presumably the breeder has seen to the vaccinations up to the time you acquired custody. Veterinarians differ in their vaccination protocol. It is not unusual for your puppy to have received vaccinations for distemper, hepatitis, leptospirosis, parvovirus and parainfluenza every two to three weeks from the age of five or six weeks. Usually this is a combined injection and is typically called the DHLPP. The DHLPP is given through at least 12 to 14 weeks of age, and it is customary to continue with another parvovirus vaccine at 16 to 18 weeks. You may wonder why so many immunizations are necessary. No one knows for sure when the puppy's maternal antibodies are gone, although it is customarily accepted that distemper antibodies are gone by 12 weeks. Usually parvovirus antibodies are gone by 16 to 18 weeks of age. However, it is possible for the maternal antibodies to be gone at a much earlier age or even a later age. Therefore immunizations are started at an early age. The vaccine will not give immunity as long as there are maternal antibodies.

The rabies vaccination is given at three or six months of age depending on your local laws. A vaccine for bordetella (kennel cough) is advisable and can be given anytime from the age of five weeks. The coronavirus is not commonly given unless there is a problem locally. The Lyme vaccine is necessary in endemic areas. Lyme disease has been reported in 47 states.

Distemper
This is virtually an incurable disease. If the dog recovers, he is subject to severe nervous disorders. The virus attacks every tissue in the body and resembles a bad cold with a fever. It can cause a runny nose and eyes and cause gastrointestinal disorders, including a poor appetite, vomiting and diarrhea. The virus is carried by raccoons, foxes, wolves, mink and other dogs. Unvaccinated youngsters and senior citizens are very susceptible. This is still a common disease.

Hepatitis
This is a virus that is most serious in very young dogs. It is spread by contact with an infected animal or its stool or urine. The virus affects the liver and kidneys and is characterized by high fever, depression and lack of appetite. Recovered animals may be afflicted with chronic illnesses.

Dogs can pick up diseases and parasites from other dogs, so be sure that your Brittany has all his vaccinations before taking him out to make friends.

Leptospirosis

This is a bacterial disease transmitted by contact with the urine of an infected dog, rat or other wildlife. It produces severe symptoms of fever, depression, jaundice and internal bleeding and was fatal before the vaccine was developed. Recovered dogs can be carriers, and the disease can be transmitted from dogs to humans.

Parvovirus

This was first noted in the late 1970s and is still a fatal disease. However, with proper vaccinations, early diagnosis and prompt treatment, it is a manageable disease. It attacks the bone marrow and intestinal tract. The symptoms include depression, loss of appetite, vomiting, diarrhea and collapse. Immediate medical attention is of the essence.

Rabies

This is shed in the saliva and is carried by raccoons, skunks, foxes, other dogs and cats. It attacks nerve tissue, resulting in paralysis and death. Rabies can be transmitted to people and is virtually always fatal. This disease is reappearing in the suburbs.

Bordetella (Kennel Cough)

The symptoms are coughing, sneezing, hacking and retching accompanied by nasal discharge usually lasting from a few days to several weeks. There are several disease-producing organisms responsible for this disease. The present vaccines are helpful but do not protect for all the strains. It usually is not life threatening but in some

Bordetella attached to canine cilia. Otherwise known as kennel cough, this highly contagious disease should be vaccinated against routinely.

instances it can progress to a serious bronchopneumonia. The disease is highly contagious. The vaccination should be given routinely for dogs that come in contact with other dogs, such as through boarding, training class or visits to the groomer.

The deer tick is the most common carrier of Lyme disease. Photo courtesy of Virbac Laboratories, Inc., Fort Worth, Texas.

Coronavirus

This is usually self limiting and not life threatening. It was first noted in the late '70s about a year before parvovirus. The virus produces a yellow/brown stool and there may be depression, vomiting and diarrhea.

Lyme Disease

This was first diagnosed in the United States in 1976 in Lyme, CT in people who lived in close proximity to the deer tick. Symptoms may include acute lameness, fever, swelling of joints and loss of appetite. Your veterinarian can advise you if you live in an endemic area.

After your puppy has completed his puppy vaccinations, you will continue to booster the DHLPP once a year. It is customary to booster the rabies one year after the first vaccine and then, depending on where you live, it should be boostered every year or every three years. This depends on your local laws. The Lyme and corona vaccines are boostered annually and it is recommended that the bordetella be boostered every six to eight months.

ANNUAL VISIT

I would like to impress the importance of the annual check up, which would include the booster vaccinations, check for intestinal parasites and test for heartworm. Today in our very busy world it is rush, rush and see "how much you can get for how little." Unbelievably, some non-veterinary businesses have entered into the vaccination business. More harm than good can come to your dog through improper vaccinations, possibly from inferior vaccines and/or the wrong schedule. More than likely you truly care about your companion dog and over the years you have devoted much time and expense to his well being. Perhaps you are unaware that a vaccination is not just a vaccination. There is more involved. Please, please follow through with regular physical examinations. It is so important for your veterinarian to know your dog and this is especially true during middle age through the geriatric years. More than likely your older dog will require more than one physical a year. The annual physical is good preventive medicine. Through early diagnosis and subsequent treatment your dog can maintain a longer and better quality of life.

INTESTINAL PARASITES

Hookworms

These are almost microscopic intestinal worms that can cause anemia and therefore serious problems, including death, in young puppies. Hookworms can be transmitted to humans through penetration of the skin. Puppies may be born with them.

Roundworms

These are spaghetti-like worms that can cause a potbellied appearance and dull coat along with more severe symptoms, such as vomiting, diarrhea and coughing. Puppies acquire these while in the mother's uterus and through lactation. Both hookworms and roundworms may be acquired through ingestion.

Whipworms

These have a three-month life cycle and are not acquired through the dam. They cause intermittent diarrhea usually with mucus. Whipworms are possibly the most difficult worm to eradicate. Their eggs are very resistant to most environmental factors and can last for years until the proper conditions enable them to mature. Whipworms are seldom seen in the stool.

Intestinal parasites are more prevalent in some areas than others. Climate, soil and contamination are big factors contributing to the incidence of intestinal parasites. Eggs are passed in the stool, lay on the ground and then become infective in a certain number of days. Each of the above worms has a different life cycle. Your best chance of becoming and remaining worm-free is to always pooper-scoop your yard. A fenced-in yard keeps stray dogs out, which is certainly helpful.

I would recommend having a fecal examination on your dog twice a year or more often if there is a problem. If your dog has a positive fecal sample, then he will be given the appropriate medication and you will be asked to bring back another stool sample in a certain period of time (depending on the type of worm) and then be rewormed. This process goes on until he has at least two negative samples. The different types of worms require different medications. You will be wasting your money and doing your dog an injustice by buying over-the-counter medication without first consulting your veterinarian.

Roundworm eggs, as would be seen on a fecal evaluation. The eggs must develop for 12 days before they are infective.

OTHER INTERNAL PARASITES

Coccidiosis and Giardiasis

These protozoal infections usually affect puppies, especially in places where large numbers of puppies are brought together. Older dogs may harbor these infections but do not show signs unless they are stressed. Symptoms include diarrhea, weight loss and lack of appetite. These infections are not always apparent in the fecal examination.

Tapeworms

Seldom apparent on fecal floatation, they are diagnosed frequently as rice-like segments around the dog's anus and the base of the tail. Tapeworms are long, flat and ribbon like, sometimes several feet in length, and made up of many segments about five-eighths of an inch long. The two most common types of tapeworms found in the dog are:
(1) First the larval form of the flea tapeworm parasite must

mature in an intermediate host, the flea, before it can become infective. Your dog acquires this by ingesting the flea through licking and chewing.

(2) Rabbits, rodents and certain large game animals serve as intermediate hosts for other species of tapeworms. If your dog should eat one of these infected hosts, then he can acquire tapeworms.

HEARTWORM DISEASE

This is a worm that resides in the heart and adjacent blood vessels of the lung that produces microfilaria, which circulate in the bloodstream. It is possible for a dog to be infected with any number of worms from one to a hundred that can be 6 to 14 inches long. It is a life-threatening disease, expensive to treat and easily prevented. Depending on where you live, your veterinarian may recommend a preventive year-round and either an annual or semiannual blood test. The most common preventive is given once a month.

EXTERNAL PARASITES

Fleas

These pests are not only the dog's worst enemy but also enemy to the owner's pocketbook. Preventing is less expensive than treating, but regardless we'd prefer to spend our money elsewhere. Likely, the majority of our dogs are allergic to the bite of a flea, and in many cases it only takes one flea bite. The protein in the flea's saliva is the culprit. Allergic dogs have a reaction, which usually results in a "hot spot." More than likely such a reaction will involve a trip to the veterinarian for treatment. Yes, prevention is less expensive. Fortunately today there are several good products available.

If there is a flea infestation, no one product is going to correct the problem. Not only will the dog require treatment so will the environment. In general flea collars are not very effective although there is now available an "egg" collar that will kill the eggs on the dog. Dips are the most economical but they are messy. There are some effective shampoos and treatments available through pet shops and veterinarians. An oral tablet arrived on the American market in 1995 and was popular in Europe the previous year. It sterilizes the female flea but will not kill adult fleas. Therefore the tablet, which is given monthly, will decrease the flea population but is not a "cure-all." Those dogs that suffer from flea-bite allergy will still be subjected to the bite of the flea. Another popular parasiticide is permethrin, which is applied to the back of the dog in one or two places depending on the dog's weight. This product works as a repellent causing the flea to get "hot feet" and jump off. Do not confuse this product with some of the organophosphates that are also applied to the dog's back.

Some products are not usable on young puppies. Treating fleas should be done under your veterinarian's guidance. Frequently it is necessary to combine products and the layman does not have the knowledge regarding possible toxicities. It is hard to believe but there are a few dogs that do have a natural resistance to fleas. Nevertheless it would be wise to treat all pets at the same time. Don't forget your cats. Cats just love to prowl the neighborhood and consequently return with unwanted guests.

Fleas can cause an allergic reaction in your dog. If you notice your Brittany scratching excessively, check his coat and start treatment.

Adult fleas live on the dog but their eggs drop off the dog into the environment. There they go

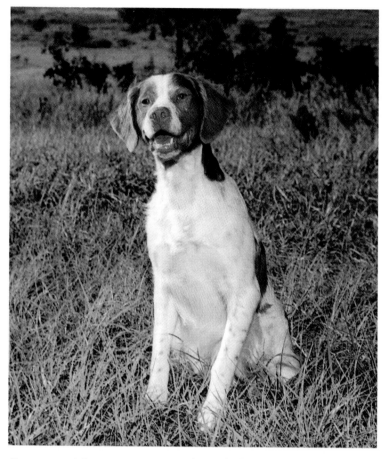

Dogs can pick up parasites like fleas and ticks while outdoors. Be sure to check your Brittany's coat after playing outside. through four larval stages before reaching adulthood, and thereby are able to jump back on the poor unsuspecting dog. The cycle resumes and takes between 21 to 28 days under ideal conditions. There are environmental products available that will kill both the adult fleas and the larvae.

Ticks

Ticks carry Rocky Mountain Spotted Fever, Lyme disease and can cause tick paralysis. They should be removed with tweezers, trying to pull out the head. The jaws carry disease.

116

There is a tick preventive collar that does an excellent job. The ticks automatically back out on those dogs wearing collars.

Sarcoptic Mange
This is a mite that is difficult to find on skin scrapings. The pinnal reflex is a good indicator of this disease. Rub the ends of the pinna (ear) together and the dog will start scratching with his foot. Sarcoptes are highly contagious to other dogs and to humans although they do not live long on humans. They cause intense itching.

Demodectic Mange
This is a mite that is passed from the dam to her puppies. It affects youngsters age three to ten months. Diagnosis is confirmed by skin scraping. Small areas of alopecia around the eyes, lips and/or forelegs become visible. There is little itching unless there is a secondary bacterial infection. Some breeds are afflicted more than others.

Hunting dogs that spend a lot of time in the field are prone to picking up burrs and thorns. A thorough examination of the coat after field work will help keep your Brittany free from injuries.

Cheyletiella
This causes intense itching and is diagnosed by skin scraping. It lives in the outer layers of the skin of dogs, cats, rabbits and humans. Yellow-gray scales may be found on the back and the rump, top of the head and the nose.

TO BREED OR NOT TO BREED
More than likely your breeder has requested that you have your puppy neutered or spayed. Your breeder's

request is based on what is healthiest for your dog and what is most beneficial for your breed. Experienced and conscientious breeders devote many years into developing a bloodline. In order to do this, he makes every effort to plan each breeding in regard to conformation, temperament and health. This type of breeder does his best to perform the necessary testing (i.e., OFA, CERF, testing for inherited blood disorders, thyroid, etc.). Testing is expensive and sometimes very disheartening when a favorite dog doesn't pass his health tests. The health history pertains not only to the breeding stock but to the immediate ancestors. Reputable breeders do not want their offspring to be bred indiscriminately. Therefore you may be asked to neuter or spay your puppy. Of course there is always the exception, and your breeder may agree to let you breed your dog under his direct supervision. This is an important concept. More and more effort is being made to breed healthier dogs.

Spay/Neuter

There are numerous benefits of performing this surgery at six months of age. Unspayed females are subject to mammary and ovarian cancer. In order to prevent mammary cancer she must be spayed prior to her first heat cycle. Later in life, an unspayed female may develop a pyometra (an infected uterus), which is definitely life threatening.

Spaying is performed under a general anesthetic and is easy on the young dog. As you might expect it is a little harder on the older dog, but that is no reason to deny her the surgery. The surgery removes the ovaries and uterus. It is important to remove all the ovarian tissue. If some is left behind, she could remain attractive to males. In order to view the ovaries, a reasonably long incision is necessary. An ovariohysterectomy is considered major surgery.

Neutering the male at a young age will inhibit some characteristic male behavior that owners frown upon. Some boys will not hike their legs and mark territory if they are neutered at six months of age. Also neutering at a young age has hormonal benefits, lessening the chance of hormonal aggressiveness.

Surgery involves removing the testicles but leaving the scrotum. If there should be a retained testicle, then he definitely needs to be neutered before the age of two or three years. Retained testicles can develop into cancer. Unneutered males are at risk for testicular cancer, perineal fistulas, perianal tumors and fistulas and prostatic disease.

Intact males and females are prone to housebreaking accidents. Females urinate frequently before, during and after heat cycles, and males tend to mark territory if there is a female in heat. Males may show the same behavior if there is a visiting dog or guests.

Surgery involves a sterile operating procedure equivalent to human surgery. The incision site is shaved, surgically scrubbed and draped. The veterinarian wears a sterile surgical gown, cap, mask and gloves. Anesthesia should be monitored by a registered technician. It is customary for the veterinarian to recommend a pre-anesthetic blood screening, looking for metabolic problems and a ECG rhythm strip to check for normal heart function. Today anesthetics are equal to human anesthetics, which enables your dog to walk out of the clinic the same day as surgery.

Some folks worry about their dog gaining weight after being neutered or spayed. This is usually not the case. It is true that some dogs may be less active so they could develop a problem, but most dogs are just as active as they were before surgery. However, if your dog should begin to gain, then you need to decrease his food and see to it that he gets a little more exercise.

All Brittanys are cute, but not all are of breeding quality. Some breeders will often sell pet-quality pups on the condition that they are spayed or neutered.

DENTAL CARE for Your Dog's Life

So you've got a new puppy! You also have a new set of puppy teeth in your household. Anyone who has ever raised a puppy is abundantly aware of these new teeth. Your puppy will chew anything it can reach, chase your shoelaces, and play "tear the rag" with any piece of clothing it can find. When puppies are newly born, they have no teeth. At about four weeks of age, puppies of most breeds begin to develop their deciduous or baby teeth. They begin eating semi-solid food, fighting and biting with their litter mates, and learning discipline from their mother. As their new teeth come in, they inflict more pain on their mother's breasts, so her feeding sessions become less frequent and shorter. By six or eight weeks, the mother will start growling to warn her pups when they are fighting too roughly or hurting her as they nurse too much with their new teeth.

Puppies need to chew. It is a necessary part of their physical and mental development. They develop muscles and necessary life skills as they drag objects around, fight over possession, and vocalize alerts and warnings. Puppies chew on things to explore their world. They are using their sense of taste to determine what is food and what is not. How else can they tell an electrical cord from a lizard? At about four months of age, most puppies begin shedding their baby teeth. Often these teeth need some help to come out and make way for the permanent teeth. The incisors (front teeth) will be replaced first. Then, the adult canine or fang teeth erupt. When the baby tooth is not shed before the permanent tooth comes in, veterinarians call it a retained deciduous tooth. This condition will often cause gum infections by trapping hair and debris between the permanent tooth and the retained baby tooth. Nylafloss® is an excellent device for puppies to use. They can toss it, drag it, and chew on the many surfaces it presents. The baby teeth can catch in the nylon material, aiding in their removal. Puppies that have adequate chew toys will have less destructive behavior, develop more physically, and have less chance of retained deciduous teeth.

During the first year, your dog should be seen by your veterinarian at regular intervals. Your veterinarian will let you know when to bring in your puppy for vaccinations and parasite examinations. At each visit, your veterinarian should inspect the lips, teeth, and mouth as part of a complete physical examination. You should take some part in the maintenance of your dog's oral health. You should examine your dog's mouth weekly throughout his first year to make sure there are no sores, foreign objects, tooth problems, etc. If your dog drools excessively, shakes its head, or has bad breath, consult your veterinarian. By the time your dog is six months old, the permanent teeth are all in and plaque can start to accumulate on the tooth surfaces. This is when your dog needs to develop good dental-care habits to prevent calculus build-up on its teeth. Brushing is best. That is a fact that cannot be denied. However, some dogs do not like their teeth brushed regularly, or you may not be able to accomplish the task. In that case, you should consider a product that will help prevent plaque and calculus build-up.

Teething puppies will chew on anything, so be sure to puppy-proof your home and provide your Brittany with safe chew toys.

The Plaque Attackers® and Galileo Bone® are other excellent choices for the first three years of a dog's life. Their shapes make them interesting for the dog. As the dog chews

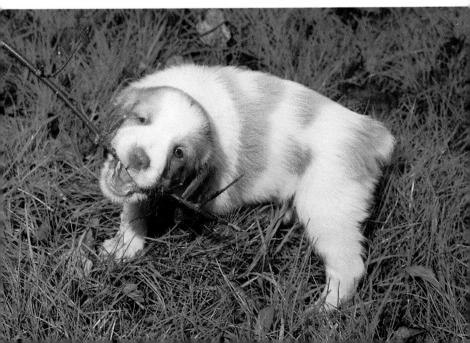

on them, the solid polyurethane massages the gums which improves the blood circulation to the periodontal tissues. Projections on the chew devices increase the surface and are in contact with the tooth for more efficient cleaning. The unique shape and consistency prevent your dog from exerting excessive force on his own teeth or from breaking off pieces of the bone. If your dog is an aggressive chewer or weighs more than 55 pounds (25 kg), you should consider giving him a Nylabone®, the most durable chew product on the market.

The Gumabones ®, made by the Nylabone Company, is constructed of strong polyurethane, which is softer than nylon. Less powerful chewers prefer the Gumabones® to the Nylabones®. A super option for your dog is the Hercules Bone®, a uniquely shaped bone named after the great Olympian for its exception strength. Like all Nylabone products, they are specially scented to make them attractive to your dog. Ask your veterinarian about these bones and he will validate the good doctor's prescription:

Nylabones® not only give your dog a good chewing workout but also help to save your dog's teeth (and even his life, as it protects him from possible fatal periodontal diseases).

Make sure that your Brittany has plenty of safe toys to chew on to keep his jaw occupied and out of trouble.

This four-week-old Brittany puppy looks perfectly content with his favorite playthings.

By the time dogs are four years old, 75% of them have periodontal disease. It is the most common infection in dogs. Yearly examinations by your veterinarian are essential to maintaining your dog's good health. If your veterinarian detects periodontal disease, he or she may recommend a prophylactic cleaning. To do a thorough cleaning, it will be necessary to put your dog under anesthesia. With modern gas anesthetics and monitoring equipment, the procedure is pretty safe. Your veterinarian will scale the teeth with an ultrasound scaler or hand instrument. This removes the calculus from the teeth. If there are calculus deposits below the gum line, the veterinarian will plane the roots to make them smooth. After all of the calculus has been removed, the teeth are polished with pumice in a polishing cup. If any medical or surgical treatment is needed, it is done at this time. The final step would be fluoride treatment and your follow-up treatment at home. If the periodontal disease is advanced, the veterinarian may prescribe a medicated mouth rinse or antibiotics for use at home. Make sure your dog has safe, clean

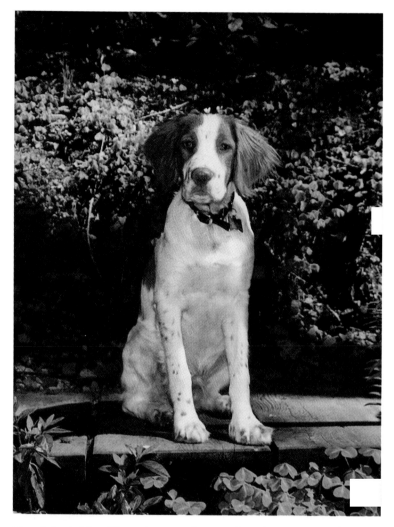

Good dental health and regular maintenance is important to your Brittany's overall health and well-being.

and attractive chew toys and treats. Chooz® treats are another way of using a consumable treat to help keep your dog's teeth clean.

Rawhide is the most popular of all materials for a dog to chew. This has never been good news to dog owners, because rawhide is inherently very dangerous for dogs. Thousands of dogs have died from rawhide, having swallowed the hide after it has become soft and mushy, only to cause stomach and intestinal blockage. A new rawhide product on the market has finally solved the problem of rawhide: molded Roar-Hide® from Nylabone. These are composed of processed, cut up, and melted American rawhide injected into your dog's favorite shape: a dog bone. These dog-safe devices smell and taste like rawhide but don't break up. The ridges on the bones help to fight tartar build-up on the teeth and they last ten times longer than the usual rawhide chews.

As your dog ages, professional examination and cleaning should become more frequent. The mouth should be inspected at least once a year. Your veterinarian may recommend visits every six months. In the geriatric patient, organs such as the heart, liver, and kidneys do not function as well as

The Carrot Bone™ by Nylabone® allows your dog to work off his desire to chew.

when they were young. Your veterinarian will probably want to test these organs' functions prior to using general anesthesia for dental cleaning. If your dog is a good chewer and you work closely with your veterinarian, your dog can keep all of its teeth all of its life. However, as your dog ages, his sense of smell, sight, and taste will diminish. He may not have the desire to chase, trap or chew his toys. He will also not have the energy to chew for long periods, as arthritis and periodontal disease make chewing painful. This will leave you with more responsibility for keeping his teeth clean and healthy. The dog that would not let you brush his teeth at one year of age, may let you brush his teeth now that he is ten years old.

If you train your dog with good chewing habits as a puppy, he will have healthier teeth throughout his life.

TRAVELING with Your Dog

The earlier you start traveling with your new puppy or dog, the better. He needs to become accustomed to traveling. However, some dogs are nervous riders and become carsick easily. It is helpful if he starts with an empty stomach. Do not despair, as it will go better if you continue taking him with you on short fun rides. How would you feel if every time you rode in the car you stopped at the doctor's for an injection? You would soon dread that nasty car. Older dogs that tend to get carsick may have more of a problem adjusting to traveling. Those dogs that are having a serious problem may benefit from some medication prescribed by the veterinarian.

If you begin traveling with your Brittany when he is a puppy, he will become accustomed to car rides in no time.

Do give your dog a chance to relieve himself before getting into the car. It is a good idea to be prepared for a clean up with a leash, paper towels, bag and terry cloth towel.

Crates are the safest way for your Brittany to travel in the car.
The safest place for your dog is in a fiberglass crate, although close confinement can promote carsickness in some dogs. If your dog is nervous you can try letting him ride on the seat next to you or in someone's lap.

An alternative to the crate would be to use a car harness made for dogs and/or a safety strap attached to the harness or collar. Whatever you do, do not let your dog ride in the back of a pickup truck unless he is securely tied on a very short lead. I've seen trucks stop quickly and, even though the dog was tied, it fell out and was dragged.

Another advantage of the crate is that it is a safe place to leave him if you need to run into the store. Otherwise you wouldn't be able to leave the windows down. Keep in mind that while many dogs are overly protective in their crates, this may not be enough to deter dognappers. In some states it is against the law to leave a dog in the car unattended.

Never leave a dog loose in the car wearing a collar and leash. More than one dog has killed himself by hanging. Do not let him put his head out an open window. Foreign debris can be blown into his eyes. When leaving your dog unattended in a car, consider the temperature. It can take less than five

The Brittany is a very adaptable dog. Once he is used to the car, he will be more than happy to accompany you anywhere.

minutes to reach temperatures over 100 degrees Fahrenheit.

TRIPS

Perhaps you are taking a trip. Give consideration to what is best for your dog—traveling with you or boarding. When traveling by car, van or motor home, you need to think ahead about locking your vehicle. In all probability you have many valuables in the car and do not wish to leave it unlocked. Perhaps most valuable and not replaceable is your dog. Give thought to securing your vehicle and providing adequate ventilation for him. Another consideration for you when traveling with your dog is medical problems that may arise and little inconveniences, such as exposure to external parasites. Some areas of the country are quite flea infested. You may want to carry flea spray with you. This is even a good idea when staying in motels. Quite possibly you are not the only occupant of the room.

Unbelievably many motels and even hotels do allow canine guests, even some very first-class ones. Gaines Pet Foods Corporation publishes *Touring With Towser*, a directory of domestic hotels and motels that accommodate guests with dogs. Their address is Gaines TWT, PO Box 5700, Kankakee, IL, 60902. Call ahead to any motel that you may be considering and see if they accept pets. Sometimes it is necessary to pay a deposit against room damage. The management may feel reassured if you mention that your dog will be crated. If you do travel with your dog, take along plenty of baggies so that you can clean up after him. When we all do our share in cleaning up, we make it possible for motels to continue accepting our pets. As a matter of fact, you should practice cleaning up everywhere you take your dog.

Your Brittany will always be happiest if he is allowed to participate in family activities, including trips.

Depending on where your are traveling, you may need an up-to-date health certificate issued by your veterinarian. It is good policy to take along your dog's medical information, which would include the name, address and phone number of your veterinarian, vaccination record, rabies certificate, and any medication he is taking.

AIR TRAVEL

When traveling by air, you need to contact the airlines to check their policy. Usually you have to make arrangements up to a couple of weeks in advance for traveling with your dog. The airlines require your dog to travel in an airline approved fiberglass crate. Usually these can be purchased through the airlines but they are also readily available in most pet-supply stores. If your dog is not accustomed to a crate, then it is a good idea to get him acclimated to it before your trip. The day of the actual trip you should withhold water about one hour ahead of departure and no food for about 12 hours. The airlines generally have temperature restrictions, which do not allow pets to travel if it is either too cold or too hot. Frequently these restrictions are based on the temperatures at the departure and arrival airports. It's best to inquire about a health certificate. These usually need to be issued within ten days of departure. You should arrange for non-stop, direct flights and if a commuter plane should be involved, check to see if it will carry dogs. Some don't. The Humane Society of the United States has put together a tip sheet for airline traveling. You can receive a copy by sending a self-addressed stamped envelope to:

Most airlines and hotels do have policies concerning traveling with pets, so be sure to research it thoroughly before making any plans.

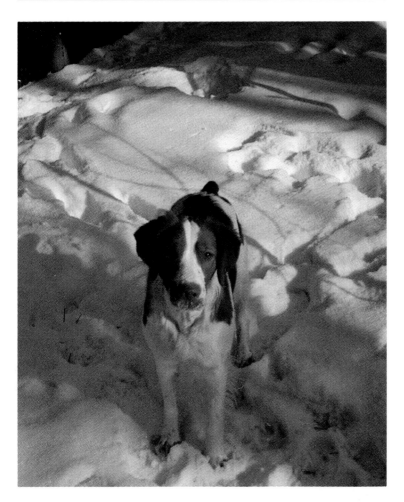

The Brittany is a hardy dog that can adapt easily to any situation or environment. Wincrest Millette Melody enjoys a romp in the snow.

The Humane Society of the United States
Tip Sheet
2100 L Street NW
Washington, DC 20037.

Regulations differ for traveling outside of the country and are sometimes changed without notice. Well in advance you need to write or call the appropriate consulate or agricultural department for instructions. Some countries have lengthy quarantines (six months), and countries differ in their rabies

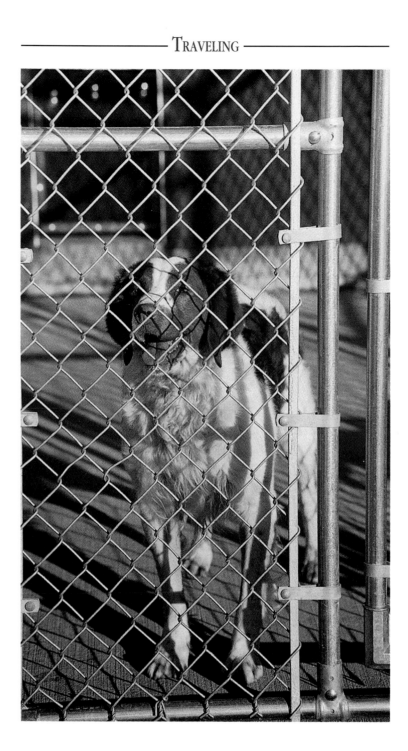

vaccination requirements. For instance, it may have to be given at least 30 days ahead of your departure.

Do make sure your dog is wearing proper identification including your name, phone number and city. You never know when you might be in an accident and separated from your dog. Or your dog could be frightened and somehow manage to escape and run away.

Another suggestion would be to carry in-case-of-emergency instructions. These would include the address and phone number of a relative or friend, your veterinarian's name, address and phone number, and your dog's medical information.

BOARDING KENNELS

Perhaps you have decided that you need to board your dog. Your veterinarian can recommend a good boarding facility or possibly a pet sitter that will come to your house. It is customary for the boarding kennel to ask for proof of vaccination for the DHLPP, rabies and bordetella vaccine. The bordetella should have been given within six months of boarding. This is for your protection. If they do not ask for this proof I would not board at their kennel. Ask about flea control. Those dogs that suffer flea-bite allergy can get in trouble at a boarding kennel. Unfortunately boarding kennels are limited on how much they are able to do.

For more information on pet sitting, contact NAPPS:
National Association of Professional Pet Sitters
1200 G Street, NW
Suite 760
Washington, DC 20005.

Some pet clinics have technicians that pet sit and technicians that board clinic patients in their homes. This may be an alternative for you. Ask your veterinarian if they have an employee that can help you. There is a definite advantage of having a technician care for your dog, especially if your dog is on medication or is a senior citizen.

If you decide to leave your Brittany at home, a reputable boarding kennel may be the right choice for you.

You can write for a copy of *Traveling With Your Pet* from ASPCA, Education Department, 441 E. 92nd Street, New York, NY 10128.

IDENTIFICATION and Finding the Lost Dog

There are several ways of identifying your dog. The old standby is a collar with dog license, rabies, and ID tags. Unfortunately collars have a way of being separated from the dog and tags fall off. We're not suggesting you shouldn't use a collar and tags. If they stay intact and on the dog, they are the quickest way of identification.

For several years owners have been tattooing their dogs. Some tattoos use a number with a registry. Here lies the problem because there are several registries to check. If you wish to tattoo, use your social security number. The humane shelters have the means to trace it. It is usually done on the inside of the rear thigh. The area is first shaved

Keeping your Brittany in a secure area outside will lessen the chances of the dog becoming lost or separated from you.

The newest method of identification is microchipping, a chip no bigger than a grain of rice that is implanted under your dog's skin.

and numbed. There is no pain, although a few dogs do not like the buzzing sound. Occasionally tattooing is not legible and needs to be redone.

The newest method of identification is microchipping. The microchip is a computer chip that is no larger than a grain of rice. The veterinarian implants it by injection between the shoulder blades. The dog feels no discomfort. If your dog is lost and picked up by the humane society, they can trace you by scanning the microchip, which has its own code. Microchip scanners are friendly to other brands of microchips and their registries. The microchip comes with a dog tag saying the dog is microchipped. It is the safest way of identifying your dog.

FINDING THE LOST DOG

I am sure you will agree that there would be little worse than losing your dog. Responsible pet owners rarely lose their dogs. They do not let their dogs run free because they don't want harm to come to them. Not only that but in most, if not all, states there is a leash law.

Beware of fenced-in yards. They can be a hazard. Dogs find ways to escape either over or under the fence. Another fast exit is through the gate that perhaps the neighbor's child left unlocked.

Below is a list that hopefully will be of help to you if you need it. Remember don't give up, keep looking. Your dog is worth your efforts.

1. Contact your neighbors and put flyers with a photo on it in their mailboxes. Information you should include would be the dog's name, breed, sex, color, age, source of identification, when your dog was last seen and where, and your name and phone numbers. It may be helpful to say the dog needs medical care. Offer a *reward*.

Make sure you have a clear recent photo of your Brittany to distribute in case he becomes lost.

2. Check all local shelters daily. It is also possible for your dog to be picked up away from home and end up in an out-of-the-way shelter. Check these too. Go in person. It is not good enough to call. Most shelters are limited on the time they can hold dogs then they are put up for adoption or euthanized. There is the possibility that your dog will not make it to the shelter for several days. Your dog could have been wandering or someone may have tried to keep him.

3. Notify all local veterinarians. Call and send flyers.

4. Call your breeder. Frequently breeders are contacted when one of their breed is found.

5. Contact the rescue group for your breed.

6. Contact local schools—children may have seen your dog.

7. Post flyers at the schools, groceries, gas stations, convenience stores, veterinary clinics, groomers and any other place that will allow them.

8. Advertise in the newspaper.

9. Advertise on the radio.

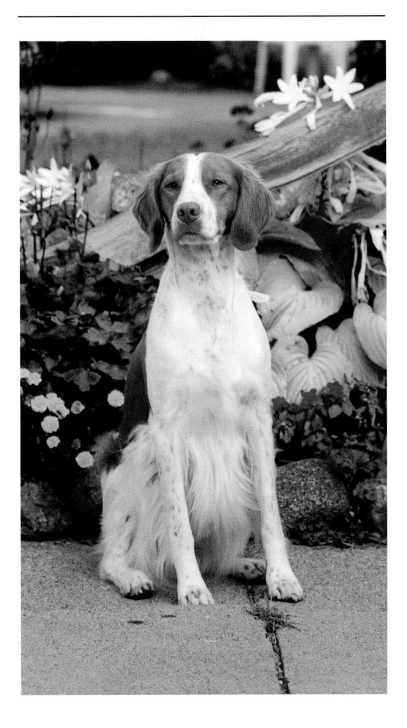

BEHAVIOR and Canine Communication

S tudies of the human/animal bond point out the importance of the unique relationships that exist between people and their pets. Those of us who share our lives with pets understand the special part they play through companionship, service and protection. For many, the pet/owner bond goes beyond simple companionship; pets are often considered members of the family. A leading pet food manufacturer recently conducted a nationwide survey of pet owners to gauge just how important pets were in their lives. Here's what they found:

- 76 percent allow their pets to sleep on their beds
- 78 percent think of their pets as their children
- 84 percent display photos of their pets, mostly in their homes
- 84 percent think that their pets react to their own emotions
- 100 percent talk to their pets
- 97 percent think that their pets understand what they're saying

Are you surprised?

Senior citizens show more concern for their own eating habits when they have the responsibility of feeding a dog. Seeing that their dog is routinely exercised encourages the owner to think of schedules that otherwise may seem unimportant to the senior citizen. The older owner may be arthritic and feeling poorly but with responsibility for his dog he has a reason to get up and get moving. It is a big plus if his dog is an attention seeker who will demand such from his owner.

Many people thrive on the devoted companionship that a Brittany can provide.

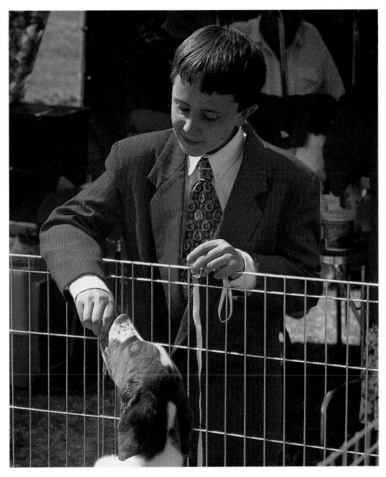

It has been found that spending time with a Brittany can reduce stress and improve your quality of life.

Over the last couple of decades, it has been shown that pets relieve the stress of those who lead busy lives. Owning a pet has been known to lessen the occurrence of heart attack and stroke.

Many single folks thrive on the companionship of a dog. Lifestyles are very different from a long time ago, and today more individuals seek the single life. However, they receive fulfillment from owning a dog.

Most likely the majority of our dogs live in family environments. The companionship they provide is well worth the effort involved. In my opinion, every child should have the opportunity to have a family dog. Dogs teach responsibility through understanding their care, feelings and even respecting their life cycles. Frequently those children who have not been exposed to dogs grow up afraid of dogs, which isn't good. Dogs sense timidity and some will take advantage of the situation.

Today more dogs are serving as service dogs. Since the origination of the Seeing Eye dogs years ago, we now have trained hearing dogs. Also dogs are trained to provide service for the handicapped and are able to perform many different tasks for their owners. Search and Rescue dogs, with their handlers, are sent throughout the world to assist in recovery of disaster victims. They are life savers.

Puppies possess an innate curiosity and can get themselves into all sorts of predicaments. Make sure you supervise your Brittany pup at all times.

Therapy dogs are very popular with nursing homes, and some hospitals even allow them to visit. The inhabitants truly look forward to their visits. They wanted and were allowed to have visiting dogs in their beds to hold and love.

Nationally there is a Pet Awareness Week to educate students and others

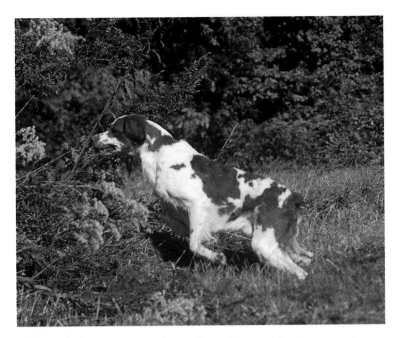

Although dogs within a breed usually exhibit the same type of personality and attributes, each dog is an individual and should be treated as such.

about the value and basic care of our pets. Many countries take an even greater interest in their pets than Americans do. In those countries the pets are allowed to accompany their owners into restaurants and shops, etc. In the US this freedom is only available to our service dogs. Even so we think very highly of the human/animal bond.

CANINE BEHAVIOR

Canine behavior problems are the number-one reason for pet owners to dispose of their dogs, either through new homes, humane shelters or euthanasia. Unfortunately there are too many owners who are unwilling to devote the necessary time to properly train their dogs. On the other hand, there are those who not only are concerned about inherited health problems but are also aware of the dog's mental stability.

You may realize that a breed and his group relatives (i.e., sporting, hounds, etc.) show tendencies to behavioral

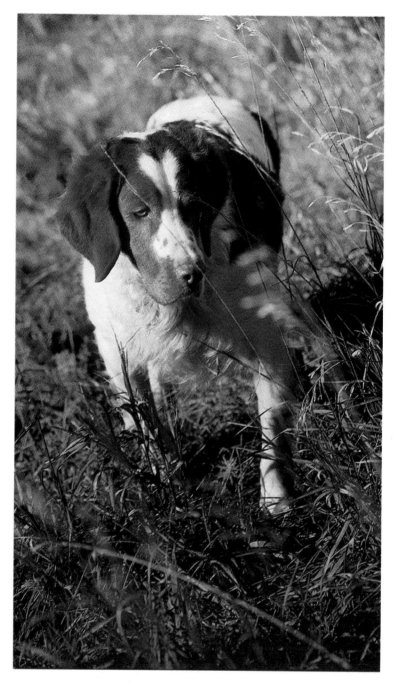

characteristics. An experienced breeder can acquaint you with his breed's personality. Unfortunately many breeds are labeled with poor temperaments when actually the breed as a whole is not affected but only a small percentage of individuals within the breed.

Inheritance and environment contribute to the dog's behavior. Some naïve people suggest inbreeding as the cause of bad temperaments. Inbreeding only results in poor behavior if the ancestors carry the trait. If there are excellent temperaments behind the dogs, then inbreeding will promote good temperaments in the offspring. Did you ever consider that inbreeding is what sets the characteristics of a breed? A purebred dog is the end result of inbreeding. This does not spare the mixed-breed dog from the same problems. Mixed-breed dogs frequently are the offspring of purebred dogs.

Not too many decades ago most of our dogs led a different lifestyle than what is prevalent today. Usually mom stayed home so the dog had human companionship and someone to discipline it if needed. Not much was expected from the dog. Today's mom works and everyone's life is at a much faster pace.

The dog may have to adjust to being a "weekend" dog. The family is gone all day during the week, and the dog is left to his own devices for entertainment. Some dogs sleep all day waiting for their family to come home and others become wigwam wreckers if given the opportunity. Crates do ensure the safety of the dog and the house. However, he could become a physically and emotionally cripple if he doesn't get enough exercise and attention. We still appreciate and want the companionship of our dogs although we expect more from them. In many cases we tend to forget dogs are just that—*dogs* not human beings.

SOCIALIZING AND TRAINING

Many prospective puppy buyers lack experience regarding the proper socialization and training needed to develop the type of pet we all desire. In the first 18 months, training does take some work. It is easier to start proper training before there is a problem that needs to be corrected.

Because of his trainability and high desire to please, many Brittanys excel at hunting and service activities.

The initial work begins with the breeder. The breeder should start

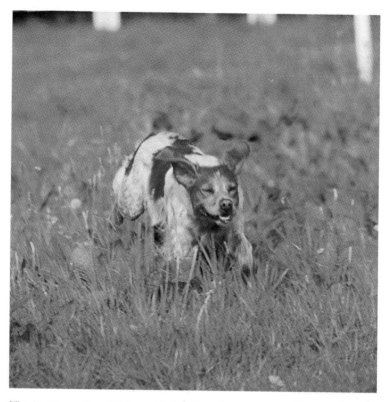

The Brittany is a high-energy dog that needs plenty of attention and exercise for his physical and mental well-being.

socializing the puppy at five to six weeks of age and cannot let up. Human socializing is critical up through 12 weeks of age and likewise important during the following months. The litter should be left together during the first few weeks but it is necessary to separate them by ten weeks of age. Leaving them together after that time will increase competition for litter dominance. If puppies are not socialized with people by 12 weeks of age, they will be timid in later life.

The eight- to ten-week age period is a fearful time for puppies. They need to be handled very gently around children and adults. There should be no harsh discipline during this time. Starting at 14 weeks of age, the puppy begins the juvenile period, which ends when he reaches sexual maturity around six to 14 months of age. During the juvenile period he needs to be introduced to strangers (adults, children and other dogs) on the home property. At sexual maturity he will begin to bark at strangers and become more protective. Males start to lift their legs to urinate but if you desire you can inhibit this behavior by walking your boy on leash away from trees, shrubs, fences, etc.

Perhaps you are thinking about an older puppy. You need to inquire about the puppy's social experience. If he has lived in a kennel, he may have a hard time adjusting to people and environmental stimuli. Assuming he has had a good social upbringing, there are advantages to an older puppy.

Curiosity may have killed the cat, but it's not stopping this Brittany! As long as they are properly introduced, most Brittanys will get along with other pets.

Training includes puppy kindergarten and a minimum of one to two basic training classes. During these classes you will learn how to dominate your youngster. This is especially important if you own a large breed of dog. It is somewhat harder, if not nearly impossible, for some owners to be the Alpha figure when their dog towers over them. You will be taught how to properly restrain your dog. This concept is important. Again it puts you in the Alpha position. All dogs need to be restrained many times during their lives. Believe it or not, some of our worst offenders are the eight-week-old puppies that are brought to our clinic. They need to be gently restrained for a nail trim but the way they carry on you would think we were killing them. In comparison, their vaccination is a "piece of cake." When we ask dogs to do something that is not agreeable to them, then their worst comes out. Life will be easier for your dog if you expose him at a young age to the necessities of life—proper behavior and restraint.

UNDERSTANDING THE DOG'S LANGUAGE

Most authorities agree that the dog is a descendent of the wolf. The dog and wolf have similar traits. For instance both are pack oriented and prefer not to be isolated for long periods of time. Another characteristic is that the dog, like the wolf, looks to the leader–Alpha–for direction. Both the wolf and the dog communicate through body language, not only within their pack but with outsiders.

Every pack has an Alpha figure. The dog looks to you, or should look to you, to be that leader. If your dog doesn't receive the proper training and guidance, he very well may replace you as Alpha. This would be a serious problem and is certainly a disservice to your dog.

Eye contact is one way the Alpha wolf keeps order within his pack. You are Alpha so you must establish eye contact with your puppy. Obviously your puppy will have to look at you.

You can often guess what your dog is trying to tell you by observing his body language.

Practice eye contact even if you need to hold his head for five to ten seconds at a time. You can give him a treat as a reward. Make sure your eye contact is gentle and not

This Brittany pup demonstrates the play bow—and indicates that he is ready for a little fun. threatening. Later, if he has been naughty, it is permissible to give him a long, penetrating look. There are some older dogs that never learned eye contact as puppies and cannot accept eye contact. You should avoid eye contact with these dogs since they feel threatened and will retaliate as such.

BODY LANGUAGE

The play bow, when the forequarters are down and the hindquarters are elevated, is an invitation to play. Puppies play fight, which helps them learn the acceptable limits of biting. This is necessary for later in their lives. Nevertheless, an owner may be falsely reassured by the playful nature of his dog's aggression. Playful aggression toward another dog or human may be an indication of serious aggression in the future. Owners should never play fight or play tug-of-war with any dog that is inclined to be dominant.

147

Signs of submission are:
1. Avoids eye contact.
2. Active submission–the dog crouches down, ears back and the tail is lowered.
3. Passive submission–the dog rolls on his side with his hindlegs in the air and frequently urinates.

Signs of dominance are:
1. Makes eye contact.
2. Stands with ears up, tail up and the hair raised on his neck.
3. Shows dominance over another dog by standing at right angles over it.

Dominant dogs tend to behave in characteristic ways such as:

Your Brittany's relationship with his littermates is essential to his socialization. He will learn to interact with other dogs by playing with his siblings.

1. The dog may be unwilling to move from his place (i.e., reluctant to give up the sofa if the owner wants to sit there).
2. He may not part with toys or objects in his mouth and may show possessiveness with his food bowl.
3. He may not respond quickly to commands.
4. He may be disagreeable for grooming and dislikes to be petted.

Dogs are popular because of their sociable nature. Those that have contact with humans during the first 12 weeks of life regard them as a member of their own species–their pack. All dogs have the potential for both dominant and submissive behavior. Only through experience and training do they learn to whom it is appropriate to show which behavior. Not all dogs are concerned with dominance but owners need to be aware of that potential. It is wise for the owner to establish his dominance early on.

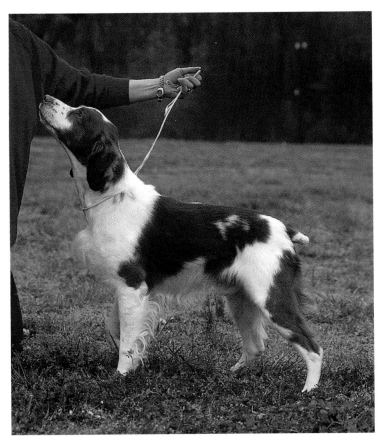

Teach your Brittany how you want him to behave. Practicing training exercises will help you establish dominance over your dog.

A human can express dominance or submission toward a dog in the following ways:

1. Meeting the dog's gaze signals dominance. Averting the gaze signals submission. If the dog growls or threatens, averting the gaze is the first avoiding action to take—it may prevent attack. It is important to establish eye contact in the puppy. The older dog that has not been exposed to eye contact may see it as a threat and will not be willing to submit.

2. Being taller than the dog signals dominance; being lower signals submission. This is why, when attempting to

make friends with a strange dog or catch the runaway, one should kneel down to his level. Some owners see their dogs become dominant when allowed on the furniture or on the bed. Then he is at the owner's level.

3. An owner can gain dominance by ignoring all the dog's social initiatives. The owner pays attention to the dog only when he obeys a command.

No dog should be allowed to achieve dominant status over any adult or child. Ways of preventing are as follows:

1. Handle the puppy gently, especially during the three- to four-month period.

2. Let the children and adults handfeed him and teach him to take food without lunging or grabbing.

3. Do not allow him to chase children or joggers.

4. Do not allow him to jump on people or mount their legs. Even females may be inclined to mount. It is not only a male habit.

5. Do not allow him to growl for any reason.

6. Don't participate in wrestling or tug-of-war games.

7. Don't physically punish puppies for aggressive behavior. Restrain him from repeating the infraction and teach an alternative behavior. Dogs should earn everything they receive from their owners. This would include sitting to receive petting or treats, sitting before going out the door and sitting to receive the collar and leash. These types of exercises reinforce the owner's dominance.

Young children should never be left alone with a dog. It is important that children learn some basic obedience commands so they have some control over the dog. They will gain the respect of their dog.

FEAR

One of the most common problems dogs experience is being fearful. Some dogs are more afraid than others. On the lesser side, which is sometimes humorous to watch, dogs can be afraid of a strange object. They act silly when something is out of place in the house. We call his problem perceptive intelligence. He realizes the abnormal within his known environment. He does not react the same way in strange environments since he does not know what is normal.

On the more serious side is a fear of people. This can result in backing off, seeking his own space and saying "leave me alone" or it can result in an aggressive behavior that may lead to challenging the person. Respect that the dog wants to be left alone and give him time to come forward. If you approach the cornered dog, he may resort to snapping. If you leave him alone, he may decide to come forward, which should be rewarded with a treat.

Some dogs may initially be too fearful to take treats. In these cases it is helpful to make sure the dog hasn't eaten for about 24 hours. Being a little hungry encourages him to accept the treats, especially if they are of the "gourmet" variety.

Dogs can be afraid of numerous things, including loud noises and thunderstorms. Invariably the owner rewards (by comforting) the dog when it shows signs of fearfulness. When your dog is frightened, direct his attention to something else and act happy. Don't dwell on his fright.

Some puppies will go through a period in which they are fearful of new things. Respect his feelings and allow him time to get used to the situation.

AGGRESSION

Some different types of aggression are: predatory, defensive, dominance,

Your Brittany will look to you, his owner, for the discipline and guidance he needs to become a well-mannered pet.

possessive, protective, fear induced, noise provoked, "rage" syndrome (unprovoked aggression), maternal and aggression directed toward other dogs. Aggression is the most common behavioral problem encountered. Protective breeds are expected to be more aggressive than others but with the proper upbringing they can make very dependable companions. You need to be able to read your dog.

Many factors contribute to aggression including genetics and environment. An improper environment, which may include the living conditions, lack of social life, excessive punishment, being attacked or frightened by an aggressive dog, etc., can all influence a dog's behavior. Even spoiling him and giving too much praise may be detrimental. Isolation and the lack of human contact or exposure to frequent teasing by children or adults also can ruin a good dog.

Lack of direction, fear, or confusion lead to aggression in those dogs that are so inclined. Any obedience exercise, even the sit and down, can direct the dog and overcome fear and/or confusion. Every dog should learn these commands as a youngster, and there should be periodic reinforcement.

When a dog is showing signs of aggression, you should speak calmly (no screaming or hysterics) and firmly give a command that he understands, such as the sit. As soon as your dog obeys, you have assumed your dominant position. Aggression presents a problem because there may be danger to others. Sometimes it is an emotional issue. Owners may consciously or unconsciously encourage their dog's aggression. Other owners show responsibility by accepting the problem and taking measures to keep it under control. The owner is responsible for his dog's actions, and it is not wise to take a chance on someone being bitten, especially a child. Euthanasia is the solution for some owners and in severe cases this may be the best choice. However, few dogs are that dangerous and very few are that much of a threat to their owners. If caution is exercised and professional help is gained early on, most cases can be controlled.

Dogs like the Brittany possess certain instinctual behaviors. Proper training is important to ensure that these behaviors are displayed in appropriate ways.

Some authorities recommend feeding a lower protein (less than 20 percent) diet. They believe this can aid in reducing aggression. If the dog loses weight, then vegetable oil can be added. Veterinarians and behaviorists are having some success with pharmacology. In many cases treatment is possible and can improve the situation.

If you have done everything according to "the book" regarding training and socializing and are still having a behavior problem, don't procrastinate. It is important that the problem gets attention before it is out of hand. It is estimated that 20 percent of a veterinarian's time may be devoted to dealing with problems before they become so intolerable that the dog is separated from its home and owner. If your veterinarian isn't able to help, he should refer you to a behaviorist.

PROBLEMS

Barking

This is a habit that shouldn't be encouraged. Some owners desire their dog to bark so as to be a watchdog. Most dogs will bark when a stranger comes to the door.

The new puppy frequently barks or whines in the crate in his strange environment and the owner reinforces the puppy's bad behavior by going to him during the night. This is a no-no. Smack the top of the crate and say "quiet"

Boredom is often a cause of problem behavior. The Brittany is an athletic dog that needs to keep busy to ensure that his energy is directed toward positive activities.

Keeping your dog occupied with toys is one way to keep him from barking or destroying things when you can't be with him.

in a loud, firm voice. The puppies don't like to hear the loud noise of the crate being banged. If the barking is sleep-interrupting, then the owner should take crate and pup to the bedroom for a few days until the puppy becomes adjusted to his new environment. Otherwise ignore the barking during the night.

Barking can be an inherited problem or a bad habit learned through the environment. It takes dedication to stop the barking. Attention should be paid to the cause of the barking. Does the dog seek attention, does he need to go out, is it feeding time, is it occurring when he is left alone, is it a protective bark, etc.? Overzealous barking is an inherited tendency. When barking presents a problem for you, try to stop it as soon as it begins.

There are electronic collars available that are supposed to curb barking. There are some disadvantages to to the collar. If the dog is barking out of excitement, punishment is not the appropriate treatment. Presumably there is the chance the collar could be activated by other stimuli and thereby punish the dog when it is not barking. Should you decide to use one, then you should seek help from a person with experience with that type of collar. Nevertheless the root of the problem needs to be investigated and corrected.

In extreme circumstances (usually when there is a problem with the neighbors), some people have resorted to having their

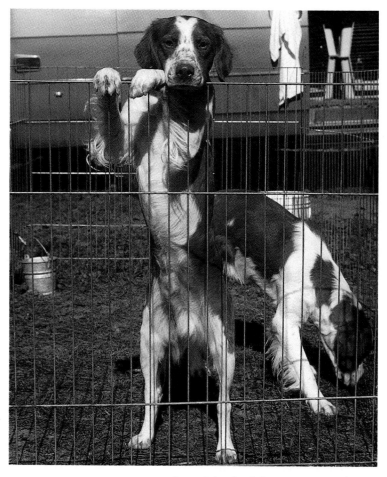

Jumping up is often a sign of affection, but your Brittany must be trained to sit for petting and attention.

dogs debarked. I caution you that the dog continues to bark but usually only a squeaking sound is heard. Frequently the vocal cords grow back. Probably the biggest concern is that the dog can be left with scar tissue which can narrow the opening to the trachea.

Jumping Up

A dog that jumps up is a happy dog. Nevertheless few guests appreciate dogs jumping on them. Clothes get footprinted and/or snagged.

156

Some trainers believe in allowing the puppy to jump up during his first few weeks. If you correct him too soon and at the wrong age you may intimidate him. Consequently he could be timid around humans later in his life. However, there will come a time, probably around four months of age, that he needs to know when it is okay to jump and when he is to show off good manners by sitting instead.

Some authorities never allow jumping. If you are irritated by your dog jumping up on you, then you should discourage it from the beginning. A larger breed of dog can cause harm to a senior citizen. Some are quite fragile. It may not take much to cause a topple that could break a hip.

A well-mannered and well-trained Brittany is a joy to own. Although you will need to take the time to teach him proper behavior, the end result is worth it.

How do you correct the problem? All family members need to participate in teaching the puppy to sit as soon as he starts to jump up. The sit must be practiced every time he starts to jump up. Don't forget to praise him for his good behavior. If an older dog has acquired the habit, grasp his paws and squeeze tightly. Give a firm "No." He'll soon catch on. Remember the entire family must take part. Each time you allow him to jump up you go back a step in training.

Biting

All puppies bite and try to chew on your fingers, toes, arms, etc. This is the time to teach them to be gentle and not bite hard. Put your fingers in your puppy's mouth and if he bites too hard then say "easy" and let him know he's hurting you. Squeal and act like you have been seriously hurt. If the puppy plays too rough and doesn't respond to your corrections, then he needs "Time Out" in his crate. You should be particularly careful with young children and puppies who still have their deciduous (baby) teeth. Those teeth are like needles and can leave little scars on youngsters.

Biting in the more mature dog is something that should be prevented at all costs. Should it occur quickly let him know in no uncertain terms that biting will not be tolerated. When biting is directed toward another dog (dog fight), don't get in the middle of it. Some authorities recommend breaking up a fight by elevating the hind legs. This would only be possible if there was a person for each dog. Obviously it would be hard to fight with the hind legs off the ground. A dog bite is serious and should be given attention. Wash the bite with soap and water and contact your doctor. It is important to know the status of the offender's rabies vaccination.

Your dog must know who is boss. When biting occurs, you should seek professional help at once. On the other hand you must not let your dog intimidate you and be so afraid of a bite that you can't discipline him. Professional help through your veterinarian, dog trainer and/or behaviorist can give you guidance.

Digging

Bored dogs release their frustrations through mischievous behavior such as digging. Dogs shouldn't be left unattended outside, even if they are in a fenced-in yard. Usually the dog is sent to "jail" (the backyard) because the owner can't tolerate him in the house. The culprit feels socially deprived and needs to be included in the owner's life. The owner has neglected the dog's training. The dog has not developed into the companion we desire. If you are one of these owners, then perhaps it is possible for you to change. Give him another chance. Some owners object to their dog's unkempt coat and doggy odor. See that he is groomed on a regular schedule and look into some training classes.

Submissive Urination

This is not a housebreaking problem. It can occur in all breeds and may be more prevalent in some breeds. Usually it occurs in puppies but occasionally it occurs in older dogs and may be in response to physical praise. Try verbal praise or ignoring your dog until after he has had a chance to relieve himself. Scolding will only make the problem worse. Many dogs outgrow this problem.

SUGGESTED READING

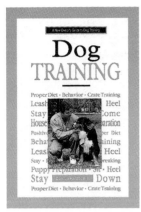

JG117
*A New Owner's Guide
to Dog Training
160 pages, over 140
full-color photos*

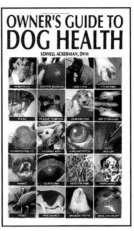

TS249
*Owner's Guide to Dog
Health
224 pages, over 190
full-color photos*

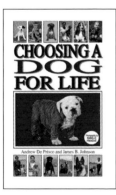

TS257
*Choosing a Dog for Life
384 pages, over 700 full-color
photos*

TS258
*Training Your Dog for
Sports and Other Activities
160 pages, over 200 full-
color photos.*

INDEX

Contrary Imaginations

CONTRARY IMAGINATIONS

A PSYCHOLOGICAL STUDY OF THE YOUNG STUDENT

Liam Hudson

SCHOCKEN BOOKS · NEW YORK

47643

First published in U. S. A. 1966
by Schocken Books Inc.
67 Park Avenue, New York, N. Y. 10016
© 1966 Liam Hudson

Library of Congress Catalog Card Number: 66-19299

Printed in Great Britain

It was *Nature* alone, which could pleasantly entertain them, in that estate. The contemplation of that, draws our minds off from past, or present misfortunes, and makes them conquerers over things, in the greatest publick unhappiness: while the consideration of *Men*, and *humane affairs*, may affect us, with a thousand various disquiets; *that* never separates us into mortal Factions; *that* gives us room to differ, without animosity; and permits us, to raise contrary imaginations upon it, without any danger of a *Civil War*.

— THOMAS SPRAT
The History of the Royal Society of London, 1667. p. 55

Contents

Acknowledgements

To a greater extent than is usual in psychology, this book reports research conducted in isolation. However, such independence is deceptive. During the last seven or eight years, I have in fact accumulated intellectual debts which are both widespread and profound. The most immediate of these is to Professor O. L. Zangwill. He has provided me with a roof for my research, and given me space in which to develop the courage of my convictions. I am also indebted to the psychologists who created the field in which I work. In England, to Sir Cyril Burt, Professor P. E. Vernon, and also Dr. R. D. Laing; in America, to Professors J. W. Getzels, P. W. Jackson, D. C. McClelland, D. H. MacKinnon and Anne Roe. If I disagree with them over matters of detail, it is in full awareness of my dependence.

In addition, a number of people have helped sort my ideas into shape: chief amongst them, Dr Michael Young. And others have commented on earlier drafts of this book: Mr R. A. Becher, Dr. K. W. Blyth, Professor Ben Morris, Mr. H. Phillipson, Dr J. D. Sutherland, Mr B. W. M. Young, and Professor Zangwill. (Although their suggestions have been invaluable, the responsibility for the text remains, naturally, entirely my own.)

I am most grateful, too, to the bodies which have given me financial support: the Ministry of Education, as it then was, who gave me a studentship from 1957 to 1960; the Department of Scientific and Industrial Research, who supported me with a grant from 1961 to 1963; and the Nuffield Foundation whose support I now enjoy.

Finally, I wish to thank the members of Staff and the pupils at the various schools and colleges where I test. The former have always received me with hospitality, the latter with friendly toleration. They have given information copiously; and I hope, if they read this book, that they will not be too disappointed with what I have made of it.

April, 1965   *King's College, Cambridge*

· I ·

Presuppositions

The aim of this book is to delineate two types of clever schoolboy: the converger and the diverger. The earlier chapters offer a fairly detailed description of the intellectual abilities, attitudes and personalities of a few hundred such boys. In the later chapters, this description is then used as the basis for a more speculative discussion – of the nature of intelligence and originality and of the ways in which intellectual and personal qualities interact. Although the first half of the book rests heavily on the results of psychological tests, and the last two chapters involve psychoanalytic theory, I have done my best to be intelligible, and, wherever possible, interesting to everyone interested in clever schoolboys: parents, schoolteachers, dons, psychologists, administrators, clever schoolboys.

There follows a little stage-setting. Psychology is a subject in which the audience should have a knowledge of the experimenter's presuppositions before interpreting his results. In this first chapter I propose therefore to declare my personal prejudices about what is good psychology and what is not. These are few and simple. The first is the conviction that much of educational psychology is trivial; the second involves a distrust of complex statistics; the third, a rejection of psychological theorizing which is unduly rigorous or precise. I hope that it will be evident from the tone of these remarks that my aim is not to lampoon my fellow psychologists, but to point to certain of the difficulties with which, as psychologists, we are all surrounded.

TRIVIAL MEASUREMENTS

First, the question of triviality. In much of what has passed for educational psychology during the last fifty years we find experimenters

absorbed, not in the problems of comprehending human nature, but of measurement. Although measurement is obviously indispensable to any science, it seems that much research becomes trivial through pursuing the problems of measurement for their own sake. These problems are often of absorbing interest, but exert an attraction unrelated to the search for insight into real men and women – and in educational research, this divorce from reality is sometimes extreme. One has visions of (and perhaps one has actually seen) 'An Investigation into Job Satisfaction Ratings among Physical Training Instructors: Part One, Methodology' and 'The Blotsky Art Appreciation Inventory: A Study of Test-Retest Reliability.'

I wish to argue that although psychologists – and mental testers especially – are known for the subtlety and variety of their statistical techniques, these are often inappropriate. At present psychology is an exploratory science, and as a consequence most of our statistical needs are simple. If – in the course of our research – we find ourselves teasing out a result with the statistical scalpel, working out our correlations to three places of decimals, this is surely a sign either of a poorly designed experiment, or of a result too trifling to pursue.

As psychologists we may point out in self-defence that not all our work is so slight. We embrace themes as elevated as any in science: the Nature of Intelligence, and Man's Relation to his Work, to name but two. But this draws a second salvo: the objection that we select the loftiest themes, yet treat them bathetically. We investigate Man's Relation to his Work with a paper-and-pencil quiz. Anyone, I sense, not hopelessly biased, must admit that this criticism has something in it. We are responsible, more or less directly, for some of the oddest effects that the urge for rationality has yet produced.[1] But intelligence is no more the ability to do quizzes, than successful marriage is the ability to give right answers to a marital adjustment inventory. There is a gap, a gulf, between tests and the more interesting aspects of human life, and it is the psychologist's job to span it. Tests are invaluable as written evidence of intelligence (or stupidity), just as

---

[1] We may buy, for example, the El Senoussi Multiphasic Marital Inventory, described by the catalogue as 'a basic instrument'; and even a paper-and-pencil Male Impotence Test, which, we are assured, 'identifies four factors . . . significantly related to male impotence,' and which has been 'extensively researched by developmental and factor analysis approaches.' Kit of 25 Tests, plus Manual, ours for $10.

examinations, reports, articles, poems or books are. The trouble, at present, is not that psychologists use tests, but that those which we do use are in an exceedingly primitive condition.[1]

My second prejudice is an extension of the first: a distrust of the purely statistical approach to psychological problems. This policy forms a powerful tradition within psychology, and is a defining characteristic of the mental testing movement. Although my own research derives to a large extent from this tradition, it is one which seems in certain respects to have led us astray.

The widespread use of mental tests, especially intelligence tests, dates back to the early years of the present century, and to the efforts of such men as Binet, Terman and Thorndike. One of the most interesting features of the research stemming from their brilliant, pioneering work is its conservatism. After an initial period of innovation and experiment, progress slackened. Instead of developing more subtle tests, psychologists concentrated on the analysis of results culled from the tests they already possessed. The result was a fine flowering of factor analytic studies on the 'structure' of the intellect: sophisticated statistics poised on testing techniques of rustic simplicity. One result of this concentration on analysis has been a remarkable stagnation in the technical sphere. The intelligence tests that we use today differ little from those employed during the First World War. By 1920, the intelligence test was already established as a cheap and useful technique for sorting the bright from the dull; yet now, nearly half a century later, the position is much the same. What is more, we are little the wiser about such tests' predictive value, despite the growth of mental testing during this period from a brave outpost on the fringe of psychology to an empire of staggering dimensions.

One wonders why progress should have been so slow; and it seems that a quality of isolation, or *incapsulation*, is the crucial one. In a variety of ways, mental testers have sealed themselves off from the

[1] Doubt is sometimes expressed not merely about the value of psychological ideas, but about the intellectual calibre of the psychologists who conceive them. We stoutly refute this, naturally. Nevertheless, the unkind saying exists: 'He who can does, he who cannot teaches. He who cannot teach teaches teachers. And he who cannot teach teachers does educational research.'

human subject-matter which would have ensured them, if not perpetual youth and perplexity, at least a livelier middle age. And in this
process of incapsulation, statistics have played an insidious part.

Looking back with the priggish sense of superiority that hind-sight
affords, one may see mental testing as an orthodoxy which has inherited both the great strengths and the relative weaknesses of the
men who founded it. Many were men of outstanding statistical gifts;
but the majority were not equally interested in the observation of
individual human beings.[1] Intelligibly, the discipline which formed
itself around such formidable men as Spearman and Thurstone was
markedly statistical in bias. Indeed, it has been suggested that the
contribution of mental testing has primarily been to the theory of
statistics itself, rather than to psychology or to education.

From the psychological point of view, the statistical bias of interest amongst mental testers has not been an unalloyed advantage.
In the first place, testers have frequently worked with excessive
impersonality. They have administered 'batteries' of tests to their
'subjects' (revealing idioms, perhaps), viewing personal contact as a
source less of insight than of 'bias'. They seem happiest when people
are at a safe distance. Many testers seem, too, to have cut themselves
off from other aspects of their culture: they display no special knowledge of books, painting, music, science, politics, administration, or
any other aspect of intelligent life in the world at large. And the
literature generated by such workers has been less stimulating than
one might have hoped.[2] Man's capacity for intelligent thought is one
of Nature's most astonishing phenomena – and we might reasonably
expect that a science devoted to its study should prove commensur-
ately fascinating. Yet we find in mental testing less a thriving area of
exploratory science, more a conservative branch of educational
technology. And it is so, I would argue, precisely because testers have
taken so little account, either of individual people, or of their intellectual accomplishments outside a technical cocoon of tests and
examinations.[3]

Thus, the statistical approach to intelligence not merely makes for
dull reading. It also suffers certain characteristic disadvantages of

[1] Binet was an important but relatively isolated exception.
[2] Indeed, it is of notorious tedium – the 20th Century's answer to psychophysics: 'Those
who desire this dreadful literature can find it.' James (1890) p. 549.
[3] There are, of course, famous exceptions, Terman's longitudinal studies being one.

method. In bulk, the mental testing literature is concerned with establishing statistical connections between one variable and another; and this is frequently achieved with technical élan. However, relatively little public attention is paid either to exceptions to the general rule, or to the frightening margins of error that small and medium-sized correlations entail. Many testers are neglectful, too, of the human situations from which their data derive. All but the best seem sometimes to forget that the subtlest analysis in the world cannot make sense of poor primary data: naïve or inappropriate tests, and children who are bored.

On this analysis, the central failing amongst mental testers has been the neglect of inconvenient evidence. Testers have committed a form of scientific solipsism, building a system so tight-knit that all forms of rude human exception are excluded.[1] And as a result of their remarkably long reign, the statisticians have left psychologists a little dazed about the proper nature of their work. Under their suzerainty, the study of intelligence has become the study of tests. This is surely wrong. For once, the plain man's view of the psychologist's task seems approximately the right one. Intelligence *does* consist in thinking efficiently, in doing jobs well. High intelligence means the ability to run an industry, do scientific research, teach, write novels, plan cities, practise politics, law or medicine, or what have you. And, in so far as he is concerned with intelligence, the psychologist's primary function is to discover what these jobs involve, and to explain why some people are good at them and others are not.

THE LURE OF THEORY

The third of my prejudices concerns theories. In psychology, these come in a bewildering variety of forms. Some are qualitative hunches, others use painstaking statistical analysis. Some concern causes; others merely seek to summarize and describe. We have the

---

[1] In this respect, a psychiatrist might see some connection between mental testing and the clinical condition of paranoias. One resists such a comparison, but it becomes disconcertingly apt when one considers not the demonstrable characteristics of mental testing but its less tangible qualities: testers' attitudes and habits of mind. Like the paranoiac, testers have evolved excellent techniques for keeping awkward facts at bay. Either they are ignored (as in the case of manifestly clever people with relatively low IQ's); or they are explained away (as due, for example, to 'motivation'); or they are removed by verbal sleight of hand (e.g., by operational definition). On this last argument, intelligence is defined in terms of IQ, and in consequence the clever person with a low IQ disappears. He is a contradiction in terms.

factor analytic (various styles), the psychoanalytic (reductive, psychodynamic, and all shades between), the behaviourist, the gestalt, the developmental, the instinctive, the social, the cybernetic, and many more besides.[1]

THE STRATEGIC OBJECTION. I now wish to offer three grounds for the belief that, as matters stand at the moment in psychology, elaborate theory-building is out of place. The first is strategic: that precisely formulated theories give rise to long drawn out battles, for and against, which are finally unproductive.

Research designed with respect to theory is also likely to be wasteful. That a theory generates research does not prove its value unless the research is valuable. Much useless experimentation results from theories, and much energy and skill are absorbed by them. Most theories are eventually overthrown, and the greater part of the associated research is discarded.[2]

Theories (Hull's theory of learning, to take an example) make claims which other workers immediately try to test. This process of testing seems, on the face of it, relatively straightforward. A rat is claimed to learn when his primary drives are satisfied: satisfy his primary drives, and see whether he learns or not. However, the design of an experiment which will test such predictions is a subtle affair, and the literature concerned with Hull's theory is a large one.[3] What usually happens in the end is that the dispute peters out inconclusively. Experimenters realize either that the theory is not sufficiently precise to test; or that it is too simple to be true. Once this stage is reached, there follows a period of patching up. Then, almost invariably, the theory is allowed to languish, and most of the research aimed to support or refute it is written off as lost.

It seems that this method of organizing psychology around a number of precisely formulated but simple theories must be a poor one:

If undue emphasis is placed on formal theories before successful research strategies have been evolved, there is a clear danger that experimental results may be regarded as evidence for or against rival theories (and nearly all of them are certain to be wrong) instead of letting the data suggest new experiments and new research strategies.[4]

[1] A survey of the varieties of psychological theory would fill volumes – and indeed has already done so. See, e.g., Argyle (1957).
[2] Skinner (1959), p. 41.
[3] Hull (1943). See, e.g., Osgood (1953), Hilgard (1956), Bugelski (1956), for discussion of this literature.
[4] Gregory (1960).

Human beings, it seems, are multifarious; and we achieve little by speculating about them without first finding out what they are like. There is, after all, little merit (and no point) in proposing general ideas about human beings if these are largely or completely mistaken. Nor is there any virtue in claiming that our idea is 'basically right' although obscured by the welter of people's individuality. It is the welter that we must observe and measure; and if we do observe, we are invariably forced to modify our initial hunches out of all recognition. It seems a matter of common prudence, therefore, if theories must be adapted continually to meet new facts, that we should not define any one theory too closely.

Some may say that this criticism is glib; that the work promoted by Hull's theory is solid, empirical research, and is therefore invaluable, either as a spring-board for the next theorizer, or simply as natural history. Whether this defence is justified in any given case, it is hard to tell. In general, though, it is unpersuasive. The back numbers of the journals of experimental psychology bulge with detailed, highly artificial studies of learning, memory and perception, which few psychologists now consult. Where an experiment is designed to test a specific prediction from a given theory, the chances of its having any readily intelligible value to later generations of psychologists is slight.

This first, strategic objection to precise theories seems to me a powerful one, and damning in itself. There are however two more, both arising from the mesmeric fascination which webs of ideas seem to exert over those who spin them. The first is that theories tend to be 'blind', leading their begetters to discover only what they expect to discover. The second is that they tend to be unsinkable – they are theories which cannot be proved wrong.

BLIND, MYOPIC THEORIES. The 'blindness' of a theory will depend to a considerable extent, of course, on the detachment of the theorizer. However, there are theories which one suspects are inherently blind, or at least 'myopic'. Factor analytic theories about the structure of the intellect are a case in point. Essentially, the aim of such theories is to show to what extent various tests of reasoning overlap; that is, to show to what extent the qualities they measure are one and the same. This is achieved by statistical analysis of the intercorrelations

between a large number of different tests. The resulting factors are, to quote Vernon, 'a kind of blurred average.'[1] They reveal the general drift of relationships in a population of people considered as a whole.

Such a method is obviously useful if one wishes to find out what is going on in a field where the data are complex and one's ignorance more or less complete – and especially so, if one can identify the factors by means independent of the original measurement.[2] On the other hand, by its nature, factor analysis is a technique which does not force us into contact with awkward exceptions. If we cannot measure a quality, or can only measure it in one way, then that quality will not reflect itself in the factor analyst's results.[3] It follows that the factor analyst is not led on continually by his data to develop new and better tests, nor to pry into special circumstances, hoping to see where his predictions went wrong.

The myopic, solipsistic nature of these statistical theories seems confirmed by the poverty of the inferences that may be drawn from them. Granted that there is a 'g' factor, a 'v' factor, a 'k' factor, an 'n' factor, and so on – what follows? The answer is that little does; and nothing, I would suggest, that cannot be deduced more accurately from other sources. We may infer, for example, that tests which measure the 'g' (or general intelligence) factor will tell us who in a class is clever and who not, but only within very wide margins of error. Yet we knew this fifty years ago, and independently of the

---

[1] Vernon (1961) p. 9. This book offers an admirably clear account of the kind of theory I am here criticizing. It is arguable that these factorial theories are not theories at all, merely high level generalizations, summarizing complex evidence. There seems, in fact, to be every kind of general statement in psychology: about data already in hand; about data which might be collected; about types, abilities, factors and syndromes; and about causes, either manifest or (more usually) hypothetical. It is not always clear, when psychologists generalize, which of these kinds of assertion they have in mind. In many cases they seem to slip from one to another and back again, without noticing the transition. The simplest course – and the one I follow – is to call any psychological generalization a 'theory', if it ventures in any way beyond the description of evidence in hand, (as, for example, is frequently the case with generalizations about the structure of the intellect).

[2] Usually, in mental testing, we cannot. We cannot trephine the skulls of schoolboys, open them like radio sets, to observe the 'spatial factor' or the 'numerical factor' at work. Such factors are statistical abstractions without physical reality – nor can they even be defined uniquely in statistical terms. They are thus quite different from the old-fashioned notion of a faculty, on which much modern talk of 'factors' and 'abilities' is now surreptitiously based.

[3] Because factor analysis is based on test interrelations. Similarly, a quality which is of great importance psychologically may appear in the analysis as trifling, because the tests used measure it very imperfectly.

factor analysis which was then in its infancy. Do we learn anything about how best to teach, about how intelligence arises, or how it can be improved? Answer: no. These, it might be protested, are tall orders. On the other hand, what we are criticizing here are not the fruits of a few isolated research programmes, but those of millions of research man-hours, spreading over four decades.

THEORIES WHICH ARE UNSINKABLE. 'Unsinkability', by contrast, is a fault not of caution but of exuberance. It is an axiom, inside science and out, that explanations must in principle be open to refutation.[1] A theorizer must offer grounds on which he would admit himself mistaken; or, even if he does not, he must look as though he could do so if we took him to task. But psychologists, pleased with a new idea, frequently elaborate it with such energy that any kind of systematic check is impossible. The chief offenders here are perhaps the psychoanalysts. Consider, for example, Adrian Stokes writing about the painter Turner. His thesis is that the form of Turner's paintings is explicable in terms of his emotional needs. The interpretation he offers is a Kleinian one, which, to the unfamiliar, is heavy going.[2] Making allowance for our ignorance, we may delay judgment, waiting for Stokes to tie his interpretation down to evidence. Here the disappointment is acute. Stokes retails the famous story of Turner on Varnishing Day at the Royal Academy, reworking his astonishing painting, the 'Burning of the Houses of Lords and Commons':

> . . . for the three hours I was there – and I understood it had been the same since he began in the morning – he never ceased to work, or even once looked or turned from the wall on which his picture hung. All lookers-on were amused by the figure Turner exhibited in himself, and the process he was pursuing with his picture . . . Leaning forward and sideways over to the right, the left-hand metal button of his blue coat rose six inches higher than the right, and his head buried in his shoulders and held down, presented an aspect curious to all beholders . . . Presently the work was finished: Turner gathered up his tools together, put them into and shut up the box, and then, with his face still turned to the wall, and at the same distance from it, went sideling off, without speaking a word to anybody.

[1] Popper (1963).
[2] For an introductory account of Melanie Klein's theories, see Segal (1964). Unfortunately, this itself is strenuous reading. The best readily intelligible books on recent developments in psychoanalysis are Brown (1964), and Guntrip (1961).

We can take it that in the act of painting, even his vast distances were pressed up against the visionary eye like the breast upon the mouth: at the same time it was he who fed the infant picture. In these embracing conceptions, no wonder that figures glue themselves on banks and bases, variegated figures, salmon-like, dully flashing films of colour, perhaps floating beneath a cloud-like architecture, perhaps pressed to the ground like the catch in baskets upon a quay, glistening at dawn. Ruskin remarked on the accumulations of bric-a-brac in Turnerian foregrounds – I would include bodies and jetsam in seas, or on an earth so flattened in some late canvases as to suggest a pavement of rippled water – and referred them to the grand confusion of Covent Garden where Turner lived as a child. An equation persists, as is well known, between nipple and phallus. The above description of Turner at work in 1835 at the British Institution may recall the couplet twice used in his incomprehensible verses entitled *The Origin of Vermilion or the Loves of Painting and Music*:

> As snails trail o'er the morning dew
> He thus the line of beauty drew.

He sought daring expedients for his sense of fitness: in the case of persons especially, I repeat, they were based on part-object models. The companions, the siblings, he projected, are often like shoals; as mere members, as mouths perhaps, they may flit about the declivities and rises of an encompassing breast, much of it out of reach as palace, torrent, ocean, mountain or murderous sky.'[1]

Admittedly, it is unfair to wrench so difficult a passage from its context – selective quotation can make nonsense of the closest argument. But even in context, one has the impression that Stokes is having his explanatory cake and eating it. He rushes ahead of us, leaving scarce a trace of ground on which we could prove him wrong. The evocation of Turner's painting is brilliant, and so too is the use of the Kleinian symbolism; but nothing more. Sneakingly, one even suspects that whatever Turner had done, Stokes would have felt Kleinian theory vindicated. The mistake is an easy one to make (I shall slip towards it continually in the last two chapters of this book) – but to be of use in psychology, such flights must be contained.

The dangers are perhaps worth spelling out in more detail, especially as they have a bearing on certain interpretations of my own. Let us assume, for the sake of an over-simplified example, that an adult's impulses to hoard money or to collect porcelain are explained in terms of his inclinations as a child to retain his faeces. One rightly objects on three counts: conceptual, factual, personal. First: collecting money (or porcelain) is not self-evidently the same activity as retaining faeces. If one is held to be a 'sublimation' of the

[1] Stokes (1963), p. 73.

other, then this connection must be demonstrated empirically. Second: when one tries to collect the relevant factual evidence, it proves exceedingly hard to find.[1] Third: one has the sense, as a hoarder of money or collector of porcelain, that the psychologist using such an explanation is seeking covertly to belittle you, your money or your porcelain. It is possible that such adult interests are a sublimation of some other impulse; that sublimation is a concept which we will be able to define well enough to examine scientifically; and that the other impulse in question is the childish one they specify. But using such explanations as this in the absence of factual evidence must seem a little high-handed.[2]

Closely related to the habit of offering irrefutable explanations, is that not of explaining but of explaining *away*. Psychologists of all persuasions seem prone to this. The confusion arises, perhaps, because an essential distinction has not yet been grasped: that between scientific explanations and exhortations or sermons on method. The first accounts for specified facts in a logically binding way; the second merely explains how such feats of explanation might be undertaken. Watson's assertion of behaviourism is a methodological sermon in this sense; and so too, although in subtly differing ways are the programmes of the gestalt psychologists and the cyberneticists. Behaviourism is not a body of knowledge, but a forceful suggestion (with illustrations) about how experimental psychologists should conduct their research. We are urged to pin our trust, quite sensibly as it happens, on Stimulus and Response; and Introspection is banished – as if it were some dubious (and perhaps Central European) perversion. Similarly, the cyberneticist does not offer us facts so much as a new language of 'noise', 'servo-loops', 'memory stores', 'input', 'output', and so on – and the idea that we look at the central nervous system as a computer. And it is interesting that although the cyberneticists' suggestions seem sensible, and although experimental psychologists have adopted them with zeal, relatively little in the way of factual discovery yet seems to have followed from them.

To say that methodological prescriptions are prescriptions is not of

---

[1] See, e.g. Sears, (1943).

[2] Eysenck (1952), among others, has pointed out the weaknesses of such explanations. It does not follow of course that because a concept is unusable that the phenomenon does not exist. I would accept what analysts describe as 'sublimation' as an integral part of our daily experience, whilst admitting that we may not yet be able to use such ideas in scientific explanation.

course to condemn them. They are often valuable, suggesting where and how we might look for explanations. On the other hand, they are easily abused. Behaviourists may slip into a dogmatic frame of mind and assert that the phenomena (whatever they are) 'are all due to conditioning'. And from an entirely different, but equally dogmatic stance, the psychoanalyst may counter that they are all explicable in terms of 'Oedipal conflicts'. Well they may be, in either case; but the difficulty is one of vagueness. As they stand, such assertions lack the precision which could render them either true or false. At best, they are declarations of intent; at worst, they are feeble efforts to sweep ignorance under the carpet. (And as a result, many of our profession perch in pre-eminence with their heads against the ceiling).[1]

THE STATISTICAL EXCEPTION

In discussing each of my three main prejudices, it seems that I have been concerned with the same problem: the evasion of a challenge which arises in all behavioural science, but which psychologists seem to face in an especially acute form. One has both to collect facts on a wide scale, and to conceive general ideas complex enough to encompass them. The real challenge of psychology lies, in other words, neither in the collection of the facts nor in devizing the general ideas, but in relating the one to the other – and the temptation is to permit an exceedingly loose fit between them. This process of relating fact to theory is, in practice, so difficult and so messy an intellectual operation that one slips away from it continually, either into webspinning and methodology, or simply by keeping one's collection of facts very small.

[1] An extreme argument, but perhaps a defensible one, is that all psychological theorizing is otiose. Skinner, for example, would have us do away with it altogether:

'When we have achieved a practical control over the organism, theories of behavior lose their point. In representing and managing relevant variables, a conceptual model is useless; we come to grips with behavior itself. When behavior shows order and consistency, we are much less likely to be concerned with physiological or mentalistic causes. A datum emerges which takes the place of theoretical fantasy. In the experimental analysis of behavior we address ourselves to a subject matter which is not only manifestly the behavior of an individual and hence accessible without the usual statistical aids but also "objective" and "actual" without recourse to deductive theorizing.   Skinner (1959) p. 96.

However, general ideas and hunches do seem to guide a psychologist's work, whether he is aware of them or not – and Skinner's faith in positive reinforcement seems a good illustration of this.

The three prejudices displayed in this chapter can be summarized, therefore, in the form of yet another sermon. There is a case, I feel, for enshrining the statistical exception. In exploratory science, the odd man out is frequently the one who foretells the next transformation in the experimenter's search for order. He deserves, therefore, to be handled with special care. Yet, as Darwin remarked, such exceptions are elusive:

I had, also, during many years, followed a golden rule, namely, that whenever a published fact, a new observation or thought came across me, which was opposed to my general results, to make a memorandum of it without fail and at once; for I had found by experience that such facts and thoughts were far more apt to escape from the memory than favourable ones.[1]

It is the death of behavioural science, or so I would argue, to be content with theories tenuously supported, and small-to-medium correlations. Our predictive control must be strong, or we enter a twilight state in which no theory is put closely to the test, and in which hobby-horses are not refuted but politely forgotten. If psychologists care about exceptions – if they *notice* them, even – progress remains a possibility.

Experimental enthusiasts may protest that although such sermons are relevant enough to psychoanalysis, the mental testing movement has standards of precision which are unparalleled in behavioural science; that one is exhorting the meticulous to be more so. Yet it seems that fastidiousness in some respects may disguise a certain hastiness in others, as the Case of the Interview proves. The meticulous are not always as meticulous as they seem.

THE CASE OF THE INTERVIEW. As an undergraduate, I received, along with many other opinions, one about the unreliability of interviews. The authorities were unamimous:

This failure of the interview is only one of many instances showing the impossibility of achieving reliable and valid prediction on the basis of subjective ratings, personal impressions, and clinical insight . . . It would appear, therefore, that the contribution of the interview may well be negative in sign, as well as small in extent.[2]

[1] Barlow (1958) p. 123.
[2] Eysenck (1952) p. 267.

. . . the interview alone is most untrustworthy for providing adequate evidence about the candidate's intelligence, attainment or future academic performance.'[1]
'It would seem that oral questioning and the interview . . . are useless for assessing ability or the results of teaching.[2]

Each of these authors referred to one piece of evidence as critical, and almost by accident, I looked it up: Himmelweit's study of selection techniques at the London School of Economics.[3] What I found there was remarkable. It was not that conclusions had run ahead of facts, rather that the two were unrelated:

In 1946, the conditions were far from good, since very large numbers of applicants had to be seen which meant that the interviews had to be brief and that not all members of the many interviewing boards were equally experienced. Furthermore, interviewers were relatively unfamiliar with ex-service candidates whose outlook and general maturity differed considerably from the usual run of pre-war students.'
'The purpose of the interview was not directed primarily at assessing intellectual ability, but more at detecting those whose personality and general background would make them capable of pursuing a course of studies, without necessarily obtaining a good degree.[4]

In other words, Himmelweit's interviews were given in abnormally difficult circumstances: they were brief; some of the interviewers had no previous experience; few of the candidates had recently done any academic work; and the interviewers were not primarily concerned, in any case, with the candidates' intellectual potentialities. Estimates of ultimate degree class can have been little more than spot judgments; and a random result is precisely what one would expect.

Yet Himmelweit's study discounted, the remaining evidence was thin. Hartog and Rhodes – to mention the most pertinent – found in 1934 that interviews based on those used in Civil Service selection at that time were unreliable. Their evidence made nonsense of that particular style of interview, but the style in question was most unsystematic.[5] For the rest, one was reduced to studies of the selection of

[1] Dale (1954) p. 151.
[2] Vernon (1956) p. 247.
[3] Himmelweit (1950), Himmelweit and Summerfield (1951a, 1951b).
[4] Himmelweit and Summerfield, (1951a), p. 73.
[5] Hartog and Rhodes (1936). The correlation between the judgments of two parallel boards was 0.41. This however is not surprising. (a) The qualities which the interviewers were asked to assess were general and ill-defined; they were simply asked to 'judge the value of the candidate's personality for the Home Civil Service.' (b) The two interviews were not standardized:

American clinical psychologists, officer cadets, and so forth; and although the results were largely unfavourable, they were by no means all so.[1]

My intention in retailing the Case of the Interview is certainly not to impugn the competence of the eminent psychologists concerned; still less to cast doubt upon their motives. Indeed, my point is precisely the reverse. Their very probity and distinction suggests how powerfully the *zeitgeist* can sway us all. The mood of educational psychologists in the early 1950's was in favour of the non-human, technical approach, and against the mystique of personal judgment. Given this, all else would seem to have followed.

THE GENERAL CHARACTER OF THE BOOK

In the light of what has already been said, the reader might well expect a book containing no tests or statistics, and no speculation of any kind – a case study, perhaps, packed with careful observations. In fact, though, as the first paragraph declares, the present research rests heavily on psychological tests. It also makes considerable use of elementary statistics. In parts, it is highly speculative; and it will certainly strike many people as trivial. At first sight, therefore, my own work is condemned as roundly as any one else's. However, such inconsistency – or even perversity – is less real than apparent. Tests seem indispensable to certain kinds of psychological investigation: they provide an empirical foundation for an argument which would otherwise be impressionistic. And although the more complex and sophisticated forms of statistical analysis seem out of place, I cannot see how the psychologist can do without statistics altogether. One can be averse to the mystique, the Number Magic, with which some psychologists surround statistics, without objecting to them generically. And similarly with theories: one can oppose web-spinning for its own sake, without condemning all forms of speculation out of hand. My objection is not to psychological theories in general – only

---

'... it was largely a matter of chance whether they struck on a topic in which a candidate felt so strongly that he was able to display his individuality.' (c) The interviews were relatively short: '... for not less than a quarter of an hour and not more than half an hour.' (d) The candidates were a small group of 16 highly selected volunteers, so the range of suitability must have been narrow. (e) The nine interviewers were eminent, but they were also somewhat old: it would have been possible, for example, for one of the two boards to have had an average age of 65.

[1] See Vernon and Parry (1949), Kelly and Fiske (1950), Taft (1955), Argyle (1957).

to those which are unduly precise or rigid, or which ignore the need
for factual verification. Good theory, on this argument, is theory
which leads fairly soon to better experiments. In all three respects –
tests, statistics, theory – I would argue not for one ideal method, but
for any approach sufficiently flexible to afford new insights and to
lend these insights factual support.

The question of triviality is not so easy. In a sense, all psychologists aspire to profound results, but find trivial ones thrust upon
them. I am no exception. My research deals with two questions; that
of differences in intellectual type, and that of thinking originally,
productively, or in any sense well. The first is moderately interesting;
the second is absorbing and profoundly important. Yet my results
seem invariably to illuminate the first of these, not the second. Such
discoveries as I have made about the originality of people's thought
are negative – or, if positive, shadowy in the extreme. The question
of originality is, in many ways, the most alluring that psychology
has to offer, but it also seems to be one of the most difficult. Consequently, although I discuss such central issues, my positive findings
about differences in intellectual type are bound to seem prosaic.

If an air of inconsistency still lingers – between the complaints of
this chapter and the tests, statistics and speculations which follow – it
is as well to acknowledge this and to make its cause explicit. My
view is that a certain sort of inconsistency is virtually inseparable
from any scientific enquiry. The scientist edges forward not (or
not primarily) by meek acceptance of his chosen discipline, but by
kicking against its weaknesses and limitations, and trying however
inadequately to overcome them. Thus a tension exists within any
research discipline, between what the research worker can measure,
and what he would like to measure. And this tension seems to me
essential to his progress – without it, his research would largely be
barren. So although this chapter rails against the practical constraints and theoretical weaknesses of psychology, the remainder of
the book describes work largely – though, one trusts, not entirely –
contained within the boundaries that such constraints and weaknesses provide. This *is* an inconsistent position, but the inconsistency
is one that I should be reluctant to avoid.

One or two other aspects of the text deserve mention. It contains,
for instance, relatively little technical jargon. This style is a dangerous

one, because stripped of their protective language, psychological theories often read like platitudes. This reduces the respect of lay readers for one's work, and is sometimes viewed by professional colleagues as blacklegging. On the other hand, plain English has two advantages. In the first place, the present proliferation of technical languages and arbitrary definitions seems to render psychology especially susceptible both to the more ephemeral forms of intellectual fashion, and also to bogus orthodoxies. Another possible advantage of plain English is that it may help to dissipate some of the distrust which exists in psychology between rival camps or factions. My own research descends from two such schools of thought: mental testing and psychoanalysis. Both profess interest (and claim expertise) in the realm of intelligent human action; yet, in this country at least, their languages and presuppositions are so dissimilar that neither understands what the other says. A typical offspring of estranged parents, I feel that some degree of reconciliation is in order: a little more discipline for the speculatively self-indulgent, and a little less for the spinsterishly scientific. My pedestrian (and perhaps puritanical) suggestion is that these two schools would enormously benefit, as would psychology as a whole, if they engineered some means of mutual comprehension through the common tongue.

The black-legging tendencies of this book are in fact centipedal. The traditional method of reporting scientific experiment is not merely to swaddle it in jargon, but to give it coat and tails. The literature is reviewed, hypotheses stated, method defined, results presented, implications discussed, and acknowledgements made – all in accordance with a rigid protocol. It has recently been protested, by a Nobel prize winner, that this form of good manners is a fraud, and a travesty of scientific thought.[1] In practice, scientific research is frequently a muddled, piratical affair, and we do no service to anyone by pretending otherwise. I have tried, therefore, to describe my research not as a neat experiment but much as it happened.

For similar reasons, the book has a somewhat personal tone; 'I' occurs frequently. This is partially a matter of verbal incompetence (avoiding the first person singular is a scientific skill all its own); partially intentional. Research, or so it is argued in Chapter 8, is very much a personal affair. It engages the individual's personality; and in

[1] Medawar (1964).

psychology there is a disconcerting tendency for the psychologists' personalities to reflect themselves in their theories, and even in their results. This being so, there seems every case for dropping the mask of objectivity in reporting psychological research, and describing the sequence of events naturalistically.

Finally, I should like to declare the intention of describing research which has no immediate practical value. This intention arises not from scientific snobbery, but from a fear that the book will seem socially useful when it is not. When my research began, I hoped that it might lead to valid tests of intellectual aptitude: tests, that is, which would tell the uncertain which career they were best suited to pursue. This may still happen. Nonetheless, the last 6 years have convinced me that the value of vocational tests in school and Universities is limited, and that their widespread use may actually be harmful.[1] I hope, therefore, that this book will not be judged as a contribution to the efficiency of any particular educational technique. My aim is not to ensure, in any direct sense, that the education of school children is carried out more effectively; rather, to use the system as it now stands as a source of insight into the ways in which children feel and think.

The plan of the book is as follows. Chapter 2 deals not with convergers and divergers, but with the background from which this work sprang – research on differences between the arts and sciences. Chapters 3 and 4 describe the converger and diverger empirically, in terms of the differences which they reveal with paper and pencil. Chapter 5 offers an interpretation of these empirical differences, showing that they conform to consistent patterns. There then follows in Chapter 6, rather an uncharitable review of the literature on 'creativity', and its bearing on my own results. Chapters 7 and 8 are speculative – the first contains some suggestions about the origins of convergence and divergence; the second some ideas of my own about the nature of originality. Statistical tables and details about tests will be found in Appendices A and B.

---

[1] My anxiety, briefly, is that the use of such tests on a wide scale will tend to reduce childrens' sense of responsibility for their own decisions. Most boys seem to choose their careers intuitively, without much conscious reflection. It may be that the very act of asking an expert for advice on this matter is a symptom of a more general anxiety. By offering to give such children advice, the aptitude tester may exacerbate their 'intellectual hypochondria' rather than helping to abate it.

· 2 ·

Arts and Science

This chapter describes the context from which the work on convergers and diverges emerged. My research began in 1957 as a study of 'Arts/Science Specialization'. As an undergraduate I had found that I was much better at some parts of intelligence tests than others: good at the diagrammatic questions, and relatively poor at the verbal and numerical ones. When the time came to apply for a postgraduate research grant, I proposed, therefore, to look into the question of verbal, numerical and diagrammatic biases in intelligence. It was pointed out to me that the problem of the Two Cultures was fashionable, and that my application would be more favourably received if my interest in intelligence was tied to the problem of the arts and sciences. Tied it duly was.[1]

My aim at this early stage was to devise tests of aptitude for arts and sciences respectively. Had I known it, the outlook was gloomy; American mental testers had been at work on this task for a decade at least – and with a minimum of success. Millions of research hours had been devoted to this problem of 'differential aptitude' before I learnt of its existence. Happily, though, my ignorance of the literature was complete: if I had had even a smattering I should certainly have tackled something else.[2]

After wasting a year meddling ineffectually with information

---

[1] My aim, presumably, was to find biases similar to my own, to see what their owners were like. Or, more realistically, to find others with a similar bias, to discover what I was like myself. The idea of relating such research to the arts and sciences was Professor R. C. Oldfield's, to whom I am indebted.

[2] No adequate, nor adequately critical, account of this American research exists. For a description of the test batteries see Anastasi (1961): and for mention of the logical issues involved see Horst (1954). Also Crawford and Burnham (1946).

theory, I had a stroke of luck. A large store of undergraduates'
scores on an intelligence test was made available to me and, re-
marking them, I found that arts specialists usually had verbal
biases of ability whilst scientists had numerical or diagrammatic
ones.[1] In psychological terms (as opposed to those of the world at
large), this was a very small, but quite momentous discovery. A
discrimination which could not be established among American
high-school students was readily apparent among Cambridge undergraduates. When I gave the same test to clever 15-year-old schoolboys, the difference in scores still held good. And there were similar
biases, too, among 13- and 14-year-olds whose academic specialization had not begun. Biases of intelligence, in other words, existed
prior to academic specialization, and were not merely by-products
of it. Possibly, arts/science aptitude was measurable after all.[2]

THE METHOD

Until recently, the character of my research changed relatively little.
Each year I visited a small number of schools, public and grammar,
and tested a group of Fourth, Fifth or Lower Sixth formers. These
were always reasonably clever boys, the dullest being well above the
national average, and the brightest among the brightest anywhere.[3]
I rarely tested more than 200 boys in any one year, or covered more
than three different schools. All the results reported in this text are

[1] I am indebted to Dr A. W. Heim for her generosity with these test results, and for her help
in other respects.
[2] Hudson (1961, 1963b). One wonders why an arts/science discrimination should show up
amongst English children, but not amongst their American contemporaries. The explanation
seems to be a methodological one. Early specialization in English schools divides children
fairly irrevocably into distinct academic groups. Consequently, the decisions which it forces
upon children are not ones which they will take lightly. Before committing himself to one
speciality or another, the English schoolboy thinks quite carefully about his abilities, interests
and ambitions. Thus, whatever its advantages or disadvantages educationally, specialization
is a great convenience for the psychologist. In England he has a number of carefully self-
selected groups to compare, whereas his American colleagues, by comparison, have to make
do with differences in marks for the various school subjects – a criterion which reveals much
less of children's true bent.
[3] I have tested, in all, at eight different schools: five public boarding-schools, one public
day-school, and two grammar schools. All are within a 100-mile radius of London; all enjoy a
high academic standing. Throughout my results, I have tried to ensure that every statistic is
based on a sample drawn half from public schools and half from grammar. In fact, though,
this precaution seems largely academic as the differences between the two types of school – as
far as my work is concerned – seem trifling. The criterion for selecting the sample was rough-
and-ready: that the boy should stand quite a good chance of reaching University if he saw fit
to do so.

based on data collected under such conditions. Of late, samples have included medical students, both male and female, and would-be undergraduates. However, members of these groups are not included in the statistical analysis, and appear only occasionally, usually for purposes of illustration.

The dangers of sampling on such a small scale need little rehearsing. A result based on a small sample may be a fluke. A discrimination achieved one year may disappear when one tries to repeat it the next. There is also the danger of basing one's results on atypical schools – what holds for Greystone College and Whitetile Grammar School for Boys in the South of England may not hold for their equivalent in the North, what holds for boys may not hold for girls, and so on.

Such objections have to be taken seriously. One must guard against them, but also prevent them from breaking one's stride. For even more important than adequate sampling is the experimenter's need to keep close to his primary data: in this case, to schoolboys. I take it as axiomatic that the research worker interested in human nature achieves little or nothing if he thinks of his sample solely in terms of dots and distribution curves. He must also be able to think of each member of his sample as an individual. Necessarily, there is a limit to the number of individuals of whom anyone can think at any one time. My own span is about 150. It so happens that this number is one which for most purposes approaches statistical respectability, and it represents, therefore, a tolerably good compromise figure. It enables one to explore briskly, without producing results which are statistically worthless. The sample accumulates year by year, moreover; and at the end of five years' research one often has not 150 boys relevant to any one discrimination, but as many as 400 or 500.[1]

---

[1] Intensive, small scale experiments of this kind involve a statistical nicety which has not been widely discussed. Let us imagine that a psychologist gives a hundred tests to a sizeable sample of schoolboys, and that they answer his tests more or less at random. If the psychologist now scrutinises his results for (let us say) arts/science differences, he is almost bound to find some. If he uses the X^2 test to assess the statistical significance of those he does find, he will doubtless find a number which reach the 5 per cent level of significance. But if the boys answer at random, 5 out of the 100 tests could be expected to reach this level of significance purely by chance – this, after all, is what 5 per cent level of significance means. Similarly, one test out of the 100 might be expected to produce a result at the 1 per cent level. The experimenter's only defence, though happily a good one, is scrupulously to repeat his work, and to make sure that the levels of significance maintain themselves from one year to the next. This is particularly important where results are unexpected. There seems a case, in fact, for eschewing low levels of significance altogether, and treating the 1 per cent level as the weakest for reported results. I am grateful to Professor P. E. Vernon who first pointed out this danger to me.

As far as tests were concerned, the backbone of the research was at first the intelligence test, but others were included even then: tests of spatial reasoning, vocabulary, general knowledge, interests and so on. With this battery of tests in hand, the prediction of boys' choices between arts and science subjects in the Sixth Form became quite easy.[1] The typical historian or modern linguist had, relatively speaking, rather a low IQ, and a verbal bias of intelligence. He was prone to work erratically on the intelligence test, accurate at times and slapdash at others; and his interests tended to be cultural rather than practical. The young physical scientist often had a high IQ, and a non-verbal bias of ability; he was usually consistently accurate; and his interests were usually technical, mechanical, or in life out of doors. Naturally, these rules-of-thumb were not perfect: a minority of arts specialist had scores like scientists, and vice versa. But, by and large, the predictions held surprisingly well, and at extremes they were virtually infallible.[2]

TWO PARADIGMS: KNIGHT AND FLEETWOOD

First, consider Knight: a delightfully friendly boy from one of the country's best grammar schools.[3] In the Sixth Form, he specialized in history and English literature, having done outstandingly well in these subjects at 'O' Level, and miserably in mathematics, general science and Latin. His interests were pronounced:

Reading, novels (modern and historical) plays, I read many. Collecting Art reproduction from the Louvre to Lewisham. Going to the pictures. I go weekly but I hope intelligently and going out to the theatre, London, old churches, and swimming with . . . friends. I sometimes go dancing. Records. I have always since I was of tender years loved History, English and Art. I have always managed to make my History interesting and 'live' it as far as possible. The same applies to

---

[1] The intelligence test was A.H.5, a test specially suited to highly intelligent groups. See Heim (1956). For details of the other tests, see Hudson (1961). 'Prediction' is here used loosely to cover two different (although statistically equivalent) operations. The first refers to genuine prediction over time: guessing in advance what someone will do before he does it. The second refers to guessing 'blindfold' after the event: in this case, identifying arts and science specialists from their scores on tests.

[2] Properly speaking 'IQ' here is a misnomer – A.H.5. scores are not applicable to the whole population. My use of the expression is therefore colloquial. The test 'profiles' for the various Sixth Form subjects are given in Table I. I only have parallels at the university level for scores derived from the intelligence test: IQ bias of intelligence, and accuracy. In these respects however the agreement between the two samples was quite close (Hudson 1960a, 1961).

[3] All the boys mentioned in the text are protected by pseudonyms.

English as books and writing has always occupied me; as for Art I suddenly discovered I could draw reasonably and Architecture and Painting fascinate me to the extent that even the largest art homeworks are a joy. My Maths and Science are non-existent.

His scores reflect his bias towards the arts in every respect. On the numerical and diagrammatic parts of the intelligence test he was abjectly weak, and his overall IQ was one of the lowest I tested. He was extremely inaccurate; and his spatial reasoning was, if anything, worse than his IQ. His verbal IQ, on the other hand, was only a little below the average for a Fifth Former; his vocabulary was well above average; and his general knowledge was quite outstanding. (This last I measured with a test consisting of factual questions about famous men from five fields: current affairs and politics, literature, painting, music, and science. Knight's scores were outstanding on each of the first four categories, but only average on the last). The majority of his form-mates mentioned him as being specially interested in literature, painting and music; not one suggested that his interests were in any way practical.

Poor test scores notwithstanding, Knight passed both history and English at 'S' Level with ease. Thus, within the context of the Sixth Form, it turns out that one of the cleverest boys has one of the lowest IQ's. Indeed, at the age of 11 his IQ of 110 was so low that in many areas of the country he would have failed the 11-Plus examination and been excluded from a grammar-school education altogether. And Knight, as I shall show, was not an isolated exception.[1]

At the other extreme from Knight, is Fleetwood, a quiet boy from the north of England, then a physical science specialist at a southern public boarding-school. Fleetwood's profile of abilities was the antithesis of Knight's. In the 'O' Level examination, he did poorly in all the arts subjects, but distinguished himself in physics, chemistry and mathematics. His interests were exclusively practical: he ran the school radio club, and was a prize-winning model builder. Yet, culturally, he was a blank. On his own admission, he did no voluntary reading whatever. He knew virtually nothing about any of the Arts

[1] Another point about boys like Knight is that they are discriminated against by University requirements in mathematics and Latin. One might argue that University arts faculties would be the death of lively boys like these – that they are better off running free. On the other hand, such boys should not arbitrarily be excluded. In practice, they often do go to University, but are dogged by their weaknesses in required subjects.

sections of the general knowledge test; and although almost all of his form-mates picked him out as specially interested in practical matters, not one of them mentioned him in another context. Summing up his own academic ambitions, he wrote:

I want to become an engineer and take the Mechanical Science Tripos. Detest Latin.

Like Knight, Fleetwood's scores reflect his talents closely: good although not outstanding, in I Q and accuracy; a very strong non-verbal bias; poor vocabulary and general knowledge; and outstanding spatial reasoning.

IDENTIFYING BOYS SUBJECT BY SUBJECT –
SOME MORE EXAMPLES

These two boys are extremes – they have been picked out to represent polar opposites. Few are so biased academically, and even fewer reflect their biases so neatly in their test scores. Between Fleetwood and Knight stretch hundreds of boys who are more versatile, and who are correspondingly less easy to identify. Identification, nevertheless, is surprisingly accurate. Taking a sample of 100 of the cleverest Fifth Formers, I once sorted them 'blindfold' into four piles, identifying them from their scores alone: those with a marked bias of ability towards the arts, those with a slight bias towards the arts, those with a slight bias of ability towards science, and those with a marked bias towards science. If I had scored them at random, thirty-five to forty individuals would have been misplaced by more than one pile. In fact, ninety-seven out of a hundred boys went either into the correct pile or into a neighbouring one. There was also surprisingly little confusion, too, between the arts specialists and the scientists. Only four out of the fifty arts boys were identified as scientists; and only six vice versa. By prevailing standards in educational psychology this was good going.[1]

Sometimes one was even able to guess which particular subjects on the arts or science side an individual boy would choose: whether, for example, a boy would choose mathematics, physics and chemistry on the one hand, or chemistry, zoology and botany on the other. Some examples show this process of identification at work.

[1] Hudson (1963b).

CANHAM IQ – *exceptionally high.*
    Bias of IQ – *strongly numerical and diagrammatic.*
    Accuracy – *high.*
    Vocabulary – *below average.*
    General Knowledge – *average.*
    Interests[1] – *Astronomy.*

There is not much difficulty about this one. Everything points to mathematics or physical science, the only discrepancy being the unusually high accuracy score – often the sign of a classicist. However, classics is ruled out both by the bias of IQ and by the weakness in vocabulary. He seems every bit as sure a bet as the paradigm physical scientist, Fleetwood.

COX IQ – *average.*
    Bias of IQ – *verbal, but not strongly so.*
    Accuracy – *average.*
    Vocabulary – *below average.*
    General Knowledge – *below average.*
    Interests – *Fishing (not fly); crosswords; making models in holidays; going for bicycle rides; Trad. jazz.*

With the more ambiguous profiles like this, one works by exclusion. Mathematics and physical science one can discount with some confidence – his bias of IQ is wrong, and his accuracy is a little low. Classics seem unlikely, too, on grounds of accuracy and vocabulary. That leaves history, modern languages and biology – or a course like geography, or politics and economics. (These last are still fairly rare for the top flight of boys, so I usually restrict myself to differentiating between the other three). History seems rather unlikely because of his interests. 'Hunting', 'shooting' and 'fishing' are frequently social observances, and do not seem to have discriminative significance. 'Model making', on the other hand, is distinctly unlike a historian. This leaves modern languages and biology, and one's only indication is a verbal bias of IQ. Thus, if I had to, I would plump for modern languages – without confidence, however.

NORTHCOTE IQ – *above average.*
    Bias of IQ – *none.*
    Accuracy – *average.*
    Vocabulary – *above average.*
    General Knowledge – *above average.*
    Interests – *Playing tennis, rackets, squash, cricket, cross-country running, athletics, golf, people.*

If anything, even trickier than the one before. Working by exclusion again, history seems unlikely, specially on grounds of IQ. Moreover, this and the vocabulary score both seem to exclude biology. This leaves physical science, classics and modern languages. Beyond this I would feel uneasy – and would resort to hunch.

---

[1] 'Interests' here refers specifically to activities outside the curriculum.

My guess, although I have not checked this systematically, is that physical scientists with presentable IQ's and good vocabularies normally have other interests besides sport. He might well be one of the able, rather aimless all-rounders who go into modern languages, or less frequently, classics. On the other hand, there is really no reason why he should not turn out to be a physical scientist.

CHRISTY   IQ – *below average.*
        Bias of IQ – *strongly verbal.*
        Accuracy – *low.*
        Vocabulary – *above average.*
        General Knowledge – *above average.*
        Interests – *Sketching, reading history and books, art, climbing, tennis, ski-ing, military history, cars.*

Another straightforward one, from the mould of my other paradigm, Knight. He classifies himself automatically as either a historian or a modern linguist. Between these, there is never much to choose, but here most of the signs indicate history: good vocabulary and general knowledge, and a variety of cultural-looking interests. The only danger sign is the interest in climbing – unusual among historians. On the other hand, modern linguists' interests tend to be scanty, and where they show enthusiasm, it is usually for social life or conspicuous consumption. If I had to guess, I would say a historian.

WERNICK   IQ – *above average.*
        Bias of IQ – *strongly numerical and diagrammatic.*
        Accuracy – *average.*
        Vocabulary – *high.*
        General Knowledge – *high.*
        Interests – *Botany, Ornithology, Chemistry (Home Laboratory), Palaeontology, Archaeology, Philately, Numismatology, Geology, Swimming (underwater), Camping.*

Not so easy. History and modern languages seem to be excluded on fairly obvious grounds; and, despite the interests, the general level of scores seems to rule out biology. This leaves classics and physical science. Of the two, the second is the better bet. Classicists rarely produce such an abundance of interests or such obviously scientific ones – and his numerical and diagrammatic bias points the same way. I would plump fairly emphatically for physical science – the kind of boy who shows real intellectual breadth, and who, one suspects, will do even better at University than he does at school.

SNEDDON   IQ – *above average.*
        Bias of IQ – *diagrammatic.*
        Accuracy – *low.*
        Vocabulary – *low.*
        General Knowledge – *low.*
        Interests – *Mechanical Engineering (Motor Cycling), Outdoor Activities.*

In addition to these scores (Sneddon was from an earlier batch) we also have evidence of his spatial reasoning, and this was excellent. He seems reasonably straightforward. Classics and history are most unlikely. His diagrammatic bias, spatial reasoning and obvious practical interests make modern languages seem improbable. ('Outdoor activities', incidentally, turned out in the interview to refer to his girl-friend). So one is left with the choice between physical or biological science. Of these, biology seems rather the better bet on account of his very poor accuracy.

THE VERDICT

Having committed ourselves, we find out what the boys really did. But to prolong the agony, let us add the clue that there is *one* biologist among them, but that he is not Sneddon. It follows that I must have blundered, not once but twice. If Sneddon is not a biologist, he must, I would argue, be a rather undistinguished, or perhaps a rather neurotic physical scientist.[1] But this does not find us the biologist. Who is he? It cannot be either Canham or Christy. It might be Wernick, especially in view of his interests in natural history, or perhaps Northcote; but the most likely candidate is Cox.

In fact, though, I was right about Cox – a modern linguist; and Northcote, as I rather suspected, was a classicist. Both Canham and Christy are true to type: physical scientist and historian respectively. The biologist, as we should perhaps have guessed from his spare-time interests, is Wernick. The point about him is that he is an exceptionally good one – the rarity, a biologist who could have done physics, or classics, but chose not to. As a token of his quality he won a Cambridge open scholarship.

The only point remaining: is Sneddon a physical scientist, and if so is he a poor one? Answer: he is a modern linguist. Happily for our self-respect, it turns out in this case that the blunder was not ours but his parents'. His father was an autocrat, determined that this, his younger son, should take over the office side of the family business. He was destined, therefore, for chartered accountancy, via modern languages. The school staff thought this a bad move, but father proved obdurate, and had his way. His son failed two subjects at 'A'

[1] I found poor accuracy scores to correlate with interview ratings of emotional instability. Some boys seemed to express their instability by being consistently inaccurate; others by being inaccurate only in patches. For a full account of all this, see Hudson (1961) for previous research, Himmelweit (1950).

Level, and when last heard of had left without finding a university place, and was being crammed by a private tutor.[1]

THE WEAKNESSES OF THE TESTS

As these cases illustrate, mistakes occur for a variety of reasons. Wernick was misjudged because he was unusually good for his subject. Others are misjudged because they are unusually weak – some mediocre physical scientists, for example, find themselves identified as biologists. Sneddon, on the other hand, was misjudged because he was doing the wrong subject. There are also mistakes which arise because the schools cannot provide for certain minority interests. At University, for example, law students' scores differ from those of students reading classics, history and modern languages; yet at school the aspiring lawyer usually has to make his choice between these three subjects.[2] It is not surprising, then, that a number of seemingly aberrant historians, modern linguists and classicists at the Sixth Form level turn out to be potential lawyers. Much the same tends to happen on the science side with aspiring architects, who, in the Sixth Form, normally have to take mathematics, physics and chemistry. Quite apart from these understandable errors, one major snag remains. The tests give little indication of how *clever* any particular boy is. They show which are the arts specialists and which the scientists, but not how successful each will be. Future open scholars at Oxford and Cambridge are frequently indistinguishable from form-mates who failed all their 'A' Levels and leave school with no glory whatever. Contrary to expectation, one can measure the bias of an individual's ability, but not the level.[3]

Take Bailey, for example. When I tested him as a Fifth Former, he was judged one of the school's best young scientists, and in his general demeanour one of the liveliest boys of his year: inquisitive, enthusiastic, musically gifted. He fulfilled his teachers' hopes, won an open scholarship in natural sciences at Cambridge, and took a

---

[1] It is interesting to note that his accuracy scores reflected this unfortunate boy's emotional condition. It was apparent from the interviews that his own uncertainty and his father's belligerence had reduced him to despondency.
[2] Law and Economics students at Cambridge are more likely to have numerical and diagrammatic biases of ability than other arts students. They are, in this respect, very similar to students studying Medicine or Geography.
[3] Hudson (1964a).

first in Part II of the Tripos. Yet his scores as a schoolboy were uniformly unimpressive. His vocabulary and general knowledge scores were presentable; but IQ and accuracy scores were lower than some 80 per cent of his contemporaries. Certainly, there was no sign in his scores of the abilities he unquestionably possessed. Another example – one of Bailey's contemporaries, Gardner. His scores were quite good by the standards of his school, but his IQ was lower than those of a third of the Fifth Formers who later became Cambridge undergraduates. Yet Gardner won an open scholarship in mathematics at Cambridge, and took Part III of the mathematics Tripos, acquitting himself with distinction and carrying off the top prize. In other words, he is one of the ablest young mathematicians of his age in England (indeed, in the world) yet from his scores one would never guess it.

Take two more examples from the mathematical field. First, Locke. At fifteen, Locke was held to be one of the cleverest boys that his public school had seen in more than a decade. In the Sixth Form, he was a brilliant mathematician – not merely accurate, but ingenious and elegant; and, as he demonstrated before he left, he could turn his hand to English essays and do competent work. Yet his scores were little better than those of the average Fifth Former. As a last example on the science side, consider Bagnall. Although not perhaps a mathematical prodigy, he was at least exceedingly academically advanced for his age, standing head and shoulders above a Sixth Form which was, on the average, three years his senior. Despite his lonely pre-eminence, there were two boys in his form with higher IQ's, and his IQ was easily his best score.

There were alarming mistakes on the arts side, too. One of Knight's form-mates, Levin, took an open exhibition in modern languages at Cambridge, and a good second in Tripos, yet his test scores do not even have Knight's redeeming excellence in general knowledge. Glancing at them, one could form no idea of his promise. Both vocabulary and general knowledge were better than average without being good, while IQ, accuracy, and spatial reasoning were all poor. His interests, too, were unpromising:

For a time I used to be very interested in model plane and boat building, and enjoyed playing with model steam, electric and compression ignition engines. Now I spend more time out of doors doing rugger, cross-country, cricket and

athletics, all . . . of which take up a lot of time, but which I enjoy very much. I
go abroad to families as much as possible. I have not finished a book for years!
(except ones required at school.)

The statistical evidence shows that these boys are not isolated
exceptions.[1] The only test which related significantly to a boy's
success at the end of his school life was the vocabulary test.[2] Future
open scholars and exhibitioners also tended to be widely read, showing interest both in literature and in current affairs.[3] The other dis-
tinguishing mark of the future open scholar, not surprisingly, is that
he is often judged by his form-mates to be exceptionally hardworking.[4]

THE MORAL

The moral of these findings is clear: that the academically successful
boy is distinguished not by his intellectual apparatus but the use he
sees fit to make of it. This is a finding which runs counter to one of
the most persistent of our assumptions about the nature of intelligence. A man with a very high IQ, it is assumed, is more likely to
become a good scientist or scholar than a man whose IQ is good but
not outstanding. A man with an IQ of 180 is thought 'more intelligent' in the everyday sense than his neighbour whose IQ is 130.
Everyone acknowledges that measured intelligence is overlaid by
other factors: hard work, good education, good opportunities, and
so on. But the underlying presupposition remains the same: 'the
higher the IQ the better'. Yet there is now a solid body of evidence,
American as well as English, which indicates that this belief is false.
It is amply proved that someone with an IQ of 170 is more likely to
think well than someone whose IQ is 70. And this holds true where
the comparison is much closer – between IQ's of, say, 100 and 130.
But the relation seems to break down when one is making comparisons between two people both of whom have IQ's which are
relatively high. The precise nature of this relation between real and
measured intelligence I shall attempt to unravel in Chapter 6.

[1] See Table 2; also Hudson (1964a).
[2] $P < 0.001$. This and all subsequent probabilities are based on the X^2 test.
[3] $P < 0.001$ and < 0.01 respectively.
[4] $P < 0.001$.

LOOSE ENDS

By the end of 1960, my work was in a state that all research workers will recognize: a modest achievement surrounded by loose ends. And it is the loose ends, not the modest achievements, which point the direction in which the work will develop. My loose ends were multitudinous. The bulk were technical – lines of analysis left unexplored. A minority were promising results at a tangent to the main course of the research. For instance: the discovery already mentioned, that the *variability* in the accuracy of a boy's work on the intelligence test correlated surprisingly well with obvious signs of emotional disturbance. There were signs, too, that such erratic performance was related to originality. A braver spirit would perhaps have abandoned the arts/science theme and plunged off in pursuit of such an alluring snippet. As it is, however, the solid work remains to be done.

A second loose end concerned boys like Knight and his friend Crouch. These boys (there were ten or eleven of them in a sample of 216) had among the lowest IQ's in the whole sample, and among the best scores on general knowledge. That the boy with high general knowledge and low IQ is an important educational type is proved by his subsequent success. Worth was for a time the only boy in the sample with a higher general knowledge score than either Knight or Crouch. At sixteen, he was lazy, and, although able, was considered by his teachers a little 'odd'. He subsequently won an open scholarship to Oxford in history, and took a first. His IQ was not quite as low as Knight's, but still belonged to the bottom 10 per cent of the sample; and like both Knight and Crouch, he was 'hopeless at maths' and could not 'abide Classics'. A form-mate of his, Peel, had a slightly higher IQ and a somewhat lower general knowledge: he took a second class in the examination in which Worth gained his first.

It seemed possible that the excellence of such boys in one form of thinking had developed as a compensation for their weakness in others. Moreover, seemingly compensatory relations were not restricted to a select group. Among arts specialists as a whole, unusually poor scores in one area went with good scores in another. If all of a boy's scores were poor, he was almost invariably very hard

working. This compensatory pattern only obtained on the arts side; it did not occur among scientists. That such compensation might in some cases have emotional roots was suggested by a case of two brothers. The Nordens were eighteen months apart in age, yet the younger – as sometimes happens – had overtaken his elder brother academically. When I saw him, the elder brother was considerably distressed. He stuttered, blushed and had facial tics. He was a historian, and doing badly, while his younger brother was a physical scientist and doing rather well. The elder brother had very low scores on all the tests apart from vocabulary and general knowledge; and his interests were exclusively cultural. The younger did quite well on all the tests except for vocabulary and general knowledge, and his interests were exclusively technical. The elder brother was an ineffectual aesthete; the younger a vigorous philistine. The elder Norden, in fact, had specialized in precisely those intellectual areas in which his brother was weakest.[1] To what extent such emotional considerations affected specialization I could not be sure, but it seemed likely that there was considerably more afoot than I could then identify.

In addition to these tempting and intelligible loose ends, one or two were fascinating but inscrutable. I found for example that among undergraduates at Cambridge, those studying chemistry differed significantly from other physical scientists in their biases of intelligence. Other physical scientists and engineers tended to be strong numerically and diagrammatically. Biologists were rather similar, but lacked numerical ability. The chemists, on the other hand, were often all-rounders, with equal strength in all parts of the test: verbal as well as numerical and diagrammatic. In this respect, their scores were like those of economists rather than those of other scientists. This oddity was found in a sample numbering over 400, and is, therefore, most unlikely to prove a fluke. Why it should exist, I have no idea; and no one, chemist or otherwise, has been able to enlighten me.[2]

[1] Looking back, I wonder whether there was not an unspoken collusion between them, some implicit agreement to cover different territory.

[2] See Hudson (1960a, 1961). Although most research emphasises the similarities among physical scientists, some recent work at the Massachusetts Institute of Technology reveals chemists as less intuitive and impulsive than physicists. How this is connected with biases of intelligence, though, I cannot see.

THE VITAL ISSUES

However, the really important loose ends were less tempting than baffling. It seemed ridiculous, in the first place, to be faced with brilliant young mathematicians and scientists, and to find them floundering on questions purporting to measure numerical intelligence. Time and again, they had lower scores than apparent dullards. This forced on one not merely a sense of the inadequacy of the tests, but of the extent to which thinking is specific. It does not follow that because two intellectual tasks look rather alike that the person who is good at one will be good at the other. Inevitably, therefore, such general notions as 'intelligence', 'numerical ability', 'verbal ability' are dangerous. My awareness of this was sharpened by a discovery about modern linguists. These boys frequently had usually poor vocabulary scores. One became used to boys with a 'flair for languages' and with vocabulary scores which placed them in the bottom 10 per cent to 20 per cent of the sample. It simply is not true that boys who are adept at learning easy words in a new language are adept (or even passing competent) at learning the more difficult ones in their own.

A less obvious but in some ways even more interesting point concerned the theoretical implications of biases in intelligence. Highly literate boys like Knight had verbal biases of intelligence not because they were necessarily very strong verbally, but because they were abysmally bad numerically and diagrammatically. Conversely, many a young philistine in the physical sciences did well on the verbal questions, but was judged to have a non-verbal bias because he did even better on the numerical and diagrammatic ones. In absolute terms, therefore, Knight's verbal intelligence was *lower* than that of many young scientists who had not a hundredth part of his literary ability or interest. It seems, in other words, that children specialize and flourish, not in terms of the absolute level of their various abilities but in terms of their bias. Each boy follows his line of greatest strength.

To the jaundiced layman, this discovery must seem commonplace. Of course, he will say, children follow their line of greatest strength. And of course a boy who follows a literary bent is bound to end up with entirely different abilities, attitudes, interests and habits of mind from someone whose initial bent is technical or scientific. Intellectual abilities do not exist in a vacuum – they evolve as a

result of growing interest in and devotion to a given line of work. So at the age of 16, a boy's intellect cannot possibly be a cluster of raw potentialities (if such it ever was). His development has already been enormously complex, and only a simpleton would pretend to understand it.

Pressing home his advantage, the layman might also point out how naïve it is to use tests which measure simple skills and expect them to correlate with the abilities of clever and relatively grown-up young men in skills which are highly complex. Of course the simple tasks will not correlate well with the complex ones. At best, the simple task shows us what a child might have made of a particular line of work if he had been interested to pursue it. But if he was not interested, the demonstration is pointless. (And specious, too, because it is the kind of prediction which it is almost impossible to disprove). What really matters is to discover why a boy is, or is not, interested in following a particular intellectual line. Why do some boys choose to use their brains, and others not? Why does one boy become an arts specialist, and his neighbour a scientist? And what leads one to continue thinking productively while his neighbour's interest peters out? These are the pertinent questions – and ones which can only be answered by giving the complexities of intelligence the respect they deserve.

Although unsympathetic to the mental tester faced with practical difficulties, these remarks are commonsensical enough. Most teachers would accept them as too platitudinous to deserve comment. Yet they condemn the assumptions that I myself employed. I approached my task with no such processes of motivation, interaction and development in mind. Rather, I tried to judge what skills a given line of work required, and then thought of tests to measure them: literary work depends on verbal skill, so the test for literary aptitude is one of verbal reasoning. Mathematics depends on numerical skill, so the appropriate test is one of numerical reasoning. And so on.

Unfortunately, by 1960, I was by no means in a position to see the full significance of my own results. My next step was governed not by searching argument, but by the most obvious deficiencies in my tests. They did not pick out the really bright child, and I felt that they should. I felt, too, that the untapped abilities might be connected with originality. It was in this direction, therefore, that I moved.

Convergers and Divergers

Chapter 2 carried us from 1957 to the end of 1960. After the usual hiatus attendant upon the examination for the Ph.D., my research effort began again in the summer of 1962. The obvious manoeuvre at this stage was to try out the American 'creativity' tests. News of these had reached England several years earlier, but had only now found their way through to me. The idea of using these was borne home especially by the work of Getzels and Jackson.[1] Their book has since received both widespread acclaim, and some waspish professional criticism. Later in this chapter, I shall make criticisms of my own (it *was* in some respects a rough-and-ready piece of research) but I am in their debt and wish to acknowledge this – both for specific techniques, and for the fresh air that they let in upon a world of musty, even foetid, expertise.

TWO TYPES OF TEST

Getzels and Jackson base their research on a distinction between two types of child: the 'High IQ' and the 'High Creative'. It is this distinction, renamed and refurbished in detail, which forms the basis of the rest of the work described in this book. Getzels and Jackson defined the difference between the 'High IQ' and the 'High Creative' in terms of scores on two contrasted types of mental test. The 'High IQ', as his name suggests, is especially good at intelligence tests, but relatively weak on tests to which Getzels and Jackson refer (to my mind regrettably) as tests of 'creativity'. The 'High Creative' is the

---

[1] Getzels and Jackson (1962). I read this book thoroughly because I was asked to review it. This mechanism for the dissemination of scientific beliefs and techniques is widespread, but only rarely acknowledged.

reverse: he is especially good at the 'creativity' tests but relatively low in IQ. The conventional intelligence test is by now familiar. This usually consists of questions in the form of puzzles. The individual is set a problem to which he is required to find the right answer; and he is frequently invited to choose this right answer from a list of alternatives. The victim knows that there is one solution which is correct, and his task is to ferret it out. His reasoning is said to *converge* on to the right answer. A typical intelligence test question might run:

> Brick is to house as plank is to . . . orange, grass, egg, boat, ostrich.

Only one of the five alternatives satisfactorily completes the analogy: 'boat'. Not all intelligence test questions rest on argument by analogy, nor are they all verbal, nor are they invariably in multiple choice form:

(a) *Which of the following words has the same meaning as the word on the left?*

   Correct . . . neat, fair, right, poor, good.

(b) *Which is the odd man out? . . . dog, cat, horse, chicken, cow?*

(c) *Which number is missing from this series? . . . 1, 2, 4, , 16.*

(d) *Add the smallest of these fractions to the second largest . . .*

$$\frac{7}{8}, \quad \frac{16}{17}, \quad \frac{1}{6}, \quad \frac{1}{34}, \quad \frac{2}{5}, \quad \frac{18}{19}$$

Intelligence test questions may also be diagrammatical: logical relations expressed in terms of patterns. And although most intelligence tests are massively biased towards the deductive, puzzle-solving type of reasoning, some (the Wechsler Adult Intelligence Scale, for example) include a wide range of material, aimed to assess general knowledge, vocabulary, and such simple skills as immediate memory. Thus, even though the scope of the conventional intelligence test is not easily defined, it does seem that nearly every item in nearly every test does have one assumption in common: that each question has only one right answer.[1] Consider now a typical question from a 'creativity' test:

How many uses can you think of for a brick?

Here, the individual is invited to *diverge*, to think fluently and

---

[1] The intelligence test on which my own results are based (A.H.5) is devoted to deductive reasoning exclusively. Questions are verbal, numerical and diagrammatic, and five 'principles' are used: series, analogies, directions, similar relations, and features in common. See Heim (1956).

tangentially, without examining any one line of reasoning in detail.[1] There are thousands of possible uses for a brick, and clearly people will differ widely both in the quantity and the quality of the uses they suggest. Here are two sets of answers: the first, it hardly needs saying, is more numerous, wittier, and more ingenious than the second:

(*Brick*) To break windows for robbery, to determine depth of wells, to use as ammunition, as pendulum, to practice carving, wall building, to demonstrate Archimedes' Principle, as part of abstract sculpture, cosh, ballast, weight for dropping things in river, etc., as a hammer, keep door open, footwiper, use as rubble for path filling, chock, weight on scale, to prop up wobbly table, paperweight, as firehearth, to block up rabbit hole.

(*Brick*) For building. For throwing through window.

Before describing such tests in detail, we face the problem of what to call them, generically. This is more important than it seems. Getzels and Jackson talk of 'High Creatives', and of 'creativity' tests, and this seems unwise: in fact, worse than unwise, positively tendentious. American workers in this field sometimes justify the term 'creative' by pointing out that the individual has to formulate his own answers, to think for himself. This equates 'creativity' with the ability to write – not a promising beginning. But even if the rationale were more convincing, it would still beg a vital question: do people who are creative in the normal sense of the word (great scientists, writers, painters, and so forth) score unusually well on these tests, or not? If they do not, describing them as 'creativity' tests is bound to mislead – the psychologists not least. In fact, neither Getzels and Jackson, nor anyone else, has yet produced evidence that could begin to justify the claim implicit in such nomenclature; and there are, moreover, good reasons (which I shall discuss later) for believing that they will not be able to do so. Calling these tests 'creativity' tests is, in other words, to repeat the error originally made with the conventional intelligence test. This, too, begged

---

[1] There is no reason, of course, why intelligence tests should be restricted to convergent material. The psychologists who compile scales of general intelligence are free to include 'creativity' tests alongside their more conventional ones; and it may be that their inclusion will increase the predictive power of the scale as a whole. For a description of the conventional intelligence test, see Anastasi (1961).

The distinction between convergent and divergent reasoning was introduced, I believe, by Guilford (1950). It is one of the distinctions built into his *a priori* model of intellectual abilities, see Guilford, (1956).

questions, as we are now acutely aware. But the terms 'intelligence test' and 'IQ' have passed so completely into everyday language that they carry with them a certain aura of sceptical doubt. The damage was done long ago, and there is little one can do but wait – matters will doubtless right themselves of their own accord.[1] With new tests, though, it seems vital that we should avoid question-begging if we possibly can. For this reason, I propose to name them technically. The 'High IQ' I shall call a *converger*; the 'High Creative', a *diverger*, and the two styles of reasoning, convergent and divergent, respectively. The new tests themselves I shall call *open-ended*. These conventions certainly do not preclude the dangers of question-begging, but they may help to keep them at bay.[2]

THE VARIETY OF OPEN-ENDED TESTS

Open-ended tests, like intelligence tests, take different forms. Indeed, the variety is already rather bewildering.[3] At one extreme are the recognizably test-like tests: *Uses of Objects* ('How many uses can you think of for each of the following objects?'); and *Meanings of Words* ('How many meanings can you think of for each of the following words?'). At the other, there are open-ended tests which are scarcely tests at all: one that I use is the *Drawing*, in which the individual is asked to illustrate the title 'Zebra Crossing'. As one might imagine, the responses are varied: naturalistic drawings of street scenes; diagrams with labels; zebras crossing railways, roads, rivers; zebras crossing themselves; and so on. I also use *Controversial Statements*. This consists of twenty-four statements of an argumentative, epigrammatic nature which boys can comment on in any way they choose.[4]

---

[1] It has been suggested that we should call IQ tests 'tests of general classification,' but this now seems more trouble than it is worth.

[2] The use of question-begging names seems to be one of the mental tester's occupational hazards. Much of the muddle over factor analysis has this vice at its root. In the past, mental testers have been prone to designate statistical dimensions with seemingly non-committal letters ('g', 'n', 'v', and so on), and then to treat these, without further justification, as if they were identical with everyday qualities: 'g', for example, is frequently taken to stand for 'general intelligence' as this is normally understood. If we slide in this slippery fashion between operational definitions and common sense, the practical inadequacies of tests tend to escape notice.

[3] No comprehensive survey exists. But see Getzels and Jackson (1962); Torrance (1962); Goldman (1964); Guilford (1964).

[4] A full description of the tests used in my own research is given in Appendix B.

In the work reported in this book, the convergence/divergence distinction is based on two open-ended tests (*Meanings of Words* and *Uses of Objects*). A boy's ability on these two tests is contrasted with his ability on the intelligence test A.H.5.[1] The other open-ended tests serve as sources of additional information, but are not used in the definition of the convergent and divergent types. This additional information is often of a kind which it is not easy, or at times even meaningful, to quantify.[2] Note is taken of humorous responses ('food for a goat'); of responses which are in some sense violent ('for drowning people in'); which make some reference to sex ('will conceal what happens in bed'); of responses which are expressed in terms of general categories and properties rather than of specific objects ('as insulation' as opposed to 'keeping an invalid warm'); and so on. In the *Drawing*, one looks for labelling, for fantastic, imaginative themes, and for pictures without people; in *Controversial Statements*, for views which seem searching or, of course, irrelevant or stereotyped. And in each of the tests, it is possible to assess, quantitatively, the rarity of any given response. Broadly, therefore, open-ended tests serve not just to indicate the fluency with which a boy reasons divergently but a large number of other qualities besides.

One of the worst snags with the various tests of divergence is that they do not correlate well with each other. Getzels and Jackson quote correlations between open-ended tests of the order of 0·3–0·4, and correlations between open-ended tests and an intelligence test of the order of 0·2–0·3. There has been dispute since among mental testers as to whether these low correlations are due to the very highly selected nature of Getzels and Jackson's sample; and whether, more generally, their results are, as they imply, incompatible with the general factor theory of intelligence. This (as I have argued elsewhere)

[1] More specifically: I score the total number of responses on *Meanings of Words* and *Uses of Objects* separately. Each test is graded A, B, C, D or E, in the proportions 1:2:4:2:1. These two grades are then averaged, and compared with the grade gained by the individual on the intelligence test. This yields a differential score which ranges from −4 to +4. Finally, these differential scores are again standardized in the usual proportions, so that 10 per cent of my usual Fifth Form sample score −2, 20 per cent score −1, 40 per cent score 0, 20 per cent score +1, and 10 per cent score +2.

[2] All open-ended tests are troublesome to score. It is often difficult, for example, to decide whether or not an answer is intended to be humorous. Nor is it clear whether 'as a container of liquids' and 'as a container for beer' should count as two uses for a barrel or only one. On the other hand, one should not find such ambiguities alarming. Where errors or inconsistencies occur, these are rarely on a scale to threaten the value of the work as a whole.

D

is an academic point, and of little interest to anyone but a mental tester.[1] These poor correlations do, however, have a practical implication which is very important indeed. If you have before you a group of clever schoolchildren, a knowledge of their scores on an intelligence test will be little help in guessing what their scores on an open ended test will be. And a knowledge of their scores on one open ended test will be of relatively little use in guessing their scores on another.

My own results confirm this, and the weak correlations apply to the intelligence test as well.[2] If one guesses at boys' grades on the second half of the IQ test on the basis of their scores on the first half, the result will only show an improvement of about 20 per cent over guesses made at random. In a similar operation, relating IQ to open-ended scores, the improvement over chance may be as low as 5 per cent. In relating one open-ended test to another, the improvement over chance may be only a little higher.[3] It follows, in dealing with a classful of Fifth or Sixth Formers, that it involves a considerable oversimplification to talk in general terms about the 'intelligence' of one boy as opposed to another, or of their 'powers of divergent reasoning'. The test scores are not homogeneous, and as a result, the use of such general notions is potentially dangerous.

What, then, must one do? Do we pool scores on a group of tests, or treat each test separately? If scores are pooled (as they are in assessing IQ) then precision is lost. If, on the other hand, we treat

---

[1] See Burt (1962), Vernon (1964), Hudson (1965).

[2] On samples of clever Fifth Formers, the correlation between *Uses of Objects* and *Meanings of Words* is approximately 0·3. The correlations between either of these tests and the intelligence test are often below 0·2. The correlations between the intelligence test and other measures which are sometimes included in an intelligence test (vocabulary and general knowledge) are again in the region of 0·2 and 0·3 respectively. The correlation between the vocabulary test and the *Meanings of Words* is of the order of 0·3 – the only difference between the two tests being that the first asks for the right meaning of difficult words, while the second, superficially similar, asks for a variety of meanings for words which are relatively simple. The correlation between the first half of the intelligence test and the second half is 0·4–0·45. The general picture, then, is one of correlations between tests which are so low as to be of little practical value.

[3] The association between two variables is usually expressed in terms of the correlation coefficient. This – perhaps it is no accident – gives the uninitiated an over-optimistic impression of the strength of that association. A correlation of 0·5 looks as though it is half-way between perfect agreement and none. However, one estimates the practical, predictive value of a correlation by squaring it. Thus a correlation of 0·5 reduces our uncertainty not by a half but by a quarter. The order of correlation which does offer a 50 per cent improvement over chance is not 0·5 but 0·707.

each test as separate, we cannot form any general concepts. The point is obviously a tricky one, and the present solution is no more than a compromise. I pool the various parts of the intelligence test, even though these do not correlate well with each other; and I do the same with the two open-ended tests. But in Chapter 4, where I interpret this broad contrast between convergent and divergent tests, I try to show that neither category is as homogeneous as I have made it seem. The fact is, then, that a boy who is a diverger (or converger) on one set of tests may not be so on another set. With this admission behind us, let us now consider convergers and divergers.

CONVERGERS AND DIVERGERS

The converger is the boy who is substantially better at the intelligence test than he is at the open-ended tests; the diverger is the reverse. In addition, there are the all-rounders, the boys who are more or less equally good (or bad) on both types of test. As a matter of convenience, I define 30 per cent of my usual schoolboy sample as convergers, 30 per cent as divergers, and leave the remaining 40 per cent in the middle as all-rounders. For the most part, my results are expressed in terms of comparisons between the two extreme groups, convergers and divergers. If at times the all-rounders seem neglected, this is not because they are unimportant, but because comparisons between contrasting groups are a convenient way of describing complex results. From time to time reference will be made to 'extreme convergers' and 'extreme divergers'. These are boys whose scores are unusually biased in one direction or the other. Working from one end of the distribution to the other, we find extreme divergers (10 per cent); moderate divergers (20 per cent); all-rounders (40 per cent); moderate convergers (20 per cent); and extreme convergers (10 per cent).

The reader will already have noted that the convergence/divergence dimension is a measure of *bias*, not of *level*, of ability. As with the measures of bias discussed in Chapter 2, it is logically possibly for a converger actually to have a higher open-ended score than a diverger, either by virtue of having a quite exceptionally high IQ score, or by virtue of the diverger's IQ being exceptionally low. This, on the face of it, should wreak havoc with the results. One of the most interesting features of the research is that it does not do so.

Once again, it is the measure of bias which produces the really striking discriminations, not the measure of level.[1]

THE CENTRAL RESULT

Initially I had hoped, as I have said, that open-ended tests would cut across the arts/science distinction, and give some reflection of boys' brightness; of their level, in other words, rather than their bias. The results were a surprise. Far from cutting across the arts/science distinction, the open-ended tests provided one of my best correlates of it. Most arts specialists, weak at the IQ tests, were much better at the open-ended ones; most scientists were the reverse. Arts specialists are on the whole divergers, physical scientists convergers. Between three and four divergers go into arts subjects like history, English literature and modern languages for every one that goes into physical science. And, vice versa, between three and four convergers do mathematics, physics and chemistry for every one that goes into the arts.[2] As far as one can tell from the samples available, classics belong with physical science, while biology, geography, economics, and general arts courses attract convergers and divergers in roughly equal proportions.[3]

This discovery, central to the argument in this book, has a number of interesting repercussions. Positively, it provides some indication of the ways in which the arts mind works; and it adds to the already formidable array of tests which can be used to predict the direction in which a boy will specialize in the Sixth Form. On the other hand, it

[1] In my most recent research, I have been using a 3 × 3 system rather than the simple converger, all-rounder, diverger one. This accounts both for differences in bias and in level. The high scoring all-rounder is clearly distinguished from the low scoring one, and so on. This is obviously more thorough, but is much more difficult to handle.

[2] Table 3. This arts/science discrimination was massively significant even on the first small sample, and it stands up to replication on samples which are larger. The 'true' arts/science discrimination is in fact sharper than Table 3 makes it seem because the minority of convergent arts specialists and divergent physical scientists often turn out to be budding lawyers and architects respectively. In Table 3, for example, one sees two extreme convergers studying history – both intend to become solicitors. Of the three extreme divergers doing physical science, two are potential architects and another is a potential archaeologist.

[3] 'Arts' during the first part of this book at least, refers rather specifically to the arts side of the English Sixth Form: forms specializing in English literature, modern languages and history. It does not include the classics; nor economics, except where this is included in a course of an obvious literary or historical bias. A 'general arts' course is usually for weaker students, and comprises a mixture of subjects such as economics, geography and history, none of which is taught at a highly specialized level.

spread doubt and disruption all around it. Either it must cause uneasiness over the recruitment and education of our young scientists; or it must undermine any research which uses open-ended tests as a measure of real originality. Conceivably, it may do both.

THE ARTS MIND

First, the question of the arts mind. The insight afforded by these new tests is seen most clearly with *Uses of Objects*. This is a test which, on the face of it, favours the boy with mechanical interests and experience: the typical young physical scientist. Yet, on this test, impractical young historians and modern linguists do as well, or better than, the physical scientists. Consider the answers given by Bolton, a young modern linguist whose interests are in no sense mechanical or technical ('playing the clarinet, singing in choir; books – mainly foreign'):

(*Barrel*) Storing beer; sitting on; using as a raft; gnawing; loud-speaker holder; as musical instrument;
(*Paper Clip*) Holding paper together; wire; pin; tooth-pick; to undo and waste time; make darts; as a button; cleaning nails;
(*Tin of Boot Polish*) Cleaning shoes; making a mess all over the place; throw as a saucer; as an instrument (musical); to put pins in; make-up; ash tray;
(*Brick*) Building; throwing; sitting on; head rest; making a fire out of doors; making a ladder; a cudgel; for using straw up.
(*Blanket*) Sleeping in; using to stifle burning; keep warm; lag pipes; round a camp fire; suffocating people; muffler and insulator for sound; for clothes;

And, by contrast, those of Poulter, an able young physical scientist of the same age and from the same school, whose interests are 'models, hand built railways, sport':

(*Barrel*) Container for liquids. Sitting on.
(*Paper Clip*) Clipping paper on when straightened as a bit of wire.
(*Tin of Boot Polish*) Cleaning shoes.
(*Brick*) Building houses, breaking windows, removing teeth (via the broken window).
(*Blanket*) Sleeping in.

Bolton is able to switch confidently from one theme to the next, and to include a number of suggestions which we might call libidinous ('suffocating people', 'making a mess all over the place') along with others which are sensible and ingenious ('as a loud-speaker holder', 'insulator for sound'). With one exception, Poulter's answers

are impersonal and pedestrian. He does not let himself go, either in the amount of material he lets fall, or in the subject-matter which he permits himself to cover. Bolton seems to express himself without embarrassment or qualification, even when his ideas are rather childish ('gnawing', 'to undo and waste time', 'making a mess all over the place', 'for using straw up'). On the one occasion Poulter ventures a little out of his shell, it is to make a carefully guarded joke – so guarded indeed that it is scarcely perceptible. In suggesting one use ('removing teeth') he refers back to another ('breaking windows') thus preventing his mildly violent sally from protruding in isolation.[1]

An interesting implication of this finding about *Uses of Objects* is that it indicates some kind of barrier or gulf between thinking imaginatively about practical matters and making things work. It seems that the arts man is free to use his imagination just because he is not committed to being practical; while the scientist's practical commitment precludes his thinking about any use for an object other than the *right*, the most conventional one. The young scientist usually is intensely practical – we know this; and most young arts specialists find engines, or any other manifestation of technology, alien. But what gives the one his skill and the other his aversion is not so much the ability to *think* practically as the commitment to (or avoidance of) practical action.

THE EDUCATION OF YOUNG SCIENTISTS

The second important implication concerns the recruitment and training of scientists in the Sixth Form at school, and later at University. Boys like Poulter are not exceptions. Most young science specialists could only produce two or three uses for each of the objects offered. These are some of the cleverest young men in the country, the central nervous systems on which the future of British science depends; yet, when asked to reason in a way which was unfamiliar, they were tongue-tied. In defence of young scientists (and those who teach them) it might be argued that science does not consist in the free play of the imagination, even over practical matters. It is a highly complex body of fact and theory which the schoolboy must master before he can hope to make contributions of

[1] The notion of protuberance from a carefully knit ring of defences is an image with obvious psychoanalytic implications, and is one to which I shall return.

his own. This is true. On the other hand, science is not entirely scholastic. Above a fairly solid bedrock of accepted knowledge, science is continuously and drastically revised. A recent survey of American physicists put the expectation of life for a theory in small particle physics at about four years, and the expectation in science as a whole somewhere in the region of fifteen years.[1] Under the present system, therefore, the work of the Sixth Form schoolboy is dissimilar to that of the mature scientist, whose research involves intuition, imagination, and the capacity to take risks, as well as painstaking analysis. Granting this, it is possible (a) that our Sixth Forms may be attracting boys who are too rigid and inflexible for research; and (b) that scientific education, instead of counteracting boys' natural inflexibility, tends to reinforce and aggravate it. Scientific education, in other words, may have become dislocated from the world of research which it purports to serve. If we teach children that science consists in learning an established body of wisdom, we may well be doing both boys and science a disservice.

Consider two further sets of answers to *Uses of Objects*: one from Poole (a modern linguist), the other from Florence (a physical scientist). Poole plans to go into 'something to do with languages – e.g. foreign administration'. Florence wants to design car engines:

POOLE (*Barrel*) To hold all liquids, sherry, port, whisky, gin, water, etc., as a wastepaper basket. For target practice with a pop-gun through the bung-hole. As a loudspeaker reflex cabinet. For barrel rolling races for charity or Rag Days. As a baby's bath or bed. As a toilet. As a washing-machine. For spin-drying (water out through the bung-hole) put it on a fast gramophone turntable.

(*Paper Clip*) To clean your nails with. To clip paper. To hold carbon paper on to the duplicate while typing. To clean the ash out of a Jetex model jet engine. To cross the points in the mains to fuse the house. To hold spectacles if they break. To use if the zip on your trousers breaks.

(*Tin of Boot Polish*) To clean boots. As a stain for your face if you're a commando. As a food on a desert island. As grease for the runners of a toboggan. As material for a surrealist painting. As stain for an electric light bulb if you want to show your etchings in the right atmosphere.

(*Brick*) To use in smash-and-grab raids. To help hold a house together. To use in a game of Russian roulette if you want to keep fit at the same time (bricks at ten paces, turn and throw – no evasive action allowed). To hold the eiderdown on a bed tie a brick at each corner. As a breaker of empty Coca Cola bottles.

[1] Schwab and Brandwein (1962), p. 20.

(*Blanket*) To use on a bed. As a cover for illicit sex in the woods. As a tent. To make smoke signals with. As a sail for a boat, cart or sled. As a substitute for a towel. As a target for shooting practice for short-sighted people. As a thing to catch people jumping out of burning skyscrapers.

FLORENCE (*Barrel*) Containing liquid or any suitable substance. To roll out – in the festive season.
(*Paper Clip*) To clip paper together.
(*Tin of Boot Polish*) Containing boot polish to clean one's shoes.
(*Brick*) Building. Smash and grab raids.
(*Blanket*) Sleeping on. Putting small fires out. (Wet blanket).

I have the impression that it is Poole, not Florence, who has the gifts of intellectual sprightliness and flexibility which we are told both science and technology so badly need. Unlike most arts specialists, Poole is good at mathematics and has practical interests (he is building a tape-recorder and develops his own films). Yet of all the boys I tested, only one of comparable divergent ability found his way into a physical science Sixth Form – and he, although 'good at chemistry', would 'rather do English':

YOUNG (*Barrel*) Drum, seat, table, boat, collecting rainwater, house, tank for any liquid, lavatory, bath, storage space for anything, bed, firewood, kennel, incinerator, hiding-place for escape or lovemaking, rolling in, rolling at, rolling over.
(*Paper Clip*) Wire, electrical contact, fastener, cuff-link, insidious weapon, pipe cleaner, making models.
(*Tin of Boot Polish*) Cleaning shoes, painting, colouring, greasing, smearing, eating if very hungry, sculpting, practical jokes, cleaning leather, shining boots, throwing at people, melt it down and experiment, musical instrument.
(*Brick*) Building houses, etc., throwing at people, windows, animals, things, weightlifting, fireplace, stopping nail from splitting wood, weapon, weight, sculpture, support, gap filler, hammer, presser, red chalk drawing.
(*Blanket*) Covering for bed, warmth, sitting on, lying on, lovemaking, roof, sail, rag, rope, sack, rolling things up in, carrying things in, stretcher, mopping things up with, modern sculpture, dog's basket.

However, it would be a mistake to draw any hasty conclusion from evidence like this. We need, I think, to examine much more carefully the nature of the task which an open-ended test presents. If we ask a young scientist like Florence to suggest uses for a barrel, we are posing him a novel problem; and superficially at least, it is one which should suit his technical tastes. On the other hand, we

have no guarantee that it will interest him. He may feel inhibited precisely because a psychologist is asking him to do something unusual; or it may be that the task itself strikes him as pointless. The fact that he does clam up is an interesting discovery (especially if he has already accepted the IQ test as worthy of his effort); but it is not one which proves that Florence is technically uninventive.

We can check this possibility directly, by looking at the open-ended responses of boys whose technical inventiveness is demonstrable. I did this recently, by giving open-ended tests to boys at a school which provides quite exceptional facilities for technical work. The aim there is to show boys how to express their spontaneous technical interests (in model aircraft, say, or model railways) in highly sophisticated form. For the most part, this technical activity is voluntary and lies outside the curriculum. It is a simple matter, therefore, to contrast the scores of boys who show an inventive flair for such work, with those of boys whose efforts are prosaic. Although this study was conducted on a very small sample it does little to cement the connection between open-ended tests and technical inventiveness. Consider Spinks, a boy of 17 who, on his own initiative, is building a computer which will optimize the speed of model racing cars around a track. It adjusts the speed of the cars automatically so that all accidents are avoided. A boy, unmistakably, of imagination and single-mindedness, his responses to *Uses of Objects* were as follows:

(*Barrel*) To hold beer in, stand on it and roll along, make a stand.
(*Paper Clip*) Use as an electrode, use as a spring.
(*Tin of Boot Polish*) Clean shoes, grease wood, use as paint to make a painting.
(*Brick*) Round it all off and make a ball, or lots of bricks, use as a powder.
(*Blanket*) Use as a tent, make a robe, make a rope, make a sack, bag, etc., make a pair of trousers or shoes.

Although Spinks turns out to be mildly divergent, and although his suggestions are quite sensible (and in one case most unusual) they are in no sense startling. One can only conclude that the test failed to catch his fancy.[1] Take another and more extreme example. Hancock, at the age of 16, has built a computer which plays the Chinese match stick game 'Nim' against all human comers. He is at the moment

---

[1] The same is true to an even greater extent of the intelligence test. He did poorly on all sections of this, and made many mistakes.

building a computer which will teach a ball to escape from a maze –
or, rather, it teaches the maze how to allow the ball to escape from it.
He is a boy of remarkable inventiveness, with great stamina and a
good theoretical grasp of what he is doing. Yet his responses to *Uses
of Objects* are few and banal:

(*Barrel*) Containing drinks. Water tub. To sit on.
(*Paper Clip*) Holding paper, etc., together. As a piece of wire.
(*Tin of Boot Polish*) Polishing boots. Tin itself as container.
(*Brick*) With which to build. As a weight, a support.
(*Blanket*) On bed.

The test, again, has failed to interest him. And, again, the same
is true to a lesser extent of the intelligence test. Although a converger,
his scores on A.H.5 are better than average only in the diagrammatic
section. The inventiveness of these boys has escaped us more or less
completely. And they are not exceptions. Of the twenty-eight boys
tested, six could be classified as showing imagination and originality
in their technical work; and six others as much more stolid, working
with great patience and precision, but without inventive flair. The
differences in test score between these two groups were slight.

IMPLICATIONS FOR MENTAL TESTING

The implications of this finding for mental testers are far-reaching.
In fact, they strike at the assumptions on which the whole edifice of
testing is based. Granted that boys like Spinks and Hancock have
qualities of technical inventiveness that our tests do not tap, we are
left with the problem of devising tests which do tap them. The
following might strike such boys as more appealing than *Uses of
Objects*:

*The research department of Fonitex Limited has produced a remarkable new plastic –
'Luminium'. It has most of the general properties of fibre glass – it is strong, resilient, and
easy to mould. But it has three important qualities in addition: it is fireproof, it is an
exceedingly poor conductor of heat, and it is luminous. Although initially in short supply,
'Luminium' promises to be reasonably cheap to produce. The company realizes that it may
have made a momentous discovery, but it is puzzled as to what to do first. Their aim is to
find uses for 'Luminium' which will show off its special qualities to best advantage. Note
down as many different suggestions as you can.*

On the other hand, there is no guarantee that a boy whose life centres
on logical computers, say, or aeromodelling, will think this Fonitex
question interesting. It may be that his mind focuses only on the

topic which he finds absorbing. If this is so, we can only hope to measure his capabilities by setting problems *within* his sphere of interest. The only way in which we can judge the abilities of a boy who is interested solely in logical computers is to judge how well his computers compute.

Yet if we allow that such specificity of interest exists (and we can scarcely deny it), we are forced to make some revealing admissions. We must envisage a spectrum of individuals, ranging from those who can apply their full energy to any task, to those who can apply themselves only when their special interests are aroused. Traditionally, the psychologist is inclined to see the second group as handicapped; and, where tests are used in educational selection, such boys doubtless stand to a practical disadvantage, in that they will fail tests which their more amenable contemporaries pass. However, research on adults suggests that the ability to channel one's interests, even obsessively, may be a condition for producing original work. (Certainly, I shall argue along these lines in Chapter 8). It may be, therefore, that the ability to turn one's hand to any task is not necessarily an unalloyed advantage. Instead of describing such people as 'brilliant all-rounders', perhaps we should view them instead as intellectually 'labile', or even as 'promiscuous'.

The analogy with sexual promiscuity is obviously unnecessarily pejorative: on the other hand, it does afford one useful insight. Intellectual promiscuity, like its sexual counterpart, may be a manifestation of adolescence. And perhaps the education we give children serves to accentuate their promiscuity quite unnecessarily. We actively encourage them to perform whatever task we put before them, and frown on a child who will not work unless he is interested. Gradually, of course (or so the parallel suggests), adolescents become increasingly discriminating about which intellectual feats they will perform, and which not. Thus the adult with clearly defined intellectual interests and values may well decline to do our tests, because he has lost the knack of applying himself at will.[1]

It would be absurd to allow this train of thought to discredit mental testing in its entirety. Most of the results upon which the

---

[1] And this, in its turn, may explain some of the relatively poor test scores which research workers like MacKinnon have found amongst men of the highest intellectual accomplishment. MacKinnon (1962a, 1962b). See the discussion of his results in Chapter 6.

generalizations of mental testers rest, are based on school children: the age at which intellectual promiscuity is at its most pronounced. Nevertheless, it points to an assumption which mental testers question less often than they ought: the assumption that we can take the interest and emotional commitment of our victims for granted.

My discovery about the arts bias of open-ended tests also has a more specific implication for recent American research on 'creativity'. The discovery that the 'High Creative' is an arts specialist and the 'High IQ' a scientist must seem a spanner in the works, a small disaster. The obvious inference is that any research which has used such tests as a measure of 'creativity' has been misconceived. At the very least, I think, we must acknowledge that the relation of convergence and divergence to originality in science will prove complex. Most American psychologists assume that an original idea in any field is, self-evidently, a divergent one. This is hard to quarrel with; it is true virtually by definition. Even in the most rigorous of the physical sciences, an original idea is one which, in some sense or other, breaks new ground. On the other hand, as Kuhn points out, this assumption misrepresents scientific research as a whole:

Because the old must be revalued and reordered when assimilating the new, discovery and invention in the sciences are usually intrinsically revolutionary. Therefore, they do demand just that flexibility and open-mindedness that characterize, or indeed define, the divergent thinker. . . . Yet flexibility is not enough, and what remains is not obviously compatible with it. . . . Almost none of the research undertaken by even the greatest scientists is designed to be revolutionary, and very little of it has any such effect. On the contrary, normal research, even the best of it, is a highly convergent activity based firmly upon a settled consensus acquired from scientific education and reinforced by subsequent life in the profession. Typically, to be sure, this convergent or consensus-bound research ultimately results in revolution. . . . But revolutionary shifts of a scientific tradition are relatively rare, and extended periods of convergent research are the necessary preliminary to them . . . only investigations firmly rooted in the contemporary scientific tradition are likely to break that tradition and give rise to a new one. That is why I speak of an 'essential tension' implicit in scientific research. . . . Very often the successful scientist must simultaneously display the characteristics of the traditionalist and of the iconolast.[1]

[1] Kuhn (1963), p. 342. This paper seems to me one of the most perspicacious yet written about the nature of science. Later in the same paper (p. 354), Kuhn goes on to suggest that American psychologists are really in search, not of research scientists, but of inventors. My evidence suggests that they will be unlikely to find even inventors with tests like *Uses of Objects*.

Granted Kuhn's contention that both convergent and divergent qualities are essential in scientific research, and granted, as he points out later, that such qualities need not neccessarily reside within one scientist (it may be sufficient that they are found in one laboratory, or even one scientific community), the task of prediction becomes bewilderingly complex. Add to this the problems of measurement – the scientist who is divergent in his laboratory will not necessarily see fit to be so on psychological tests – and the psychologists' difficulties appear insurmountable. At any rate, we would be wise to approach the problems of scientific originality with circumspection. And although my discovery of an arts bias in tests of 'creativity' may seem damaging, the inferences that we can draw from it are bound to be guarded.[1]

IN CONCLUSION

In this chapter, I have tried to show that two fields which we previously considered separate – research on differences between the arts and sciences, and research on 'creativity' – are in fact intimately connected: indeed, that the two topics have, unwittingly, been confused. This is a familiar occurrence in psychology and, depending on where one happens to be standing at the time, evokes irritation or amusement. However, the worlds of aptitude testing and 'creativity' research are now linked, whether we like it or not; and they might be said to illuminate each other's deficiencies. Much 'creativity' research, though spirited and ingenious, has been impoverished by a disregard for the complexity of original thought, and for differences between one type of originality and another. Aptitude testing, in contrast, has suffered from rigidity and unimaginativeness. Now that the empirical connection between the two fields is established, both seem to have suffered from over-simplification. Images of cross-fertilization are, admittedly, an integral part of current scientific cant. We tend to talk as though men from different disciplines have only to meet to produce, not babel and incomprehension, but new light. In scientific, as well as social, reality, matrimony is not easy, and there is certainly no guarantee that the wedding of (in this case) the

[1] See Chapter 6.

flamboyant to the painstaking will automatically spawn a new discipline which is at once eloquent and precise. Still, joined the two fields unavoidably are – and there is hope that a nuptial optimism may buoy us up, if not for a generation, at least until the end of this book.

· 4 ·

A Network of Connections

Besides differentiating arts from science, the converger/diverger distinction also correlates with a wide network of other variables, some of them intellectual, some personal. A number of these relationships have already been established by Getzels and Jackson; but the present results cover a somewhat different range of material and are in many respects more detailed. One group of such connections concerns certain of the open-ended tests. As a matter of definition, of course, divergers are usually better at these tests than convergers: they suggest more meanings for words, more uses for objects, and so on. But apart from their sheer quantity, the responses of the two types of boy differ qualitatively.

OPEN-ENDED TESTS

RARITY. First, there is the question of rarity. Nearly everyone suggests that a barrel be used to store alcoholic refreshments of one kind or other; very few suggest that it be used in constructing a spin dryer. Most people think that bricks can be used in a smash and grab raid; few for sharpening knives. Divergers are roughly three times as likely to produce such rare responses on *Uses of Objects*, and on the *Drawing*.[1] This suggests that divergers scan a wider range of ideas before selecting their responses. Some of the rarer themes for the *Drawing* are certainly ingenious and far-fetched:

a zebra playing noughts and crosses
an airbound zebra crossing Basingstoke at 2,000 feet
a pedestrian crossing formed from a dead zebra skin

[1] P < 0·001 and < 0·005 respectively. These and all subsequent discriminations are summarised in Table 4. A 'rare' response is defined as one produced by 1 per cent of the sample or less, and an 'unusual' one as one produced by less than 10 per cent and more than 1 per cent.

a morality: boy crossing a zebra crossing (labelled 'Public Schools'), making for shops (labelled 'Sound, Lazy Career', etc.) and being menaced by a speeding truck (labelled 'Labour Policy')

a cross-Channel race across the backs of swimming three-tailed zebras

By comparison, the converger is usually content with a naturalistic drawing of a street scene, zebras crossing roads, or diagrams – all of them popular themes. Some convergers set out quite clearly to be straightforward, to avoid imaginative frills. Others appear to find their choice of a theme daring, when in fact it is conventional. A zebra crossing the road is a joke, but it is one which occurs to quite a lot of people. It is in fact the most popular theme of all, and one which convergers chose two to three times as often as divergers.[1] By contrast, the diverger is not content with discovering a joke or incongruity. He refines and elaborates upon his original idea until he feels confident that he has thought of something which makes his effort unique. Convergers and divergers differ, in other words, not so much in the quantity of their humour as in its quality.[2]

PEOPLE. A further interesting point about the *Drawing* concerns people. The convergers are more likely than the divergers to omit people,[3] and have a special taste for deserted 'lunar' street scenes.[4] Conversely, the divergers tend to populate their pictures, even when humans are irrelevant to the action.[5]

FANTASY. One implication of Getzels and Jackson's research was that the 'High Creative' child had a taste for the bizarre; and the results on the *Drawing*, where utility is not a consideration, would certainly seem to support this. On the other hand, rare responses are not necessarily far-fetched. On *Uses of Objects*, for example, they are, as often as not, quite sensible. These are the suggestions for a

---

[1] $P < 0.05$.

[2] There is a difference in the frequency of humorous drawings, but it is too small to be significant, even on a sample of 249. In this respect, my results do not tally closely with Getzels and Jackson's (1962).

[3] $P < 0.01$.

[4] $P < 0.05$.

[5] It might be argued that this particular difference arises from the converger's inability to draw. However, convergers seem to draw as well as divergers, if not better; and, in any case, there appears to be no connection between draughtsmanship and the inclusion of people.

barrel which occurred only once in a sample of eighty-four Sixth Formers:

sand pit	art medium
making cider or beer	road block
play pen	changing room
rabbit hutch	beehive
dove cote	roller in conveyor belt
exit in garden wall for pet	incinerator
vase	stage prop
pot rack	storing grass
dolls crib	holder for spades, brushes, etc.
children's toy chest	roller as transport
lamp shade	for bingo
hoops for swords	door stop
putting loudspeakers in	see-saw
shop window dressing	armour
boiler	containing corpses
ark	suicide

Not all of these ideas are practicable; nevertheless, the general tone is not one of unbridled fantasy. The diverger's capacity for the bizarre is, in other words, merely one manifestation of a more general conceptual freedom.

'GENERAL PHYSICAL PROPERTIES', 'PARTICULAR OBJECTS', AND INTERESTS. The next point of difference seems at first a detail, but has fascinating implications. I had assumed that scientists (and hence convergers) were prone to analyse material objects in terms of their physical properties rather than of their particular functions. Faced with a barrel, a scientist would tend, both by nature and by training, to analyse out its properties in general terms: a container for liquids and solids; buoyant; combustible; a resonator; rollable; two or three feet high and quite heavy; consists of iron hoops as well as wood; top and bottom will knock out; a bung-hole in its side; could be sawn into halves; et cetera. Conversely, I viewed the arts specialist as lacking this capacity for abstraction, and tending to think of objects in terms of specific uses: a barrel contains beer, whisky, gin, vinegar, potatoes, grain, flour, cement; for pickling fishes; for drowning the Duke of Clarence in; for living in, like Diogenes; as a lavatory; for making speeches from; and so on. Thus, although the arts specialist might be expected to produce more

suggestions, and even more ingenious or amusing ones, it would be the scientist who produced the searching physical analysis.

This assumption is false. The differentiation is precisely the reverse. Divergers, not convergers – arts specialists, not scientists – analyse objects in terms of general categories. Roughly half the divergers (and half the arts specialists) gave 'general physical property' uses for a barrel, whereas only a third of the convergers (and a third of the scientists) did so.[1] Paradoxically, too, responses in terms of general physical properties were most frequent among historians, where one would least expect them, and least among the physical scientists, where one would expect them most.[2]

We could guess, from Chapter 2, that divergers would have cultural interests, and convergers ones that are practical and out-of-doors; and this is what happens.[3] Typically, the diverger's interests outside the curriculum are reading, current affairs and the arts, whereas the converger concerns himself with cars, radios, model building, climbing, camping, natural history, canoeing and so on. He eschews the arts, with the single exception of music. Also the diverger tends to have a broad range of interests, while the converger's range is narrow.[4]

The paradox, therefore, is tight-knit. The boys who think most fluently, inventively and, it seems, analytically about physical objects are those least likely to have an interest in controlling them. The boys whose whole way of life is centred on the control of their physical environment, either literally or conceptually, are the least likely to think about it in any but conventional, prosaic terms. This discovery accords neatly with the poor open-ended scores already reported (in Chapter 3) amongst boys who are outstandingly technically inventive. The simplest explanation is that the task strikes such boys either as alarming or as unusually trivial – and there is, doubtless, truth in this. But it also seems possible that we are making a false assumption in *expecting* technically-minded boys to analyse ordinary objects in general terms. This, after all, is not how they think when pursuing their own special lines of interest. A boy

[1] P < 0·005.
[2] Modern linguists produce slightly less than the historians, as do the biologists. Classicists, as so often, belong with the physical scientists.
[3] P < 0·001.
[4] P < 0·001.

devouring knowledge about computer circuitry is not analysing the transistor in terms of its general physical properties; he is learning to exploit one or two of its *special* properties. And he assimilates his knowledge not by working each step out from first principles, but by absorbing an enormously elaborate system or 'rhetoric' of conventions relatively uncritically. It is arguable, in other words, that thinking of an object in terms of its general physical properties is relevant in science and technology only occasionally, and at the very fringe of knowledge; that the scientist thinks in this way only when his current repertoire of conventions fails him.

VIOLENCE. The next important area of differences between convergers and divergers concerns the expression of violence. Convergers are much less likely than divergers to produce uses for objects involving aggressiveness, or to produce violent themes for drawings.[1] Turton, an extreme diverger and rather an unsuccessful student, comes as close to unbridled violence as any:

... to drown someone in ... to put on someones nose ... to fire from an elastic band at someone ... to slap in someones face ... to throw at someone ... to de-rail a train with ... to throw through a window ... to sink a boat ... to smother someone with ...

However, most expression of violence is more devious. The majority either feel no aggression, stifle it, or express it in a form which seems to them intellectually respectable. Robinson, a form-mate of Turton's, illustrates diverger's aggressiveness more typically, and also reveals some of the ways in which this emotion is harnessed to civilized purposes:

(*Barrel*) Putting any liquid in, rolling in, bran-tub, using as a latrine, water-butt. (*Paper Clip*) Clipping paper, picking your teeth, opening a lock, completing electrical circuits, hair clip, keeping your trousers up, cleaning ears and nails, playing with. (*Tin of Boot Polish*) Polishing shoes, make-up, putting boot polish into, keeping things in, smearing over students who ask damn fool questions. (*Brick*) Building, throwing, breaking windows, knocking people out, fetching off the bottom of swimming-pools, providing work for people.

[1] $P < 0.001$, and < 0.05 respectively. There is, incidentally, a strong connection between inaccuracy on the IQ test and violence in the *Drawing*. Out of twenty-seven boys with high accuracy scores, only one did a drawing involving violence; $P < 0.005$. The topic of accuracy seems a likely one for further research.

(*Blanket*) Sleeping in, wearing, eating, ripping up, suffocating people with, covering things, blocking up a broken window, making rope with, muffling cries, preserving virtue.

His suggestions are firmly personal, and although not especially ingenious, range quite freely. Sex and aggression are both present, although both are partially veiled by pedantry ('muffling cries', 'preserving virtue'). Also, he suggests a somewhat messy fate for myself ('smearing over students who ask damn-fool questions') – voicing a resentment which many seemed to share, but few made explicit.[1]

However, the question of violence is not simple. In fact, the broad distinction between convergers and divergers conceals one of the most intriguing discrepancies that I have yet come across. A few boys make suggestions which seem, to the adult eye, unusually violent, gruesome, or cruel – and these boys are not divergers as one might expect, but *convergers* and all-rounders.[2] Obviously there is no absolute criterion of what is morbid or warped, but certain of these responses seemed quite different in quality from the relatively harmless violence which most divergers produce (often in lieu of wit). I therefore prepared a short-list of forty responses, including all of those which to my eye could conceivably qualify as morbid (and several relatively harmless-seeming responses as well, to make weight); and this I circulated to a wide variety of adults, asking them to pick out the dozen or so which struck them as the most gruesome, cruel or warped. Although a number of people clearly disliked the task, and others found (rightly) that the judgment was a very crude one, a fair measure of agreement was reached. Certain suggestions were picked out by almost everyone, others by almost no one.[3] The following are the twenty-five most frequently selected. They are set out in order of estimated 'morbidity', highest first, with the

[1] Robinson's aim in life, perhaps revealingly, is to become a clergyman. Few boys declare such an aim at the age of 16, but of those who did, almost every one revealed some violence in his responses to the open-ended tests.

[2] This result, interesting in itself, also provides a useful example of a research worker's disinclination to pursue exceptions. I noticed that one or two of these boys were convergers fully two and a half years ago, but could not account for them, and left them on one side. Only recently did I pursue the discrepancy systematically.

[3] The questionnaire is reproduced in Appendix B. The rank order given here is based on the estimates of eighty independent, adult judges. Nearly all of these were graduates or undergraduates; and they represent a tolerably good, if not precisely balanced, cross-section of the thinking public.

convergence or divergence of their perpetrators in brackets afterwards – the minuses being divergers and the convergers pluses.
Asterisks denote boys occurring in the list for a second time. Some
suggestions were offered, in almost identical verbal form, by more
than one boy:

1. To put spikes round the inside and put someone in and roll the barrel along the ground. (*Barrel*) [o, o]
2. Smash sister's head in. (*Brick*) [+1]
3. Wrapping up dead wife so as blood does not stain car seats. (*Blanket*) [+1]
4. For stuffing dead, headless bodies in, see A. Hitchcock. (*Barrel*) [o]
5. To remove from baby sister's bed in mid-winter while asleep. (*Blanket*) [+2]
6. To use (full of nails) to torture people. (*Barrel*) [+1]
7. Smother my sister. (*Blanket*) [+1*]
8. Close the lid on someone and roll him over cliff or something. (*Barrel*) [+1]
9= To make people sick with by putting small quantities in their food. (*Tin of boot polish*) [o*]
9= Suicide. (*Paper Clip*) [−2]
11= Suffocating a person to death. (*Blanket*) [+1]
11= Fill with stones and rol¹ it down a hill on to somebody to squash him. (*Barrel*) [o]
13. To tie to cats and drown them in ponds. (*Brick*) [+1, +1, o]
14= As a weight to remove a pistol after committing suicide. (*Brick*) [o]
14= Hitting and killing people. (*Brick*) [o]
16. Murder by smothering. (*Blanket*) [+2, −1]
17= Nailing up one's study-mate inside. (*Barrel*) [−1]
17= Attaching to unwanted cats. (*Brick*) [o]
19= To put a cat in when half full. (*Barrel*) [+2*]
19= Unrefined torture. (*Paper Clip*) [−1]
21. As a thumbscrew. (*Paper Clip*) [−1]
22= Strangle somebody. (*Blanket*) [o, −1]
22= Suffocating an animal. (*Blanket*) [o]
24. For suffocating someone. (*Blanket*) [various]
25. Drowning someone in (i.e. Duke of Clarence) (*Barrel*) [−1, o]

Although here and there responses may strike one as too high in
the list or too low, the general effect is unmistakable: responses get
progressively less gruesome, cruel or warped the lower down the list
one goes.¹ At the top end of the scale, the suggestions are not merely

¹ Differences of opinion over such a matter may arise from a number of sources. The
quotations are lifted out of context, and, in some cases, their impact seems distorted. Also,
people differ in the weight they ascribe to ideas drawn from novels, films or television –
some feel that such suggestions 'really don't count'. And, likewise, judges differ in the weight
they place on the various components of 'morbidity': the cruel, the gruesome, and the
warped.

ghoulish, they seem to reflect both alarming attention to detail, and, in some cases, considerable ingenuity. And, equally unmistakably, convergers and all-rounders dominate the upper sections of the list. The first diverger occurs in ninth place, and seems in fact to be an instance of a suggestion distorted by its lack of context. This boy's open-ended responses are given in full in Chapter 5, and the reader may feel – as I certainly do – that 'suicide' seems less morbid a suggestion there than it does in isolation. The next divergers do not occur until we are two thirds of the way down the list; but from then on they outnumber convergers in the proportion three to one. The most 'morbid' responses from divergers all seem relatively innocuous when one compares them with the first half-dozen or so in the list. 'Suicide' seems relatively harmless when set against 'to put spikes round the inside and put someone in and roll the barrel along the ground'. 'Murder by smothering' is less specific than 'smash sister's head in'. 'Nailing up one's study-mate inside' – from its context almost certainly more lighthearted than it seems in isolation – is mild when compared with 'Wrapping up dead wife so as blood does not stain car seats'.

In short, then, convergers are less likely to produce violent responses than divergers – but when they do produce one, it is much more likely to be really ghoulish.[1] Although an extraordinarily interesting result, it is not clear what construction should be put upon it. Statistically speaking, there is little question of its being a fluke; nor, I think, can it be entirely explained away as a joke. Doubtless, a number of these morbid suggestions are offered as jokes, or in an effort to shock: but we have still to explain why the converger's sense of humour takes this form. We also have to explain a connection between what I have called 'morbidity' and emotional disturbance in certain of the boys concerned. I have no systematic information about boys' social adjustment, but two of the boys in my sample I know to have been in difficulty. One of these, Gregory, is an unusually able scholar, but has been involved in crime of quite a serious nature. Nevertheless, he has reached University with considerable distinction, and did well on all the tests I

---

[1] The distribution of violent responses – when plotted against convergence and divergence – is therefore U-shaped. Bringing out such non-linear relations in statistical terms is not simple. There seems no question, however, that the finding is highly statistically significant. The question is briefly discussed in Appendix A.

gave him (being quite outstanding, incidentally, in vocabulary). He is jointly responsible both for the top suggestion in the list already given, and for an equally unsettling idea: No. 9 – 'to make people sick by putting small quantities in their food.' Sharing top place on the list with Gregory is Adkins, who expressed a similar idea to Gregory's in slightly different form: 'For rolling people down a hill in when it has got spikes inside.' Although form-mates, and although the idea seems likely to have cropped up in their schoolwork, Gregory and Adkins are dissimilar in personality, and produced their responses independently. Where Gregory seemed thoroughly capable, Adkins was markedly emotionally withdrawn; to such an extent, in fact, that academic work became more than he could manage, and he left school with only the most meagre examination results behind him.

A third reason for taking the present finding seriously, and perhaps the best, is the fact that suggestions like Gregory's and Adkins' have been selected as 'morbid', not merely by myself and other psychologists, but by quite a large sample of physical scientists (quite a high proportion of whom are bound to be convergers).[1] If Gregory's and Adkins' suggestions were no more than examples of convergent wit, then judges specializing in the sciences would presumably rate them differently from judges specializing in the arts. Yet this does not happen. The rank orders for arts and science judges turn out to be fairly similar. Certainly, in my view, there is no question that the result deserves detailed interpretation of some kind, and I shall offer one in Chapter 5.

HUMOUR. The next point to turn to is that of humour. Getzels and Jackson's work leads one to expect that divergers will be more likely than convergers to be witty. Their 'High Creative' sometimes runs to elaborate and sustained fantasy, both comic and bizarre. I found, surprisingly, that although this distinction did exist among English boys, it was not very marked.[2] Indeed, the fabric of schoolboy humour seems subtly to transmogrify itself in mid-Atlantic. There

---

[1] The panel of eighty judges included thirty-two mathematicians, engineers and physical scientists.

[2] For humour in *Drawings* the difference was too slight to be significant; on *Uses of Objects*, $P < 0.001$.

are no instances in my scripts of the elaborate, wisecracking constructions with which Getzels and Jackson's book abounds. Here, for example, is the first part of a 'High Creative's' autobiographical sketch:

I was born into an academic family. My father is a professor. I was born in Tampa, Fla. at the home of my Uncle Henshaw. My family has changed with the introduction of my brother. At present my family is not extraordinary except that my brother has two heads. My parents do not quarrel (nor have I ever seen them do so). The other day when my brother fell down a manhole we all (including aged Uncle Henshaw who was visiting us then) pitched in to flush him down to the sanitary canal and then fished him out. . . .[1]

By comparison, English boys' humour is fragmented, guarded, elliptical, and sparse. For the most part, references to violence (or occasionally sex) serve, but every now and again one finds something a little more complex:

Bricks are used to build houses; break windows or warm beds if hot. Hot bricks are very useful for cats. Cats love them and they dance with delight at the prospect. Bricks are also used as people. E.g., Your a brick.

One has the feeling, reading this last effort that the boy concerned is using an elusive whimsy to mock at the question and the questioner. But even this wintry level of amusement is reached only occasionally; and, in fact, four hundred odd scripts have revealed only one sustained piece of fantasy – the drawing already mentioned of the cross-Channel zebra race (a reference, incidentally, to No. 11 of *Controversial Statements*).[2] This was surrounded with odds and ends of captions:

Every year there is a race from England to France. Every zoo in the country rounds up its Zebras and drives them into the English Channel to form a sort of bridge (see Illustration). Then the *handlers* walk over the Channel by stepping from Zebra to Zebra. On the return journey the Zebras walk over the men, and who can blame them . . . England . . . France. . . . Aerial view of annual zebra crossing race. . . . Not only horses have three tails.

I shall return to this drawing, and the draughtsman, Tarry, in the next chapter. For the moment, one fact is salient: that both this and the preceding quotation were from the work not of divergers,

[1] Getzels and Jackson (1962) p. 100. Uncle Henshaw turns out, apparently, to be fictitious.
[2] See Appendix B, and discussion in Chapter 5.

but convergers – and extreme convergers at that. Overall, divergers are more likely to make jokes than convergers; but some of the sharpest wit comes from boys at the other extreme. Although superficially anomalous, this finding can be fitted into a consistent interpretation, as I try to show later.[1]

'MESSY' RESPONSES. Perhaps it is in this next category rather than either of the previous ones that we come closest to spontaneous emotional expression. Some of the uses suggested for a tin of boot polish were messy:

To put underneath peoples shoes so as to make a nice mess.
To make a mess of someones bed.

These are the province of the divergers.[2] Normally, they are expressions of aggressiveness, but occasionally (as in the first example) messiness is advocated for its own sake. If questioned, most 15-year-olds would doubtless tend to view such answers as childish; in psychoanalytic terms they are obviously regressive. It seems safe to conclude, therefore, that the diverger is more likely to indulge impulsive and infantile ideas, whilst the converger is more guarded. It is not clear, all the same, precisely what these impulses are, nor what it is that the converger guards against. Psychoanalysts might identify the smearing of boot polish with the smearing of faeces. However, this may be an over-simplification. In the first place, there is the question of dirty-mindedness. Messy responses have about them a ring of innocence which is quite different from the flushed, knowing way in which schoolboys of 15 normally refer to excrement. Is this innocence a defence? Or is the analogy with faeces a false one? Secondly, there is the question of aggressiveness:

Used at CCF camps for blacking behinds.
For slapping in someone's face.

Boot polish is usually smeared with aggressive intent – the first quotation referring euphemistically to the practice of forcibly blackening boys' genitals with boot polish, and thus humiliating them.

---

[1] As well as the more conventional type of joke, there is an additional category of response, presumably intended to be *risqué*, but ringing with unconscious implications: (*a barrel*) 'very useful when a dirty old woman takes your clothes when you are swimming starkers'. Unfortunately, there are not enough of these to warrant a statistical comparison.
[2] $P < 0.001$.

So the aggressive feelings may be the 'basic' ones, and the smearing merely incidental. Conversely, the aggression may serve as a defence against illicit sexual desires, illicit desire to play with excrement, or some other desire. Or, possibly, it constitutes the welling up of a true sadistic sexuality. In short one does not know. We reach here the gap which separates our relatively simple theoretical concepts (anal regression, sadism, the libido and so on) from the diversity of real human behaviour. For the time being, perhaps, the question of what it is that the diverger expresses and the converger does not can be left vague. Sufficient to say that there is an expressive freedom in the one and a corresponding constraint in the other.

ATTITUDES

MINORITY ATTITUDES. The next broad area in which differences occur is that of attitude. On *Controversial Statements*, for example, divergers are the more likely to hold attitudes shared by only a minority of their peers.[1] Statement No. 7 is Bernard Shaw's remark:

Money is indeed the most important thing in the world; and all sound and successful personal and national morality should have this fact for its basis.

The majority of boys express hostility:

Bunk!! The happiest people are not always the richest. Happiness of the world's population is the most important thing.
There are better things even in this day and age than money.
Rubbish!
Unfortunately the influence of money is everywhere.
The world goes round on love, and you cannot buy true love at any price.

Only one boy in six expresses agreement with Shaw, and almost never a converger: only three in a sample of 119. It is plain, too, from the content of the answers that where divergers take an unusual line, it is frequently, although by no means always, because they have avoided a stock response and have tried to come to grips with ideas they do not understand. With Statement No. 7, comments can broadly be divided into three categories: (a) the popular, high-minded stereotype ('Money is the root of all evil'), (b) the relatively unpopular pragmatic stereotype ('You can't get far without it, mate'), and (c) answers which try to deal with the point Shaw was making:

[1] $P < 0.005$.

This is a statement with a twofold meaning. Firstly if a man has a lot of money he is not always happy. Happiness is an essential in life, and sometimes it cannot be found in money. In the case of starving people, however, money is the only means by which they can obtain food.

This is a muddle. Nevertheless, in the last sentence, it does alight on a vital point, and one which almost every other member of this highly accomplished sample missed.

This quality among divergers is clearly important. They do produce statistically unusual attitudes, but not – as Getzels and Jackson might imply – because their views are unrealistic or far-fetched. On the contrary, their attitudes are unusual precisely because they avoid the high-minded stereotype, and choose instead either the pragmatic stereotype, expressing a cynical acceptance of the facts, or a comment which suggests that they have read the original statement closely enough to see what it is about. In other words, the diverger owes his greater flexibility not to a lack of detailed concern with facts or logic, but to his relative freedom from the tendency to see the world in terms of preconceived patterns. To some extent, however, this freedom on the diverger's part is tied to the subject-matter in question. He seems to think more incisively than the convergers about human issues, but is prone to lapse into general comment when faced with a logical puzzle or conundrum :[1]

No horse has two tails;
Every horse has one more tail than no horse;
Therefore; every horse has three tails.

There are some other interesting differences to be found:

With the single exception of Homer, there is no eminent writer, not even Sir Walter Scott, whom I can despise so entirely as I despise Shakespeare. . . .

The whole weight of English education leads children to accept Shakespeare as a genius. To question this, in some homes and some schools, is little short of blasphemy. Naturally, not many boys in my sample did so; only nine out of 119. Of these, five were divergers, none convergers.

It would be most unfair to exclude South Africa from the next Olympics. Its internal politics are none of our business.

Most boys were opposed to exclusion, almost invariably on the

[1] $P < 0.05$.

grounds that 'you can't mix sport and politics'. Only a handful were in favour; and again, they were more likely to be divergers than convergers. The majority simply compartmentalized the one topic from the other. The stock response to this statement was not that exclusion was unwise, rather that it was unthinkable. The emotional functions of such compartmentalizing and the more conventional form of stereotyping are presumably very similar.

AUTHORITARIANISM. Divergers are also much more likely to have views which are liberal and non-authoritarian. Information about this comes from two sources. First *Controversial Statements*. On this test, divergers tend to favour the United Nations' intervention in the Congo, and freedom in their choice of reading; and to show hostility to apartheid, Boy Scouts, and compulsory membership of the Combined Cadet Force. They are also much more likely to admit that they are unhappy at school.[1] This liberal atmosphere permeates nearly all their opinions. There are, however, two telling exceptions – Statements Nos. 5 and 6:

Human nature being what it is, you can't run a boys' school without corporal punishment.

The English country gentleman galloping after a fox – the unspeakable in full pursuit of the uneatable.

On these two topics, both of which involve physical pain, (or cruelty, depending on your point of view), the divergers' liberalism breaks down. They are more likely to approve of hunting and caning than to disapprove. This incongruity becomes even more pointed when one looks at the results of the *Personal Qualities Questionnaire*. Among other differences, one finds the divergers more likely than the convergers strongly to approve of 'fondness for animals.'[2] Divergers, in other words, approve both of hunting animals and of being kind to them; thus they are more capable than convergers of containing strong feelings – even when these conflict. As with apartheid, divergers show how capable they are of entertaining conflicting systems of value (in that case, the rights of coloured people in South Africa, as against the non-political nature of sport).

[1] $P < 0.001$, when all the *Statements* touching on issues of freedom, authority and conservatism are pooled to form a Liberal/Authoritarian Scale. See Appendix B.
[2] $P < 0.05$.

Faced with a paradoxical situation, they are more likely to grapple with it, less likely to side-step. In psychological jargon, they are more tolerant of ambiguity.

These findings about the converger's conservatism and conformity – so far a matter of qualitative judgment – are confirmed on the *Personal Qualities Questionnaire*. This avoids any danger of interpretative bias by being in multiple-choice form. It lists thirty qualities, of which boys are asked to approve or disapprove; and it was compiled with five characteristics in mind: authoritarianism, rigidity of attitude, social conformity, freedom of emotional expression, and defensiveness. As it happened, only the first three groups of qualities yielded a discrimination; but on these three, the differences were consistent and marked.[1] Convergers are more likely to approve of being obedient, and having a low opinion of themselves; and to disapprove of being independent of their parents. They are more likely to approve of accepting expert advice, and having set opinions; more likely to disapprove of being highly imaginative, and of artistic sensitivity. They are more likely to approve of mixing well socially, of being a good team member, of being personally neat and tidy, and of being very well mannered; and to disapprove of 'arty' clothes and bad language. Convergers also seem more likely to disapprove of being highly strung; and more likely to approve of having a 'stiff upper lip'. With almost every individual quality, the differences were consistent and in the expected direction, but relatively slight. Only one quality separated convergers and divergers in any striking way: being highly imaginative. Almost everyone seemed to approve of this quality, but divergers were nearly four times as likely to approve of it strongly.[2]

Returning to *Controversial Statements*, we find that convergers and divergers differ not only in the content of their attitudes, but in the manner in which they are expressed. Divergers tend to express themselves more emphatically, even at times with vehemence. First an extreme diverger, second an extreme converger:[3]

[1] See Appendix B for a complete list of qualities and the groupings employed. The items given here are those in the authoritarianism, rigidity and conformity scales which contribute to converger/diverger discrimination. P < 0·005, < 0·001 and < 0·01 respectively.

[2] P < 0·001.

[3] The first of these boys, Wilson, I shall return to in Chapter 5. Both incidentally, later won open awards at Oxford, one in classics, the other in medicine.

Absolute Rubbish! Typical of the Englishman with his narrow minded prejudices.
. . . Beatniks are just a lot indolent, parasitic yobs. . . . Rubbish! . . . Typical low
class trash like the *Daily Express*. . . . Clearly a case for a mental home. Perhaps a
warped mentality or even just a 'Bolshie'. Reminds me of a 12-year-old trying to
impress a grown up audience. . . . Rubbish! It is everyone's moral duty to strive
for Right, whether in England or the North Pole. . . . Definitely! We have reached
the moon, so why not the 3-minute mile? . . . A scandal! . . .

The recent Pilkington Report has praised the B B C, and called for a reorganisation
of the I T V. . . . The scouts has been for a long time a way of leading an outdoor
life. Often people find that such a life is not to their taste, by this means. Many
would not otherwise experience these pleasures, and so would miss such enjoy-
ment. . . . This is probably true, because many points of religion are able to be
interpreted in several ways. It is often impossible to tell which is correct, therefore
if only one opinion survives, it will be regarded as the truth. . . . The British Royal
Family is a symbol of British power, few countries now have this form of govern-
ment, which in early days was almost universal. The fact that the abolition of such
a system would save the taxpayers a considerable sum of money, does not warrant
such a drastic break with tradition, which is greatly respected. . . .

The difference between these scripts is, admittedly, a matter for
qualitative judgment. Sticklers for quantification may turn to the
Personal Qualities Questionnaire. In this, the individual chooses
between five comments, two emphatic ('strongly approve', 'strongly
disapprove'), and three relatively non-committal ('mildly approve',
'mildly disapprove', 'don't know'). The diverger, as one might
expect, is more likely to use the two emphatic categories; the converger to judge mildly, or say that he does not know.[1] On the other
hand, it is interesting to note that the converger is much more likely
to be emphatic on a multiple-choice test than an open-ended one.
He can express himself strongly, in other words, when the response
is defined for him; not when he does not know quite what is expected
of him, and has to formulate his response for himself.

THE INTELLIGENCE TEST

The last group of connections concerns the intelligence test. Naturally, as a matter of definition, convergers usually have higher
intelligence test scores than divergers. Moreover, their superiority
extends not merely to the diagrammatic and numerical parts of the
test, but to the verbal ones, as well.[2] And one might deduce, on the

[1] $P < 0.05$.
[2] $P < 0.001$, in all three cases.

strength of Chapter 2, that they also differ in the biases of their IQ's. We would predict that divergers have verbal biases of intelligence, whereas convergers' biases would be non-verbal. In my first reports of this research, based on a small sample, this certainly seemed to be the case.[1] However, and to my great surprise, I found that when I attempted to replicate this finding on larger samples, it dwindled to insignificance.[2] This discovery is an odd one. Arts specialists tend to have verbal biases. Arts specialists tend to be divergers. Yet verbal biases amongst divergers are slight.[3] What the explanation is, I do not see. Nevertheless, the finding is a convenient one, because it helps to answer an objection frequently raised to open-ended tests: namely, that they favour the verbal boy and penalise the non-verbal. This seems unfounded. Convergers have, as I have said, higher scores than divergers on the verbal questions in A.H.5; they do not differ significantly in their vocabularies; and now we find that they do not differ significantly, either, in the biases of their intelligence. In other words, it is not the verbal nature of tests like *Uses of Objects* which put convergers off; rather the fact that they are open-ended.

In addition, we find that convergers are much more accurate on the intelligence test – in the language of the schoolroom, the converger is a 'disciplined' worker, the diverger not.[4] Remembering the link established in Chapter 2 between inaccuracy and emotional instability, it is now tempting to conclude that as well as being more 'disciplined', the converger is also more 'stable'. However, the relationships is a complex one. Originally, two accuracy scores were derived, one from each half of the intelligence test. The lower of these was called 'worse accuracy', and the discrepancy between them 'range accuracy'. In Chapter 2, it was 'range accuracy' which correlated so surprisingly well with ratings of boys' apparent insta-bility. Here it is 'worse accuracy' which discriminates well, whilst 'range accuracy' discriminates poorly.

---

[1] Hudson (1962, 1963 a).

[2] Analysing this result in detail, I find that convergers do have a significant bias towards disgrammatic questions, but not to numerical ones.

[3] There is, of course, no logical contradiction here. Correlations between A and B, and A and C have to be quite high before a correlation between B and C is entailed.

[4] $P < 0.001$.

CONVERGERS AND DIVERGERS DIFFER AMONG THEMSELVES

Thus far, I have concentrated on the respects in which converger and diverger differ – and inevitably my account has been a distorted one. The unwary might well conclude that one converger is much like another, and divergers likewise. Anyone who has tried to measure human behaviour knows that this is not so. A considerable variety exists; and there is little point in pretending otherwise. Such differences are most marked – or, at least, most obvious – among the divergent. Boys who are good at the open-ended tests are good in various ways. There is a tiny minority of boys, for example, who are fluent but impersonal: no violence, no jokes, no levity of any kind.

Uses for a Barrel
 (1) Containing Liquids.
 (2) A slop bucket.
 (3) Table (or support for same).
 (4) Chair.
 (5) Lampstand.
 (6) Christmas Tree support containing earth.
 (7) Wastepaper basket.
 (8) 'House' for dog or cat or other pet.
 (9) Strawberry growing.
(10) Rain-water but.
(11) Decoration for walls of restaurant/cafe.
(12) Pontoon for a raft.
(13) A window dressing in a shop.
(14) A support for sawing wood on.

Uses for a Paper Clip
 (1) Keeping loose papers tidily.
 (2) Holding two surfaces while glue sets.
 (3) Modelling.
 (4) A hook for attatching a knife to trousers, etc.
 (5) A key-ring.
 (6) A weight to correct the centre of gravity of a model airoplane.
 (7) Lock picking.
 (8) A length of wire for binding objects.
 (9) A device for extracting objects from sink holes, etc.
(10) Trade object for primitive peoples – used as a personal ornament.

Uses for a tin of Boot Polish
 (1) Ceaning shoes.
 (2) Making various leather objects more suple.
 (3) Preserving and cleaning leather chairs.

(4) Makeup in a play.

(5) A lubricant.

(6) A pigment for colouring.

(7) Dried-up boot polish for brass rubbings.

Uses for a Brick

(1) A building material.

(2) A support for scientific aparatus.

(3) A paper-weight.

(4) A weight to hold down such things as a tarpaulin or roofing-felt on a roof.

(5) Cleaning the inside of a cement mixer.

(6) A hammer.

(7) A weapon for hitting or throwing.

(8) Breaking glass in a jewellry raid.

(9) Firebrick in household grates.

(10) A general support.

A Blanket can be used as or for

(1) A Bed cover.

(2) Part of a bed.

(3) A wall hanging.

(4) Chair cover.

(5) A place to sit in picnics.

(6) Fire fighting – cutting off oxygen from flames.

(7) A carpet.

(8) A cusion.

(9) A blind to exclude light from a room.

(10) A lying space for a pet.

(11) Lagging of pipes and boilers.

(12) Lagging a car radiator.

(13) An object of clothing.

(14) Wrapping up clothing, books, etc., to make easier their carrying.

(15) Escaping from fire both by making a rope and by jumping into a blanket held taught by other people.

(16) Muffling loud noises.

This boy, Fordham, though exceptionally fluent, is in no way personal. Every suggestion is pedantically phrased, written and numbered – showing that emotional uninhibitedness, although usually a concomitant of fluency, is by no means necessary to it. In spite of his fluency, Fordham 'feels' like a converger.[1] As fluent, but

[1] Is it fanciful, I wonder, to see his spelling mistakes as a chink in the armour of repression, especially in the first suggestion for 'boot polish'? The connection between this and the qualities of 'anal obsession' which a psychoanalyst would see in the rest of his work seems to me rather interesting.

quite different in tone, is Wilson; his suggestions rain down, seem-ingly written without a moment's reflection:

(*Barrel*) Water barrel, wastepaper basket, overflow tank, raft, storage of fish, beer, etc., life-buoy, hiding-place, shooting, camoflage, weapon.

(*Paper Clip*) Torture, tie-pin, nose-clip, hold papers, weapon, suicide, cuff-links, collar-stud, picking locks, fastening a strap, clean your ears.

(*Tin of Boot Polish*) Clean shoes, black one's face, disguise, poison, dye clothes, cosh, bullet, use tin for knife or tops of petrol tanks.

(*Brick*) Robbery, weapon, smash windows, buildings, weight, ruler, plumb-line, ballast, sign-post, sign.

(*Blanket*) Warmth, stop fires, sick people, fire blanket to jump into, to protect hands when smashing windows, clothes, suffocate people with, ladder, rope, hat, cap, trousers.

Between Fordham and Wilson lie other divergers who effect a better balance between poise and uninhibitedness – Allan, for example, a divergent physical scientist:

(*Barrel*) Keeping a liquid or solid in, i.e. grain, water, drink, playing with (roll down hill inside), fire bullets through it, suck water out to get a vacuum, growing flowers in, source of metal rings, mould for concrete filler, wastepaper basket, source of firewood.

(*Paper Clip*) Clipping pieces of paper together, holding things (forceps), pinching skin, unwind and use as short bit of wire, putting through a hole on the end of the inner section of a spring tape measure while changing tape.

(*Tin of Boot Polish*) Cleaning shoes, straps, etc., emptying out and using as a tin to keep oddments in, using as a source of metal.

(*Brick*) Building with, weight, throwing through a window, throwing at some-thing in a temper.

(*Blanket*) Putting on a bed, suffocating a fire, item of clothing, source of wool when unravelled, curtain, insulating block of ice, filtering water in bulk, padding, catching people jumping from window, bumping people on.

And quite apart from the question of sheer fluency, there are boys like Wildash who are distinguished less by the ideas they express, than by the manner in which they express them:

(*Barrel*) Well, clearly, one keeps things in them – beer to gunpowder. There is the minimum of decency secured by taking out the head and foot and holding the staves and hoops round one's middle. Diogenes lived in one – presumably a large size – and they make splendid water baths. I have rolled down a hill inside one, but would wish to build handles inside and padding before I repeated this. The staves make splendid skis or sleigh runners, while the hoops are good for sword blades if suitably cut and bent. I know a man who uses barrels as loud-speaker enclosures, but this is more visually than auditorally effective. And they can be used as seats

and tables. I have floated about in one, which is better than rolling down hill, but less directional.

(*Paper Clip*) There are two sorts of paper clips. The wire ones one can use whenever one wants a bit of wire; the nice brassy ones with unfolding wings I used a lot in aeromodelling. Unfolded and twisted they made nice looking airscrews; bent and put into the wings they were fine undercarriages. They are fine emergency collar-studs, given that one knows how to fold them. And occasionally I clip paper with them; or try to – ever tried to restore to paper-clipping service an emergency collar-stud?

(*Boot Polish*) Blacking boots and the faces of enemies. The empty tins are useful as tins with an airtight lid. Various practical jokes and (my main use) as a lubricating and refurbishing material for old shellac 78 RPM discs. The tins are splendid things, light, tight, strong, and easy to conceal. And the material they are made up of is easy to chop up and use as sheet metal, again for modelmaking in particular.

(*Brick*) I suppose the standard 9″ by 4″ by 3″ stock-brick. These are a great political force in some places, split in half and used to express the feeling of the electorate. They are very handy as ballast or other in weighting functions. Ground to powder and mixed with water, the red type at least is a good raddle, for frescoes. But I like bricks only as static parts of houses: they are too heavy to be handy utensils.

(*Blanket*) Tent, sail, rug, towel, clothing, catch cloth (to break a fall), smoke-signal maker, window curtain for clandestine operations, moth cafeteria, thing for sleeping in.

Emotionally, worlds separate Wildash and Fordham; the one flamboyantly self-confident, the other meticulous, impersonal and closed. One suspects, in fact, that Wildash embodies the typical scientist's stereotype of the typical arts man: somewhat unbuttoned and prone to padding. By comparison, Fordham is a robot, the converger without his inflexibility. Similarly, differences are detectable among convergers. They are by no means as universally inhibited as my recital of evidence has made them seem. They are sometimes witty, as I have shown; sometimes very shrewd; and occasionally emotional. I do not intend to skirt round these exceptions – they afford, in fact, a wealth of insight into the workings of the convergent mind, and will be discussed in the next chapter. There, I shall attempt to interpret the differences between the two types; and, at the same time, I shall try to fit exceptions into the interpretative web. One danger of this policy is that I may fall into the opposite mistake; I may allow the exceptions to blur the broad distinction already established. Perhaps I should end, therefore, by reaffirming the diversity of intellectual behaviour which the convergers and divergers encompass. At the one extreme, a mathematical

near-prodigy, with an IQ well within the top 10 per cent of the Cambridge population, and open-ended responses as follows:

(*Barrel*) Keeping wine in, playing football.

(*Paper Clip*) Keeping papers together, repairing page of a book.

(*Tin of Boot Polish*) Cleaning shoes (when empty) keeping pins, etc.

(*Brick*) Building things, throwing.

(*Blanket*) Keeping warm, smothering fire, tying to trees and sleeping in (as a hammock), improvised stretcher.

And at the other end of the scale, the slightly awe-inspiring spectacle of a fluent mind in spate:

(*Barrel*) For storing old clothes, shoes, tools, paper, etc. For pickling onions in. For growing a yew-tree in. For inverting and sitting on. As a table. As firewood chopped up. As a drain or sump for rain-water. As a sand pit. At a party for games. For making cider or beer in. As a play-pen for a small child. As a rabbit hutch, inverted with a door out of the side. On top of a pole as a dove cot. Let into a wall as a night exit for a dog or cat. As the base for a large lamp. As a vase for golden rod and michaelmas daisies, as an ornament, especially if it is a small one. With holes cut in the top and sides, either for growing wallflowers and strawberries in, or for stacking pots, and kitchen utensils. As a proper garbage can or wastepaper basket. As a ladder to reach the top shelves of a high bookcase. As a casing for a home-made bomb. Sawn in half, as a doll's crib. As a drum. As a large birds nest.

(*Paper Clip*) For holding papers together. To clean wax out of one's ears. Red hot, to bore holes in a cork. Unwound, as a pin or needle for rough work. To clean the dirt from between floorboards, and from under finger-nails. As a fuse wire. As a keeper for a magnet. As a safety-pin. As a hair clip. As a tooth pick. As a stylus for working on wax or in clay. As a fish-hook. With a thread passed through it as a sort of hook. As a charm on a necklace or bracelet. As a collar for a pet mouse, or as a ring for a bird's ankle. To tie labels on with. Unwound, to clear out a small hole, bind something together, or as solder wire. As a sort of shoe-lace. As a tie-pin. As a means of barter. As a counter in a game of cards. As a piece of a board game such as draughts. As confetti. To sabotage a clock. To match with a spring. To make into chain mail.

(*Tin of Boot Polish*) To polish boots. To stain wood. To create a diversion in the household. To put into an enemy's shoe, glove, hat, etc. As theatrical make-up. As an artistic medium. As ink. As glue. As something to throw. As a storage place for smuggled jewels. As a fuel in an oil lamp. As a deodorant, with holes in the lid. As a lubricant. As a puck in ice hockey. Or as a quoit or ball. As an ashtray. As a beer-mat, or hot plate for a jug. As a building brick. As a stepping stone.

(*Brick*) As a weight. As a weapon (missile). As a grindstone and sandpaper. To build with. To make a flower-bed edge. To keep something from blowing away. To make a bookshelf out of. As a hot water bottle. As a paper-weight. As a book end. As a bolster to level a table or something similar. Instead of an asbestos mat on the

stove. As ballast. As rubble. As a tile to pave a courtyard. To block a drain. To break a window. As a hammer. As an ornament. As a draught excluder. As a scourer. As a ruler, or a set square. As a stepping stone. As a practical joke as in a cake or as a present. As a nutcracker.

(*Blanket*) As a bedcover. As a drape. As a curtain. As a straitjacket. As a turban. As a carpet. Instead of a lawn. To cover a car. To dun a cow. As fuel. To line a garbage can. As wallpaper. As a tablecloth. As a convenient way of storing wool. To smother somebody. As a fishing net. As a hammock. As a dishcloth. As a flag. As a sunshade or umbrella. As a tent. As a pillow, or cushion. As a target in archery or shooting. As a saddle. As a back drop. As camouflage, depending on colour. To evoke national feeling (also depending on colour). As a fence. As a mulch for a flower bed. As a lampshade. As upholstry or padding. Cut into strips as a rope. As a sail. Impregnated with oil, as the skin of a small boat. As a shroud. Something to write on or as an artistic canvas. As protective coverings to wrap a present or breakables.

· 5 ·

Rival Systems of Defence

In this chapter I shall try to unify all the factual evidence about convergers and divergers into relatively simple patterns. To some extent this is bound to be a speculative venture; and certain subtleties of detail, to say nothing of margins of statistical error, may be overlooked in the search for an all-embracing scheme.

I shall, in fact, have three points to make. In the first part of the chapter, I shall use boys' autobiographical scripts as the basis for a general point: that all schoolboys are, in some sense or other, 'defended'. Throughout the American Literature on 'creativity', the diverger (or his equivalent) is seen as emotionally 'open', the converger as defensive or 'closed'. I with to argue that both are defended; that convergers and divergers differ, not in being defended or open, but simply in the defensive style or policy which they employ. My second step will be to outline the defensive policies of convergers and divergers respectively – contrasting them, and considering the strengths and weaknesses of each. Lastly, I shall discuss the defects of the interpretation I have offered, and suggest ways in which new and pertinent information might be collected.

THE AUTOBIOGRAPHIES

It goes without saying, of course, that a request for autobiographical information is bound to seem intrusive – especially if it comes from a psychologist, and even more so, perhaps, if it is open-ended:

Use this page to write a brief autobiography. There is no special form which this ought to take – just describe those aspects of your life which seem to you interesting or important.

What a boy writes down will depend, not just on his character and

habits of mind, but on his personal reaction to the intruder – on his impression of myself as alarming or safe, sympathetic or unsympathetic; and, more diffusely, on his preconceptions about psychologists as a whole. Although the *Autobiography* provokes defensiveness, the way in which a boy frames his answers is often revealing, nevertheless, about the way in which he thinks. One sees which defensive style a boy adopts when challenged. Some boys, as Getzels and Jackson observed, restrict themselves to recitations of factual detail. Others are facetious, academic, wry, ostentatious, or openly hostile. Some are circumloquacious; others exceedingly brief. Whatever the tactic, one nearly always has the sense of an elaborate screen being placed between boys' private feelings and the world at large.

The first example illustrates well, I think, the pervasive form of convergent restriction. The boy concerned has outstanding academic gifts; he entered one of our great public schools as a scholar, and has dominated his contemporaries ever since:

I was born in D——, a medium-sized town in ——shire. I can remember little until about an age of 4. Then I started to go to a small school down in the middle of the town, where I learnt a few things like how to add, subtract, multiply, divide, etc. Our house was some way away from the actual town, and some way above it. Usually I used to catch a bus down there, but occasionally I walked with my two brothers, one two years older than I, one four years my elder. Most often it would be up from school that we walked, and it was, in fact, a surprisingly long way. But of course I did not spend all my time at school. My father owned a factory near M——, thirty miles away, and there he went five days out of every seven. Sometimes, during the holidays, we would go with him, but most often we would be left to entertain ourselves. Our most frequent form of entertainment was in the form of walks over D——. This is a very extensive moor, and one could walk long distances over it. At best it could be called bleak; but somehow one never found this when one was actually walking on it. A great thrill to us young ones was climbing D—— Tower, from which we could get a very extensive view as far as B——. My father's brothers also owned another factory actually in the town of D——. Most Saturdays we would go down there with our father, and go climbing all over the place, and getting a very complete thrill from it. Once every Christmas there was a party at my father's own factory, and we would go there every time. I can remember that we always used to get sugar in our tea there, which we loathed! ... In 195-, my father decided to sell the factory and move down into ——shire, near S——. There we have been since January, 195-. Near our home is the farm which has been the family property for over a century. At the beginning of 195- it was being farmed by an old tenant, but he decided to give up in May. So my

father took over, not really knowing anything about agriculture. Since then he has greatly improved the farm, and my brothers and I spend a lot of time there in the holidays, especially during the corn harvest. Between January and July of 195– I went to a nearby day-school, and began a study of Latin and French. In September I went to A——, near W——, and there I spent four years, coming top of my form most terms, but not doing as well in games. However, I did have some success in athletics, and won several cups. In May, 196–, I took a scholarship to —— at the age of 11, and came second. Since September, 196–, I have been at —— coming top in my form every term. This term I took 'O' level, and I am pretty sure I got eight 'O' levels. I also got the top Senior Scholarship. I am most keen at tennis and athletics, still, and I do not do too badly in them.

This boy's expressions of feeling seem somewhat flat and mechanical – 'getting a very complete thrill,' for example, is an oddly dissociated remark for a 15-year-old; and from his other work, one notes how careful he is to avoid controversy. Some of his answers to *Controversial Statements* distil indecisiveness to the point of self-contradiction:

(*Human nature being what it is, you can't run a boys' school without corporal punishment.*) There are other ways of punishing boys apart from corporal punishment. Asceticism is a perfectly good method of punishment. Some boys do not care at all about beatings. But with human nature being what it is, school boys will need to be punished, but whether corporal punishment is the most effective method is questionable.
(*Aeroplanes and sports cars – not paintings and music – are the twentieth-century's works of art.*) This is really quite true. But the twentieth century does produce music and paintings, but most of both are pretty foul. In any case, aeroplanes and sports cars are not really works of art, but everyday commodities.
(*The happiest years of your life are spent at school.*) This if one thinks hard, is quite true in most cases. For at school one is wholly catered for, especially at boarding-school, so one has no worries. But in 'after-life' all the worries are one's own.[1]

This boy's defences seem both unconscious (in the sense that they are automatic) and all-enveloping. He does not fend others off explicitly – rather he lives a life reduced to rule.

[1] It is interesting to see how muddled even the cleverest 15-year olds are when considering a topic outside the curriculum. Boys who work with elegance and precision on Latin verses or mathematics are children again when confronted with a task which is unfamiliar. Only rarely does one come across remarks made with candour or asperity:
(*The happiest years of your life are spent at school.*) A fallacy that has recently, thank goodness, become extinct. Probably originated because one tends to forget past unhappiness, and in retrospect it would be very easy to think of innocence, friends, lack of problems, expressing a sort of yearning to escape from one's present situation.
(*The Boy Scout movement is the ideal means of learning to enjoy an outdoor life.*) UGH!!! Refuge for dim-wits and seedy homosexuals who are devoid of other interests.

My second example is the work of a diverger: a clever boy, although not as academically distinguished as the first:

Born 194– (September 28th to be exact) in a hospital in H—— (I think). Lived in a pad W—— way until I reached the ripe old age of 4. Looked after well by my dear old ma during the war when we had flying bombs and all that jazz coming over. Anyhow my dad got a job up Brum way so we packed our bags and moved up there in Feb. 194–. Lived in a pad in S——, a very la-de-da area, until May, 195–. Went to P—— school (wonder if that old drag of a head is still there), and passed the 11 plus to a very posh grammar school on the outskirts of the city. I did quite well there and got into a rugby team. My dad got another job in L—— in May, 1957, so we moved to C—— that month. I am still living there. I came to —— in the third year and got thrown into 5α. I soon made a lot of friends and in the next year I was in Lower B which was a great form to be in and continued into Upper B with the same blokes. I got all my nine 'O' levels and went into the Sixth Form where I am now taking History, English and Economics. I have had quite a good life really, but it has had its ups and downs like anybody's. I was a good quarter-miler when in Upper B, but I can't get my form back. Still, I'm not losing any sleep over that. I've got a taste for jazz, both trad and modern, so no one can say I'm not cultured. I suppose the turning point in my life was when I got the 11 plus and got to grammar school. That probably affected my whole life.

This boy, Stamford, hedges himself round with a highly self-conscious use of slang. Reading it, one is not sure whether he thinks it impressive, or is using a language which he thinks stale and feeble to express his disregard. Certainly, in conversation, he left one with a strong impression of churlishness and resentment.[1] Getzels and Jackson quote a much more florid example of the same kind of thing, written, again, in laborious slang:

I was transferred from another world or "hatched" as you might call it, at a very young age (0 for a fact). I called my mammy and she came runnin'. Den dat dok came an' he done took me and ah' squealed with fright. O' course I couldn' see anythin' anyhoo. (I was done borned in dat place dey call "Bellview", now what would ah' be doon' dere?) Den I grown up fur' three (3) yer' before my brudder was bornded. He is de' durndist critter ah' eveh' saw podnah'. At this time in my life you can see I played a cowboy, with my mudder as a injun. She never was the same cause ah used to hit her with a frin' pan. . . .[2]

The archness of this script places a barrier between the boy (or girl) and the interrogator. It acts, in a sense, as an elaborate decoy;

---

[1] One expression of this resentment was to wear the badge of the National Socialist Party of Great Britain in a school with a strong CND movement. Protest against protest, as it were.
[2] Getzels and Jackson (1962), p. 100.

and in much the same ambiguous way as Stamford's slang. One also finds, especially amongst young classicists at public schools, the opposite of slang – pedantic academicism. Yet both, one senses, fulfil much the same defensive function:

I have no strong religious beliefs but incline to Unitarianism; I am a convinced Social Democrat and agree with Gaitskell on most political matters. . . .

This from a tiny 15-year-old, seemingly preadolescent, yet waspish as a don. Another gambit is brevity:

Born at the age of three – premature birth – date 1984. Joined Dan Dare's space fleet at age of twelve. Emigrated to Mars and died. Born 13th March, 194-. Died later. Started school at age of $4\frac{1}{2}$. Took 11+ exam 1 year early and passed at age of $10\frac{1}{2}$.

Idiot (harmless)! Convinced I am Napoleon. Do not like horse meat. Very ambitious. Would like to be an actor.

These two scripts were from an extreme converger and all-rounder respectively. The next is from a diverger, and illustrates yet another tactic – a wry (and sometimes appealing) detachment:

My life is divided into three parts: one at school, one at home and one in my mind. . . . At school. . . . I eat as much as possible and play the guitar, banjolele and drums. When not doing these I am either doing Corps which is compulsory or doing games which are also. . . . The one at home is much the same except the food is better and there is no work. . . . The one in my mind is completely wonderful but unattainable. It consists of being a much sought after guitarist and of having the attentions of an anonymous girl who is saved from danger etc. at much trouble by the author.

However, the overwhelming impression that one carries from most scripts is less one of explicit defensiveness, more one of bewildering, boring detail:

. . . when I played for W—— Juniors Primary school team and had an undefeated season (played left half). Next year I vice-captained the side in another undefeated season, winning the H—— challenge cup. In the summer I captained the W—— Primary School's Cricket XI. Although quite reasonable at school I was soon susceptible to examination nerves. However I passed the 11+ exam and came to this school.

10–15 years. Going into a C form (3c) I started well. Captained the school 3rd form cricket XI and got into the 3rd form rugby team at scrum half. In the fourth form I worked harder and was promoted to 5A (from 4c²) but in doing so lost my cricket captaincy due to a slight argument with the cricket master who had insisted that I play for a draw when a win was still possible. We almost lost. In the 5th form had a good school year but exam position dropped during the

summer (cricket again). In the Remove however I had a poor academic year but a good sport year, captaining the colt's hockey team and vice captain of the cricket XI. At this age I had my 1st girl friend, what a fiasco! She didn't like taking 3rd place to (1) sport and (2) work. In my G.C.E. year I did not work hard and scraped 7 'O' levels. (Maths, English, History, French, German, Latin and Physics). Sport once again in this year. In my first possible year I got into the 1st XI as opening batsman and wicketkeeper. I received the bat for the most promising player. Huh! *1st year sixth*. Here I have relaxed completely and am satisfied with average exam marks. I got my colours in the 1st XI Hockey team and in the 1st XI Cricket team, which I captained. My father, a keen cricketer, has just died and this may affect my future at the school. I now have a steady girl friend. I want to do V.S.O.[1]

Although it remains a distant prospect, Turton brings us as close to ingenuousness as most:[2]

Born 194–, april 18th–. First walked at age of $2\frac{1}{2}$ on beach at J——. First injury $3\frac{1}{2}$, split open knee on doorstep. Went to school aged 4 yrs 11 months at private school, S—— park, E——, had much religion pumped into me there and grew to disbelieve it there. Had first real friction with teacher at the age of 9 when was hit over the head with my fathers oak ruler which broke. I did not complain about the teacher but a friend did and got told to mind his own business. Was first caned age 11 for being out of school in dinner hour, taking bus numbers of all things! Did best ever academically at this tender age when I came first in three subjects and fourth in overall classification. General position in form around 7–12th. Lowest ever 19th at Easter and 20th at summer exams. Passed 11 plus, very thrilled with this, and received prize at prep. school speech day. Had a bicycle as a reward next Christmas. ever since been very keen on cycle racing. Was interested in all forms of transport from age of 10 onwards, especially railways and aircraft. By the time I was 13 knew more about the latter two than many friends of 17 & 18. First kissed a girl seriously when I was 13 (what a laugh to look back on) when the lights fused at a Christmas party. At about the age of 14 I began to formulate ideas on politics, perhaps they were juvenile ones but I realised for the first time the futility of reactionary Conservatism. At about this time I also began to become interested in railway photography although I didn't own an expensive camera until a year ago. I had my first mild sex experiences in the summer of 196– when I was nearly 15 and have gradually progressed in my relationships with girls until the present time although I am not obsessed, I don't think, by sex and have not yet reached the ultimate. Academically I have never particularly shined but have not completely failed either although I have at times come pretty low. I think I am about average. I am now a member of CND and would like to see, in a vague sort of way the setting up of a perfect communist state although this is nearly impossible in practice.

[1] This boy, an all-rounder, eventually went up to University, to read social sciences.
[2] We have already met him in Chapter 4.

These illustrations could be duplicated many times over; and serve, I hope, to make my point. Whether it is through flamboyance, allusiveness, open hostility, academicism, or unconscious all-enveloping restriction, almost all boys, it seems, set some distance between themselves and the outside world. And although a number do discuss their private lives, they do so archly, or as if discussing some interesting technical device. In dealing with their written work, one is tempted to confuse the more exuberant and outspoken forms of defensiveness with genuine openness. There are, however, one or two exceptional cases which suggest by contrast how thick the normal 15-year-old's armour may actually be. And, conveniently for my argument, both the most striking of these come, not from divergers, but from all-rounders. After dozens of scripts written by boys striking one posture or another, their relative directness comes as something of a surprise:

... I moved up the school very quickly, and had 2 yrs in the top form. I won a number of prizes. My father was very willing to help me in work during the holidays; this no longer occurs. My brother was more easy going than me; I was rather studious, and didn't enjoy myself much; the young headmaster, who would probably have been happier farming, was pretty useless at teaching and discipline. I got 'beaten up' a great deal by the boys and was very unhappy most of the time. At 13 I took the scholarship exam, and got 11th. I was extremely confident my first year here and was almost a stoic, in the proper sense of the word. I came fairly high (3rd the last term of my first year). My confidence, however, was shaken, and I have been fairly unhappy recently; I think I have now emerged rather more stable.

I was born at W—— on 1st April 194- (what a date!) Nothing worth recording occurred until when I was about 3 I fell in the next door neighbour's water-tank and caused a great flap, the third in my life. The first came when I was vaccinated as a baby and was snatched off my mother's lap by the girl next door, who obviously thought a lot of me. The second came on my 3rd birthday when Podge, our cat, got stuck in a rat trap and broke his leg and tail. He was all right after a time, though. Just as well because my parents knew that if anything happend to him I would have raised hell. On June 5th 195- I started at K—— Primary school. Nothing of much importance occurred there for a few years so I shall switch to other matters. That Christmas I went to the circus for the first (and only) time in my life. At this time I first met a friend of my father's and his daughter Rosemary, who was a year younger than me. I shall have more to say about her and her young sister Ann later on. The first 2 years of my school career passed without incident. When, however, I reached the top infant class I formed my first 'attachment'. Unfortunately, I had a rival and lost her. That repulse made me

buckle down to work and got me, eventually, my place at this school. In 195- I passed my 11+ and came here, after waiting a long while for my interview. After a few weeks I settled down, and again did quite well. That year my parents, thinking 'Oh! he knows how to speak French!' took me on the continent. The following year at school my career continued with its usual ups and downs. That year in the holidays I grew rather attached, in a friendly sort of way to the girl next door. This, however, was also doomed to destruction after 2 years. Passing to the next school year, on May 1st 195- at the school founder's day service I passed out without visible cause. Nothing further happened until in September my cousin got married and at the wedding I saw someone I claimed then and still do now to be the most beautiful girl I have ever set eyes on. The following summer after a year at school I went to N—— for the 3rd and made more friends who were extremely glad to see me the following summer. At this time too my affection for Rosemary was on the point of blossoming out. Unfortunately it was a little one-sided. My feeling did not change in spite of a few repulses and a constant strain between us. Once I admitted to Rosemary that I was fond of her. This was untrue. As Ann had guessed I was more deeply in love than I cared to say.

It would be a mistake, obviously, to see either of these two scripts as entirely open. On the other hand, they do have a directness of expression about emotional matters which makes the average run of autobiographical comment seem contrived. The ingenuousness of the second, particularly, is sufficient to embarrass the average 15-year-old (and many adults). And our very uneasiness in the face of such work suggests how much we take defensiveness for granted. One wonders, therefore, if the imagery of the 'defence', the 'barrier', and the 'screen' is the right one. The impulse for self-protection seems to have invaded so much of some boys' lives that their every move is coloured by it. They present less a Siegfried or Maginot Line, more a countryside laced with trenches. Not so much a shell with soft marrow, more bone all through.[1]

I should like now to use this autobiographical material as a background to the main polemic purpose of this chapter: my contention that we can unify the evidence about convergers and divergers by considering each as the embodiment of a different defensive system. This case is one that has to be argued, not merely against readers' scepticism, but against a solid psychological orthodoxy. As I have already remarked, the American literature on

---

[1] The second quotation is from a boy who suffers severe physical handicaps. One wonders whether he is emotionally open precisely because his disabilities disqualify him from physical toughness, the aggression (and fear of aggression) which play a central part in most schoolboys' lives.

'creativity' treats the diverger as emotionally open and the converger as closed. The case for the American point of view, it must be admitted, is quite a strong one. Glancing down a list of the differences between convergers and divergers in Table 4, familiar distinctions press themselves upon one. Convergers strike one as inhibited, divergers as uninhibited; convergers seem reluctant to let themselves go, divergers less so. These are the metaphors of everyday language; but they have found their way too, into the reflections of eminent psychologists:

Openness to experience: extensionality. This is the opposite of psychological defensiveness, when to protect the organization of the self certain experiences are prevented from coming into awareness except in distorted fashion. In a person who is open to experience each stimulus is freely relayed through the nervous system, without being distorted by any process of defensiveness. Whether the stimulus originates in the environment, in the impact of form, color, or sound, on the sensory nerves, or whether it originates in the viscera, or as a memory trace in the central nervous system, it is available to awareness. This means that instead of perceiving in predetermined categories (trees are green; college education is good; modern art is silly) the individual is aware of this existential moment as it is, thus being alive to many experiences which fall outside the usual categories (*this* tree is lavender; *this* college education is damaging; *this* modern sculpture has a powerful effect on me).

This last suggests another way of describing openness to experience. It means lack of rigidity and permeability of boundaries in concepts, beliefs, perceptions, and hypotheses. It means a tolerance for ambiguity where ambiguity exists. It means the ability to receive much conflicting information without forcing closure upon the situation.[1]

Openness to experience, defensiveness, restriction, inhibition; all these notions seem at first sight to summarize the differences between convergent and divergent patterns. Or, at least, they do so until one looks at the evidence in detail.

THE CONVERGER

Let us begin with the converger. Two of his characteristics seem to me to stand out from the evidence. The first is his concentration upon the impersonal aspects of his culture, both in school and out. The second, the caution with which he expresses his feelings. At some stage in his life he seems to have turned his back on the sphere

---

[1] Rogers (1959), p. 75.

of personal relations, and focused all his attention on areas where people and personal emotions are least likely to obtrude. In a sense, of course, this picture is misleading. The typical converger is not a recluse in a laboratory; indeed, he may be very sociable. On the other hand, there is an important sense in which the converger seems to have limited both his emotional involvement with other people, and the extent to which he is open to the more unruly kinds of feeling. One suspects (to take an interpretative step) that the converger uses some sort of mental barrier against thoughts and feelings which unsettle him. And the use of such barriers seems to secure him an area of security, within which he is free to pursue his interests, unhampered by emotional disruption.

If we accept this idea of a mental barrier, a great deal about the converger makes sense. We note, for example, that his reactions to controversial issues are often stereotyped, and that he is prone to compartmentalize one topic from another. Both habits of mind serve, presumably, to minimize the uneasiness which ambiguous or conflicting ideas create; and both may be seen as defences against anxiety.[1] Both stereotyping and compartmentalizing serve to keep unpleasant conflicts at bay, and do so by the primitive expedient of ignoring them. It is interesting, too, that the converger's attitudes tend to be conventional, and authoritarian. It seems, in other words, not merely that he is willing to observe codes of conduct, but that he positively enjoys the security which rigid systems of belief engender. And not only do the converger's defences protect him from controversy; they also, as I have said, serve to limit the expression of his feelings. With the single exception of extreme or 'morbid' violence, every differentiation reveals the converger as the more discreet in the expression of what he feels. We can only prove, of course, that it is the *expression* of his feelings which is at issue here, but it seems reasonable to assume that his emotional responses themselves are under rigid control. Many convergers, one suspects, do not stifle strong, disorganised feelings – they fail to experience them.

The converger's restriction affects his thinking as well as his personality and interests. He is disconcerted by open-ended tests, not

---

[1] Gordon (1962). These terms have certain technical implications that I wish to avoid. I intend to use them as they occur in plain English: 'defence'—a protection; 'anxiety'—uneasiness or worry.

simply because they offer emotional possibilities which he distrusts, but, particularly, it seems, because they offer a task which lacks a single right answer. The converger seems to dislike ambiguity, even when it is stripped of its more obvious emotional overtones (as, for example, in *Meaning of Words*). If we compare his relatively poor showing on the open-ended tests with his excellence in IQ (and with his adequate performance on the vocabulary test), we see how he comes to specialize in work which enables him to be unambiguously right or wrong. And we should recognize, too, that the ability to think in highly conventional terms may be of the greatest importance to a young scientist in his work. Far from being a fault, it may be essential that he should accept massive bodies of conventional knowledge on trust; not merely assimilating it as a chore, but thoroughly enjoying it. As Kuhn suggests, the scientist must be a 'traditionalist' before he can hope to become a 'revolutionary'.[1]

One's general impression, then, is that the converger goes out of his way to avoid stress and controversy, especially that associated with people. Some convergers seem blank as far as the personal aspects of life are concerned. Others, whilst aware of the world of turbulent emotion, keep their reactions to it carefully in check. In almost every case, too, one senses that these emotional and intellectual habits are of long-standing. Far from being trivial by-products of interest or education, they appear deeply rooted in the growth of a boy's character.

My guess, then, is that convergence is a defence. The child turns his back on all those human issues which might upset him. He also seems to compartmentalize one broad area of his life from another: 'thinking' is compartmentalised from 'feeling'. This is a policy with characteristic strengths and weaknesses. Its chief virtue is that the person concerned is able to zone his preoccupations, coping with them one by one, rather than having to handle them simultaneously. He can think unhindered by emotional disruption; and then turn to his emotional life, and deal with as much of that as he sees fit. The individual consists, 'inside', not of a homogeneous emotional and intellectual fabric, but of a number of more or less disconnected

[1] Kuhn (1963). The authoritarian strain in the average converger's attitudes may, therefore, have an important adaptive function. The young scientist who questions everything, and totally distrusts authority, may stand at a crippling disadvantage.

elements. One would also predict certain weaknesses: that the converger's emotional relations will remain undeveloped; that he will think about personal matters only in highly conventional terms; and that if his internal defences are inadequate, his equilibrium may be wrecked completely by eruptions from the private sector.

CONVERGENCE TURNED TO GOOD ACCOUNT

Thus far, the converger has been interpreted as someone whose restrictions limit the scope of his experience, but permit him, within these limits, great intellectual freedom. His defences serve, on this argument, to demark an enclave. For many of the more profoundly defensive convergers, this model would seem to serve. On the other hand, there are convergers whose qualities demand a further interpretative refinement. In this section, I shall describe briefly a converger who displays quite exceptional wit and inventiveness. These qualities are usually the province of the diverger, but when they are produced by a converger, the result is sometimes outstanding.

Unquestionably the most imaginative response that I have seen to the *Drawing* is the three-legged zebra race mentioned in Chapter 4. Tarry the draughtsman is, quantitatively speaking, a model of convergence.[1] Yet he manages to brighten even his answers to *Meanings of Words* with a drawing or two, and a few cryptic verbal touches – (bit) 'Thing in horses mouth (not its tongue)'; and in *Uses of Objects*, his only suggestion for a blanket is 'will conceal what happens in bed'. Although personally shy and retiring, on paper he is sharp and at times peppery. He is severely right-wing on political issues ('The most dangerous man in the world is the educated African'), and shows a characteristic hostility to infringements of liberty, either intellectual or social. Everything he writes radiates his own brand of defensiveness – a natural extension, it seems, of his shyness. Often he picks questions to pieces rather than answering them; and when he does answer, the reader still cannot tell whether he means what he says. Barely once does he commit himself. Although his comments are often shrewd, he always leaves the initiative, the task of saying something positive, to someone else. In short, he seems a

---

[1] His I Q placed him in the top 1 per cent of the grammar school population; both his open-ended scores were below average.

familiar English type: the sceptical, reactionary individualist. His gifts assume a butt, someone willing to stick his insensitive neck out:[1]

(*A man ought to read just as inclination leads him; for what he reads as a task will do him little good*).
Some men's inclination leads to things other than reading.
(*No horse has two tails; Every horse has one more tail than no horse; Therefore, every horse has three tails*).
This is an interesting point. Why shouldn't a horse have three tails. Live and let live. If horses had three tails they would not need to use one anothers tails. Which all goes to prove that the horse, not the dog, is a man's best friend. He can lend us a tail in time of need.
(*Truth, in matters of religion, is simply the opinion that has survived*).
Why bring in the bit about religion?
(*Happy the man with an interest to pursue in his spare time*).
Therefore he has no spare time.[2]
(*Their Royal Family costs the British taxpayers some £2,000,000 per annum*).
So what! British Railways lose twenty or thirty times as much.
(*The Public Schools should be public – not private*).
They are in America. Do we want to degenerate completely into a little America?
(*It would be most unfair to exclude South Africa from the next Olympics. Its internal politics are none of our business*).
Yes. And let's have South Africa back in the commonwealth instead of Ghana. Shoot Nkrumah somebody.

Although convergers are defensive, it is a defensiveness which is not incompatible with wit and inventiveness. Indeed, in cases like Tarry's, defensiveness seems actually to cause originality, albeit originality of a special brand. Thus, the absence of constraint may not be the only source of novel or searching ideas: these may stem, as they evidently do in Tarry, from resentment well harnessed. Instead of removing himself to the centre of his defensive enclave, Tarry gives us the impression of skirmishing continually with the unruly forces outside – but sniping, as it were, never fighting hand to hand.

---

[1] In this sense his intellectual position is parasitic. It is interesting that despite the forceful impression that Tarry gives of himself on paper, he seems to pass unnoticed by his form-mates. As part of the testing routine, each boy is asked to list the five or so boys in his form who seem to him outstanding in a number of ways: widely read, mechanical interests, interest in the arts, interest in current affairs, interests out of doors, hard working. Almost everyone is mentioned once or twice by someone else, even if not more often. Tarry is one of the rarities: a boy mentioned by no one at all.
[2] A point which he, almost alone, perceived.

CONVERGENCE AND THE EXPRESSION OF VIOLENCE

I have already discussed my evidence about 'morbidity' in some detail, and pointed out that whatever reading we put on such data, some serious explanation is required. My aim now is to suggest one way of looking at this evidence, consonant with the picture of the converger that I have sketched so far.

Whether or not I am right in interpreting what goes on 'inside' the converger, one point seems established beyond much dispute. Namely, that there are processes of restriction or inhibition active in the converger, and that these prevent him from expressing (and probably experiencing) a wide range of the feelings to which the diverger is open. And it seems to me that this idea of a restrictive or inhibitory mechanism helps to explain the data on 'morbidity'.[1] I would suggest (scarcely a novel idea) that the process of inhibition creates tension; and that this tension is greatest when the repression of a particular impulse is only half complete. As an illustration, consider the temptation to swear when one stubs a toe. The publican, easy going in such respects, swears volubly, and thinks nothing of it. The priest, brought up to abjure foul language and incontinence of any kind, does not swear, and, again, thinks nothing of it. The man who does experience tension on such occasions is, let us say, the psychologist; the man who believes that swearing is wrong, but whose convictions on the matter are relatively weak. His impulse is to swear, but he tries not to. The tension on such occasions is sometimes extreme. In rather the same way, conflict occurs within political states not when any one force – the monarch, or the Army, or the middle class, or the proletariat – is all-powerful, but when two or more such forces acquire sufficient power to become mutually threatening.

Obviously, the causes of the tension that I envisage in the converger are not as simple as stubbing one's toe; and what they are I shall not for the moment hazard a guess. What I do wish to point out is the possibility that elaborate ideas arise as by-products of such

---

[1] 'Mechanism' is here used figuratively, and without physiological connotation. Inhibition is a concept which psychologists use with abandon; it occurs in many contexts, meaning something slightly different in each. In common between most usages, though, is the idea of two systems, or forces, within an organism, one producing action and the other dampening it down. The dampening, stultifying system is the inhibiting one.

tension. The boy who experiences both a powerful impulse, and the need to control it, may try to dissipate some of the resulting tension by exploring and elaborating trains of thought which others lack the energy to pursue. Just such a train of thought may be one involving extreme violence or cruelty. The converger who suggests taking a blanket off his sister's bed in midwinter whilst she is asleep has bothered to explore an idea which no other boy in the sample has touched upon. And it is of some interest that 'morbid' responses occur most frequently not at the extremes of the convergent/divergent spectrum, but amongst all-rounders and mild convergers. This suggests that in divergers the process of inhibition is too weak to create much tension, whilst in most extreme convergers, the inhibition is so successful that little tension remains.

This discovery of 'morbid' responses amongst all-rounders and convergers is an intriguing one; and not solely for the light it throws upon the internal processes of convergers and divergers. It also has implications for the theory of creative thought. Originality in most spheres would seem to depend, amongst other qualities, on persistence: on the pursuit of a given train of thought far beyond the limits that the ordinary citizen can countenance. And the evidence about 'morbidity' offers an interesting clue as to where the roots of such persistence may lie. Clearly it would be a simple-minded error to confuse the answers to paper-and-pencil tests with writing a novel, say, or conducting a scientific experiment. Nevertheless, it may be that all elaborate and persistent thought has analogous origins. If the tension is chronic, and its cause integral to an individual's personality, there is no reason why the resulting drive to think should not crystallize into a style of life. The habit of thinking, of pursuing ideas for their own sake, may be a by-product of the individual's need to keep the irrational elements of his personality under control.

THE DIVERGER

In many respects, the diverger is the converger's opposite. He flourishes on the open-ended tests which convergers dislike. He moves naturally towards the human aspects of his culture – literature, politics – and shuns the technical and practical. He is liberal in his attitudes; and seems less prone than the converger to accept beliefs on trust, or to think in conventional terms. And, above all, he seems

actively to enjoy the expression of his personal feelings; or, at least, to enjoy expressing his feelings about matters which are personal. Where the converger avoids personal discussion, the diverger positively seeks it out.

Up to now, we might be excused for seeing the diverger as fortunate, and the converger as less so. However, the diverger's position has its weaknesses. The chief of these lies in his reaction to precise, logical argument. He is weak at this, and in some cases, seems positively alarmed by it. Where the converger enjoys precision, the diverger views it as a trap. In caricature: the converger takes refuge from people in things; the diverger takes refuge from things in people.

This is, though, an over-simplification of the diverger's position. A crucial quality of the diverger is the way in which he *manifests* his emotions. He is willing, even eager, to reveal what others prefer to keep hidden. It may be that his show of emotions is the spontaneous upsurge of what he has inside him. But I feel fairly sure that it is often a form of display. Wilson is an extreme diverger of confetti-like fluency:

I like smart clothes. I like to be fashionably dressed. I buy my clothes at Simpsons, Austin Reed, and Aquascutum. I like London because it is expensive. I like tapered trousers, striped shirts, bootees. I like dates, girls, smoochy night-clubs. I like the 'Establishment'. I like *Beyond the Fringe*. School bores me. I prefer blondes. I love dancing. The Twist is way out, man. I like good food. I like chicken curry and pilau, I like paiella and octupus. I love caviar, and vol-au-vent. I love crepe-suzette. I love truffle and patte de foie. I love travelling. I have been to India, Africa, France, Egypt, Switzerland, Italy, Spain, Germany, America, Morocco. . . . I like fast cars. I like Jaguars, E-types, Aston-Martins, and Lagondas. I like friends, lots of them. I like people. I like parties. I like jazz, modern and trad. I like King Oliver, Bechet, Shelly Manne, Benny Goodman, Ory, Satch, Krupa, Barber, Nichols, Morton, Ottilie, Ray Charles, Connie, Dutch Swing College. My favourite horn is the clarinet and trumpet. I like New Orleans, and Mississippi style real hot. I love sketching. I prefer drawing portraits, preferably girls. I dislike Modern Art. I am at heart liberal. I like films. I love B.B. She sends me. I shall marry when I am 26. I hope to have a girl and a boy. I adore girls.

Yours A. L. S. Wilson.

This effusion is slightly disconcerting. Initially, one suspects bravado; but surveying the rest of the evidence about Wilson, one feels less sure. His opinions reflect less bravado than a sincere, if slightly hollow, vehemence:

Absolute rubbish! Typical of the Englishman with his narrow minded prejudices.
. . . Rubbish! It is everyone's moral duty to strive for Right, whether in England or
the North Pole. . . .

The fluency of his work suggests a mind rushing from one association to the next, without pause for analysis or reflection. Some of his
opinions are expressed so hurriedly as to be confused:

Blood sports are ridiculous. If England is all for equality whatever colour or caste,
to carry this *ad absurdum* a fox with their red coats should be allowed the rights of
the individual to a certain extent obviously, being an animal.

He is prone to comment by association rather than to bother with
logic ('Reminds me of Managing Directors at the Mayfair Hotel,
whisky and soda in hand' . . . 'Reminds me of a 12-year-old trying
to impress a grown-up audience'); and to say 'it is so obvious that
no explanation is necessary', or 'if I were to attempt to answer this
question in full, I would have to write a book'.

In general, Wilson's thinking seems to have about it certain manic
qualities: rapidity, a hectic emphasis, and a preoccupation with
conspicuous consumption – the *labels* of hedonism, as it were. (He
writes, 'I like Jaguars, E-types . . .', using two evocative names almost
as if he had failed to realize that they referred to the same object.)
Also, he is exceedingly inaccurate on the non-verbal parts of the
intelligence test, on which he does poorly, although accurate on the
verbal parts, which he does well. My impression is that he may be
using his outspokenness as a mask, or, perhaps, as a source of reassurance. One's sense of discontinuity is heightened by the incongruity of Wilson's open-ended responses and his personality in
the classroom. There, he seems the opposite of manic: suave and
self-contained, a young adult in a roomful of children. And, somewhat astonishingly, he is not a historian or modern linguist, but an
exceedingly hardworking classicist, gifted enough to win an open
award at Oxford. It seems, in other words, that the open-ended
tests have tapped a *persona* which is normally kept under close constraint.

Wilson illustrates a general point about divergers: that emotional
pyrotechnics may be complex in origin. Emotions may be displayed
as a mask, hiding the individual's true feelings; as a source of self-
reassurance; as a way of gaining social approval; or for a number of

other reasons.[1] There is no guarantee that because an emotion is expressed, it reflects unambiguously what is felt. The diverger sometimes has the air of a boy whose real feelings are buried, or lost, and who reassures himself of his capacity for pleasure by a reiteration of its external signs. He may express an emotion, yet drain it, as an actor does, of its proper experiental content. The diverger feels more freely than the converger, but not necessarily more fully.

If we grant that the functions of emotional expression in the diverger, his 'openness', may be defensive, we can next consider how these defences are arranged. Emotionally, divergers seem to differ from convergers in two respects. Where the converger compartmentalizes his intellectual life from his personal one, the diverger attempts a synthesis. And where the converger creates an enclave, blocking out all disruptive personal feelings, the diverger tries to contain it, to colonize the whole jungle. The merits of the diverger's approach are considerable. His emotional life may be more abundant than the converger's, and may also seem to him of greater significance. And, granted that he places relatively little reliance on arbitrary conceptual barriers, his thinking about personal matters is likely to be the more efficient. Certain weaknesses of the diverger's position we already know: he is weak at close, impersonal or technical argument, perhaps because he cannot dissociate his personal life from his intellectual one. And we suspect, too, that the diverger may achieve his emotional freedom at the price of a certain hollowness. He can always go through the moves of discussing and analysing personal relations, and of expressing his private feelings; but his experience of the emotions in question may become shallow and intellectualized. Further difficulties for the diverger may arise, too, from his very neglect of convention: relatively unprotected by social conventions, his emotional life may become chaotic.

DISCUSSION

The nature of the forces at work 'inside' convergers and divergers is unlikely to be either simple or readily intelligible; and suggestions about it are bound to be a matter of guesswork. Throughout, I have

---

[1] Scott Fitzgerald once remarked:

The strongest guard is placed at the gateway to nothing. . . . Maybe because the condition of emptiness is too shameful to be divulged. (1955), p. 138.

taken up the language of 'defences', and implied that wherever an intellectual or emotional 'split' or discontinuity exists, it serves to keep the individual's anxiety at bay. And behind this language of 'defences' and 'splits' there lurks a further assumption: that the processes I am discussing are vitally important and enduring features of the individual's internal landscape. It might be argued – on the contrary – that the differences between convergers and divergers, the whole network of connections described in Chapter 4, are relatively superficial side-effects of, let us say, differences in teaching, and that they have little dynamic significance. What evidence have I that the language of defences is justified?

As matters stand at present, this objection cannot be refuted. It may be that patterns of convergence and divergence are of relatively short standing in adolescents; and, a different point, that they can be shown to follow from the diverse educations that such boys receive. Arts education may cause boys to become divergers; and science may cause boys to become convergers. Personally, I should be surprised if something of this kind did not occur.[1] It seems perfectly reasonable to envisage school-teaching as a process of personal as well as intellectual inculcation. The young scientist, coming into contact with science specialists for the first time, may well find support for prejudices and presuppositions which until then had merely lurked at the back of his mind. The men who teach him science will encourage him to ignore the warm sprawl of emotion in which arts men wallow, and to reason with complete impersonality. Conversely, those who teach the budding arts specialist may reassure him (as he had long suspected) that scientists are narrow and philistine, and that all the paraphernalia of mathematics and logic is unnecessary to the conduct of a civilized life. Both arts and science teaching look like systems of cultural indoctrination and it would be odd if they had no effect.

However, I am not willing to accept that the minds of the clever 14- or 15-year-olds are *tablae rasae*, open to whatever habits the

---

[1] I have evidence that convergent and divergent patterns are already marked amongst 13-year-olds who have just arrived at public school. On the other hand, the overlap between the two types of ability seems greater at this age than it is at 15–17. Intelligence and open-ended scores correlate rather better with each other amongst 13-year-olds than they do two years later. This suggests that convergent and divergent patterns differentiate themselves increasingly throughout adolescence.

teacher may choose to instil. There is evidence (I shall discuss it in Chapters 7 and 8) that marked bents towards science, for example, exist long before the specialist teacher gets to work. These are found within the first four or five years of life, and are frequently pronounced by the age of 9 or 10. So, the Sixth Form teacher plays upon the convergent or divergent *predispositions* of his pupils – predispositions which reach back into childhood, and, perhaps, have their roots not in school at all, but in the home. Nor am I willing to believe that 15-year-olds are highly malleable. It seems most unlikely that convergers could easily be turned into divergers; and vice versa. On the other hand, it would be of the utmost interest to discover to what extent these configurations could be changed, and under what conditions.[1] Under what conditions could extreme convergers like Tarry be induced to produce forty suggestions for a blanket rather than just one? Could he do so with half an hour's practice, or half a term's? Would he do so for a financial reward: 10s. say, or £100? Would he do so when slightly intoxicated? Or only with an experimenter he thoroughly trusted? Similarly, with divergers. One would like to discover whether they can evaluate ideas that they produce. Also one wonders under what conditions they could be brought to enjoy convergent skills: mathematics, chess, or logical puzzles? The project is an alluring one, and not solely for the light it would throw upon psychological theory. It opens a prospect of educational research designed specifically to overcome children's resistance to particular kinds of thinking. The results might eventually place teaching upon solid technical foundations, and, at the same time, create a psychology of intellectual types which was both empirical and relevant.[2]

THE QUESTION OF 'DYNAMICS'

Finally, what of the question of 'defences'? What evidence is there that the characteristic patterns of the converger and diverger are any

---

[1] Crutchfield's (1962) experimental studies of conformity would seem to be relevant here; and also perhaps the work of Parnes and Meadow (1963).

[2] One's guess is that such research could make good use of programmed instruction; but that it might also demand techniques more akin to group psychotherapy. (See Abercrombie (1959), for pioneering venture in this direction.) Once established, such research should presumably be able to create a two-way traffic with psychotherapy proper – drawing inspiration from the psychoanalytic sphere, but also providing invaluable knowledge about how to change the behaviour of normal individuals.

more than configurations, the products of habit and convenience? How do we know that issues of internal security are at stake; that the conceptual architecture of these boys is military and not civil? Insight into this question is bound to come from attempts to change convergers' and divergers' habits of thought experimentally. For the time being, the data are relatively thin. Although the general tendency of the evidence about convergers and divergers suggests that defensive mechanisms are at work, and although this suggestion has behind it the whole weight of psychoanalytic thought, there is relatively little evidence in these chapters which could not be interpreted without the use of such psychodynamic ideas. The most convincing single piece of evidence seems to me that concerning 'morbidity'. I cannot see how one would make sense of this material without invoking some notion of inhibition, repression, or control. For the rest, we are concerned with individuals like Tarry and Wilson; and some would reject this as anecdotal. For those who, like myself, find illumination in individual cases, two further deserve mention. Both concern students at the very limit of convergence, the extreme of the extreme.

The first is very slight indeed – no more than a detail. It concerns Canham: a boy we have already met in Chapter 2. His score on the intelligence test was the highest in the sample; and his score on Part 2 of the test one of the highest ever achieved.[1] His score on *Uses of Objects* was one of the lowest: only eight suggestions in all. Yet one of these suggestions was a violent one – a blanket: 'for suffocating people'. His interests are heavily technical, and it is interesting to see that his remarkable diagrammatic ability reflects itself in the way he tackles mathematical problems. Wherever possible, he solves these not numerically or algebraically, but in terms of diagrams, patterns and spatial models. On paper, then, he gives the impression of massive defensive restriction, with the occasional violent, libidinous impulse leaking through. And in class, apparently, he is prone to behaviour which fits this model precisely. Normally quiet and withdrawn, he will occasionally, and without the least provocation, make a remark, in a loud voice, of hair-raising sexual indelicacy. This has no obvious explanation, and seems unrelated to any other aspect of his life at school.

[1] He attempted thirty-four out of thirty-six questions, getting them all right.

The second anecdote is only a little more substantial. Miss Wilkinson was one of a sample of medical students tested at the very beginning of their training. She was an extreme converger, scoring an A on the intelligence test and E on both of the open-ended ones. Subsequently, she became one of the best pupils of her year: diligent, cooperative, quick-witted and cheerful. But at the beginning of her second year, she suddenly announced that she was abandoning medicine for matrimony. During the summer vacation, she had gone abroad, met a man many years her senior, and, falling profoundly in love, determined to marry without delay. Her impulse to marry seems to have been overriding; and out of character with the rest of her behaviour. Although she returned to college for a short while, and her tutors advised her strongly to stay on, she soon left and married. In one sense, this story is heartening: a triumph of romance over the depressing virtues of caution and conformity. In another, it offers a good illustration of what happens when a converger's defences are breached. I would argue that, as the extremity of her convergence suggests, her repression of the irrational elements in her character was unusually fierce. The greater the threat, the more rigid the defence. And, the more rigid the defence, the greater the freedom enjoyed within it. Until, that is, something unusual causes an irrational need to erupt. Once this happens all equanimity is lost.[1]

Miss Wilkinson's romance suggests that the convergent defence involves a tightly interlocked system of weaknesses and strengths, risks and advantages. The intellectual freedom that exists within a defence seems to increase as the rigidity of the defence increases. But, presumably, defences are not rigid for rigidity's sake; they are rigid precisely because the irrational impulses which they stem back are unusually potent. The greater the intellectual freedom, therefore, the greater the risk of sudden and overwhelming disruption. Conversely, the greater the permeability of someone's defences, the less their freedom to ratiocinate, but the less, too, their risk of complete collapse. The looser the defensive network, and the wider the emotional range encompassed within it, the less the danger of any one disruption proving disastrous. On this argument, we would expect divergers to experience difficulty not just in logical argument,

---

[1] Miss Wilkinson's family background – she grew up apart from her father – might well have produced in her a strong need for paternal security.

but also in the day to day business of organizing and concentrating upon their work. The converger, on the other hand, would be more likely to present a picture of effortless concentration – overthrown completely, in one or two cases, by emotional crises. And the converger would also be particularly prone, or so we would predict, to breakdown at University if he felt that his intellectual system was inadequate; if, for whatever reason, he found that his grip over what he had to learn was slipping.[1]

The weakness with all such interpretative efforts as this is the rapidity with which they stray out of their factual depth. Frequently, the relevant data are not available; and, in many instances, we should not know how to recognize them even if they were. The difficulties, in other words, are not just factual, but conceptual, too. We do not know how to talk about personal experience except in terms of naïve metaphor. In such a confusion, there is a grave temptation to argue from the extreme case to the normal one – indulged, in this chapter, to the hilt. The design of the research as a whole is one which neglects the all-rounder, the boy in the middle. One tends to see him as the conflux of two quite different systems of personal organization. He may well be (in Chapter 7, I shall argue that in some cases he is), but we do not know. The trouble with the all-rounder, as with the average man, is that he offers us few toe-holds, few loose ends at which to prize. Inevitably, we are drawn to boys at extremes, and to use them as sources of insight into the forces at play in the sample as a whole. This is regrettable; but beggars cannot be methodological prigs.

What remains unclear is why, by the age of 14 or 15, convergers and divergers should be as different as they are. Why does one boy choose one defensive strategy and his neighbour the other? The idea of other people acting as a source both of anxiety and of comfort is

---

[1] There is evidence to suggest that this is a frequent cause of breakdown amongst undergraduates at Cambridge; but no evidence, as yet, that students who do break down in this way are convergers. It would be of interest to know whether, when they break down, convergers and divergers suffer different neurotic symptoms. It is arguable, for example, that convergers would suffer from anxiety, and divergers from hysteria. It would be interesting to know, too, whether convergers and divergers differed in the nature of their dreams. One might predict that convergers are more likely to forget their dreams rapidly and completely. There seems a strong case, therefore, for relating future research on convergers and divergers to that of clinical psychologists who deal with adolescents therapeutically.

not hard to grasp; but what, for example, is the precise emotional significance of the 'one right answer'? In Chapter 7 I shall offer what I hope are informed guesses, not as explanations but as signposts towards areas which might profitably be explored. Meanwhile, in Chapter 6, I wish to discuss certain more practical issues; in particular, the relation of my results to 'creativity'.

· 6 ·

The Question of Creativity

I wish now to discuss a topic tangential to that of convergence and divergence: originality, or as psychologists have it, 'creativity'. Whatever the logical connection between convergence or divergence and originality, psychologists are prone to view the topics as one and the same. Many psychologists, particularly American ones, see the diverger as potentially creative, and the converger as potentially uncreative. My own view, and my thesis in this chapter, is that the two topics must be carefully distinguished, otherwise we cannot begin to see how subtle the interconnections really are. I shall offer a commentary on the recent American research on 'creativity' and, in doing so, try to distinguish between certain beliefs about creativeness and the evidence from which these are supposed to spring.

'Creative', it must first be established, is an adjective with widespread connotations:

'Tell me, how did you happen to get into inspirational writing?' He pondered for a moment before replying. 'Well, it was sort of a call,' he said reflectively. 'I had my own business up in Hollywood, a few doors from Grauman's Egyptian, on the Boulevard. We eternalized baby shoes – you know, dipped them in bronze for ashtrays and souvenirs. The work was creative, but somehow I felt I wasn't realizing my potentialities.'[1]

In some circles 'creative' does duty as a word of general approbation – meaning, approximately, 'good'. It is rather the same with its derivative noun, 'creativity'. This odd word is now part of psychological jargon, and covers everything from the answers to a particular kind of psychological test, to forming a good relationship with one's wife. 'Creativity', in other words, applies to all those

[1] Perelman (1959), p. 472.

qualities of which psychologists approve. And like so many other virtues – justice, for example – it is as difficult to disapprove of as to say what it means.

As a topic for research, 'creativity' is a bandwagon; one which all of us sufficiently hale and healthy have leapt athletically aboard. It represents a boom in the American psychological industry only paralleled by that of programmed learning. Thus a topic, interesting in its own right, becomes fascinating, too, as an example of scientific fashion at work. One of the odd features of such vogues is that the ideas on which they are based are often old ones. That for programmed learning began some twenty-five years after Pressey invented the teaching machine; and the 'creativity' movement's heritage is longer still. Real creativity, excellence in the arts and sciences, has been a centre of psychologists' curiosity since their subject began. The present burgeoning is not a new phenomenon, but a return to a subject which has titillated the psychological fancy for a hundred years or more. Yet, apart from the vast increase in the scale of such research, and the generalization of 'creativity' to cover all aspects of human life, the work of the last fifteen years does also reveal a slight shift of focus: away from the romantic, humanistic figure of the artist-genius, towards the successful physical scientist. The causes of this shift are not fully understood. But two factors, at least, one can distinguish: a diffuse cultural ground-swell, elevating the scientist from the status of technician to that of culture hero; and a more specific concern on the part of the American nation with the state of their armaments industry. The first, though real enough, we can only guess about. The second factor can be traced to some extent to Sputnik.[1] This alerted American opinion, official and otherwise, to the emergence of Russia as a major technological force; and stimulated a search for more first-rate, home-grown physical scientists. The result has been the investment of previously unheard of sums of money in the quest for scientific talent.

Here, though, one meets an intriguing paradox. On the face of it, one would expect this preoccupation with physical science, and more specifically with scientific productivity, to tell against the 'tender-minded' progressive traditions within psychology, and to tell in favour of the 'tough-minded' scientific behaviourists and mental

---

[1] Roe's work, however, and much of Guilford's, was published before Sputnik, not after.

testers. In fact, though, the overriding character of the 'creativity' literature is one of enlightened, progressive humanism: we read not of ruthless conditioning for sophomores, but of sympathetically oriented teachers nurturing the creative impulse. This deserves a better explanation than I can offer. My guess would be that the post-Sputnik scare put the prevalent 'hard' scientific disciplines within psychology to a test which they failed. Mental testers were expected, and perhaps expected themselves, to apply scientific method to the problem of the original scientist and to produce a practical solution. (Psychologists understand their fellow men and scientific psychologists understand them scientifically). But in this case the trick did not work. In terms of their test scores, good scientists turned out to be virtually indistinguishable from mediocre ones.[1]

One wonders how the mental testers could have deceived themselves about the potentialities of their tests. Or were they so deceived? My belief is that during the 1930's and 1940's mental testers did in fact slip gradually away from the difficulties of prediction and explanation, into a state of false academic calm; and that this lapse was partially induced by the factor analytic theories which had been in vogue for the previous twenty years.[2] But, whatever the true account of all this, the 'creativity' movement has served in practice as a platform for the 'progressives'; and it represents the end of the isolation of the mental testing discipline from the rest of psychology. It has encouraged, too, a spirit of speculation, and of co-operation between one discipline and another. Mental testers and psychoanalysts publish cheek by jowl, and so, too, do sociologists, anthropologists, demographers, administrators, teachers, historians of science, cyberneticists, and many more besides. That a state of scholastic divorce from reality should be superseded by one of hectic freedom is surely to be applauded. At least the dangers of the situation are apparent. Under the old régime, critics could rarely master the necessary (or unnecessary) technical paraphernalia with which the concept of intelligence was surrounded; and, hence, tended to keep their doubts to themselves. Nowadays, it is clear to most, with or without technical knowledge, not only that the 'creativity' boom is, itself, a manifestation of fashion, but that the assertions of the psycho-

---

[1] Roe (1953); MacKinnon (1962a, 1962b). Also Harmon (1958, 1959).
[2] These have already been discussed in Chapter 1.

logists concerned are frequently expressions of a particular psychological tradition rather than of dispassionate fact.[1]

SIX MAXIMS

What is left after a fashion has swept through a particular area of psychology is usually a handful of important new facts, and what might be described as 'research maxims'. These are influential, imprecise and often misleading views about the general drift of events in a field of research. In the sphere of 'creativity', I detect six:

(1) That the conventional intelligence test is outdated.

(2) That in place of the conventional intelligence test, we now have tests of 'creativity'.

(3) That despite the existence of 'creativity' tests, the factors which determine an individual's creativeness are personal not intellectual.

(4) That originality in all spheres is associated with the same personal type – the diverger.

(5) That convergence is a form of neurotic defence, while divergence is not. Divergence leads to all the good things in life, personal, as well as professional; convergence achieves the second at the expense of the first.

(6) That conventional education is antipathetic to the diverger. Hence it jeopardizes the nation's supply of creative talent. Hence education should become more progressive.

Few psychologists would stand by any one of these maxims without qualification. Nevertheless, they have currency in popular thinking on the subject, and in the minds of psychologists when they are off their guard.[2]

(1) THE DOWNFALL OF THE INTELLIGENCE TEST. That the conventional intelligence test has failed to predict who will do

[1] An interesting discussion of the various psychological approaches to creativeness is given by Miller (1964). He distinguishes five: (i) The tradition, strong in mental testing ten years ago, that creative thinking is logical thinking. (ii) Associationism. (iii) Gestalt psychology. (iv) The psychodynamic approach, emphasizing the role of the unconscious. (v) The cybernetic. It is the fourth of these, I suggest, which is the dominant one, and the one which gives the 'creativity' literature its progressive tone. A remarkable (if somewhat alarming) instance of the cybernetic approach is Simon's work on the use of computers to solve mathematical and scientific problems. Simon (1962).

[2] Lest I be thought to attack straw men, the reader is recommended to read any handful of the dozens of books and hundreds of articles published during the last ten years with the word 'creativity' in their titles. A number are listed amongst the references at the back of this book.

H

outstanding work in science (or any other field) there is little question. MacKinnon's work is the most telling in this respect. He finds little or no connection between adult IQ and adult achievement above a minimum level, which lies somewhere in the region of IQ 120. That is to say, nearly all of his eminent men and women produced scores above this level; but amongst them, the relation between IQ and originality was virtually nil. A mature scientist with an adult IQ of 130 is as likely to win a Nobel Prize as is one whose IQ is 180. MacKinnon comments:

> Over the whole range of intelligence and creativity there is, of course, a positive relationship between the two variables. No feeble-minded subjects have shown up in any of our creative groups. It is clear, however, that above a certain required minimum level of intelligence which varies from field to field and in some instances may be surprisingly low, being more intelligent does not guarantee a corresponding increase in creativeness. It just is not true that the more intelligent person is necessarily the more creative one.[1]

A similar point was made ten years earlier by Roe:

> Indeed there are a number of subjects for whom none of the test material would give the slightest clue that the subject was a scientist of renown.[2]

Admittedly, all such evidence about famous adults suffers a crucial weakness – the one already discussed in Chapter 2. Such men may have abilities which they do not choose to display. Or alternatively, they may only think efficiently when they care profoundly about what they are doing. Either way, it is quite likely that the greater a man's achievements, the less intellectually 'promiscuous' he will become. Evidence about adult abilities needs therefore to be viewed with circumspection. (If we ask a man to show us his braces, and he refuses, it does not follow that he supports his trousers with string.) On the other hand, we can by no means discount such evidence. And if anyone nurtured the belief that intellectual distinction was related closely to IQ, MacKinnon's evidence must disabuse him.

However, the intelligence test cannot be discarded. Tests of this kind perform perfectly well the function for which they were originally conceived: the rapid and impersonal assessment of intel-

---

[1] MacKinnon (1962b), p. 488.
[2] Roe (1953), p. 52. Roe here refers not just to intelligence tests but to a whole battery of testing techniques: the Rorschach and Thematic Apperception projective methods, Minnesota Multiphasic Personality Inventory, and Strong Vocation at Interests Blank and so on.

lectual ability in the population as a whole. As Getzels and Jackson remark, the IQ test is probably the best single measure we have.[1] American Army psychologists showed that tests performed their task surprisingly well during the First World War; they have continued to do so ever since. British research on the 11-Plus examination proves this. Over a wide spectrum of ability the intelligence test gives quite a good indication of a child's ability at school.[2] Difficulties arise only when the IQ is thought of as a precise measure of mental 'horsepower'. It is nothing of the sort; nor has factual evidence ever suggested otherwise. The chances of Smith (IQ 90) passing GCE 'O' Level are much lower than those of Jones (IQ 110). But it does not follow that all boys of IQ 110 will do better at 'O' Level than all boys of IQ 90. Nor does it follow that because professional people score well on IQ tests that the more successful professional people have higher IQ's than the less.

The relation of IQ to intellectual distinction seems, in fact, highly complex. As far as one can tell, the relation at low levels of IQ holds quite well. Higher up, however, it dwindles; and above a certain point, a high IQ is of little advantage. However, there are differences between one occupation and another, the relationship dwindling lower down the IQ scale in some subjects than in others. In the arts, for instance, it seems to peter out lower down than in science. For practical purposes, therefore, it might be fruitful to distinguish, for each occupation or subject, both the IQ levels above which a strength in IQ is not an advantage in real efficiency; and also lower limits, below which a weakness in IQ becomes incapacitating. Where one sets such limits depends, of course, on the criteria one has in mind. For argument's sake, we might define success academically: a good second class degree at Oxford or Cambridge; or, in more worldly terms, a successful novel or a good piece of scientific research. Granting these standards, I would guess that the lower limit in science lies in the region of IQ 115; and that a high IQ is of little advantage above IQ 125. The lower limit for the arts escapes me,

[1] Getzels and Jackson (1962), p. 3.

[2] Just how valid the 11-Plus is, it is not easy to tell. Vernon (1957) argues that the error involved is 5 per cent either way: or, to express the same statistic in different terms, that a quarter of the grammar school places each year are awarded in error. However, this estimate is certainly too favourable. It is based on correlations between the 11-Plus and GCE 'O' Level results, themselves a poor index of true intellectual ability.

because the 11-Plus ensures that few boys with IQ's below 110 enter my sample in the first place. It probably lies somewhere in the area of IQ 95-100; and the upper point in the region of IQ 115.

Why should this relationship between IQ and real accomplishment peter out? Obviously, no one knows. But there are two simple explanations. First, (as the third research maxim asserts), that above a certain level of IQ, motivation is of overriding importance. Second, that the intellectual skills measured by IQ tests are too simple – and that if they were based on more complex skills, their predictive effectiveness would increase. As illustration of this second point, take the analogy of spelling. A man who cannot spell at all cannot write a novel. But once his ability to spell reaches a certain level, the restrictions which his inability imposes upon him largely disappear. Some of the most eloquent and literary of novelists, Scott Fitzgerald for example, spelt atrociously. In the same way, Einstein was comparatively only a mediocre mathematician, and Darwin was virtually innumerate. It may be that this argument applies to intelligence tests as well. However, this proposition, as I shall try to show later in this chapter, is not as simple as it seems.

Returning once more to the first research maxim, it seems that the downfall has affected not the IQ tests, but certain naïve and mystic notions about them: the belief that, armed with such tests, the psychologist could probe the innermost recesses of our minds, and predict our future accomplishments unerringly. In fact, they are a useful technique for measuring a particular kind of reasoning, and tell us, cheaply and quite accurately, which members of the normal population are, broadly speaking, clever, and which not. Responsible mental testers may protest that they, as responsible testers, have never suggested otherwise. But this would be disingenuous. Thousands of psychologists have been suggesting otherwise for several decades; and, moreover, have neglected to collect the evidence that would prove their suggestion (and the implicit power which it bestows on the tester) false. It has taken us fifty years to discover (or, at least, to publicize) what could have been ascertained overnight: that there are highly intelligent men and women who are not particularly good at intelligence tests; and men and women who are outstandingly good at intelligence tests who are not outstandingly

good at anything else. We can scarcely now complain if our enemies take this failure as evidence of our lack, either of candour, or of native wit.

(2) 'CREATIVITY' TESTS. Open-ended tests are known throughout the United States as 'creativity' tests. Yet, as far as I can discover, there is scarcely a shred of factual support for this. The nearest we come to direct evidence is in the work of MacKinnon.[1] He found that creative scientists, architects and novelists were prone to give unusual responses to a word association test; indeed, that unusualness of mental association was one of the best indices of an individual's originality in his professional work. However, the correlation is not high ($r = 0.50$ amongst architects), and applies particularly to associations which are unusual as opposed to rare. The highly creative members of MacKinnon's samples produced, it seems, not bizarre or remote associations, but relatively ordinary ones in large numbers.[2] He also found differences between creative and non-creative on the Barron-Walsh Art test. On this, the creative were much more likely to prefer visual patterns which are complex and asymmetrical.[3]

The issue of whether 'creativity' tests measure creativeness has been further confused by certain commentators. Getzels and Jackson have been taken to task for suggesting that the kind of ability measured by their open-ended tests is not closely linked with IQ. In this they follow Guilford, the factor analyst, who claims to have isolated a very large number of intellectual factors, convergent and divergent reasoning being only two among them.[4] This assertion has caused a rapid closing of British ranks, and some American ones, too. Ostensibly, the point at issue is whether or not Getzels and Jackson's work refutes the general factor theory of intelligence. Burt, particularly, has argued that it does not.[5] He is doubtless correct; but seems, in his eagerness to defend the general factor theory, to have

---

[1] MacKinnon (1962a, 1962b). His research is described in more detail below.
[2] MacKinnon (1962b), p. 490. MacKinnon defines an unusual association as one produced by less than 10 per cent and more than 1 per cent of the normal population: a rare association as one produced by 1 per cent or less.
[3] MacKinnon, op. cit., p. 488. Barron (1958).
[4] Guildford (1956).
[5] Burt (1962); also Vernon (1964).

missed a vital point. Whether or not they express it with sufficient clarity, the import of Getzels and Jackson's evidence is not that the general factor theory of intelligence is mistaken, but that for many practical purposes, it is irrelevant. The crucial fact, it emerges from Getzels and Jackson's work and my own, is that a knowledge of a boy's IQ is of little help *if you are faced with a formful of clever boys.* The boy with the lowest IQ in the form is almost as likely to get the top marks as the boy with the highest. It is this simple, but disruptive, implication that English critics of Getzels and Jackson have overlooked. They land, claws extended, on a technical red herring.[1]

(3) PERSONAL FACTORS NOT INTELLECTUAL ONES ARE CRUCIAL. This, of all six maxims, is the one with the best factual foundation. Long ago, in the context of Terman's Genetic Studies of Genius, Cox remarked:

> ... high but not the highest intelligence, combined with the greatest degree of persistence, will achieve greater eminence than the highest degree of intelligence with somewhat less persistence.[2]

Roe concurs; and so, too, does MacKinnon:

> Our data suggest, rather, that if a person has the minimum of intelligence required for mastery of a field of knowledge, whether he performs creatively or banally in that field will be crucially determined by nonintellective factors.[3]

If they are right, the policy of devising new and better tests of high grade intelligence is a mistaken one. What we need, instead, are better tests of personality. Although this is a sensible deduction from the evidence, it is not logically binding. It does not follow, because we have not found a test of reasoning which predicts research

---

[1] Where this leaves us regarding factorial theories of mental ability, I am not sure. If one wishes to predict or explain the behaviour of any individual or group of individuals, what one needs are good primary data: pertinent tests, and detailed evidence about the choices the individuals actually face. If a boy wishes to study either mathematics or biology, one needs norms showing his chances of success in either field. Where the general (or any other) factor theory of intelligence comes in to such a process of detailed prediction I cannot quite see. Factorial theories of the intellect may be a useful stimulus to the construction of new tests, as they clearly have been in Guildford's case; but my impression is that for explanatory or predictive purposes they are unhelpful. In all probability, though, the minimum IQ score for comprehension of the general factor theory's significance is very high, and I do not meet it.

[2] Cox (1926), p. 187.

[3] MacKinnon (1962b), p. 493.

ability, that such a test could not be devised. There may still be a case for better tests of reasoning: as they now stand mental tests are, after all, primitive affairs, and the skills they test are exceedingly simple. When we ask a scientist to complete a verbal analogy for us, or a numerical series, we are asking him to perform a skill insultingly trivial compared with those he uses in his research: when he grasps a theory; reviews the facts for which it is supposed to account; decides whether or not it does so; derives predictions from it; devises experiments to test those predictions; and speculates about alternative theories of his own and other people's. In all these manoeuvres he exercises skills of a complexity greater than we can readily comprehend.

And these intellectual operations are beyond us not simply because they are too complex. They depend, firstly, on huge accumulations of experience; and, secondly, upon the fact that the individual concerned cares intensely about what he is doing. Without training and experience, these complex skills do not exist. As I have remarked in Chapter 2, mature reasoning does not occur in a vacuum, but at the end of a lengthy and subtle development. Before he enters his training, the scientist (or, of course, any other brainworker) has potentialities rather than accomplishments. What matter, at this stage, are the factors which predispose him to pursue a given line of work, and enable him to benefit from it. Once he has become a mature scientist our ability to measure his intellectual skills with tests (rather than by reading his published works) becomes academic. The whole point of testing, in other words, lies in measuring those qualities which predispose a man to follow a particular bent. Some of these may be a matter of intellectual ability; but, in all probability, the majority do lie – as Cox, Roe, and MacKinnon suggest – within the sphere of personality.

(4) DIVERGERS ARE POTENTIALLY CREATIVE, CONVERGERS ARE NOT. Much writing on creativity rests on the assumption that creative people are open, flexible and unconventional, and that the uncreative are inflexible and authoritarian. On this argument, it is the divergers (and perhaps all-rounders) who break new ground, while the convergers plod along cautiously in the rear. My own evidence suggests that this assumption is mistaken. Moreover, the

two outstanding studies of originality amongst adults, those of Roe and MacKinnon, indicate that the relation between divergence and creativeness is bound to be complex.[1] Both studies were based on famous people who subjected themselves voluntarily to psychological examination. This encompassed details of personality, attitude, and biography, as well as intellectual ability. Roe restricted her sample to scientists (physical, biological and social); MacKinnon included architects and writers as well. Both command attention as studies of individuals who are distinguished beyond any reasonable doubt. 'Creative', in the context of these studies, for once carries its true connotation, their subjects being amongst the most able and intellectually productive in the world. I shall discuss their findings more fully in Chapters 7 and 8. For the time being, it is enough to note that the findings of these two remarkable pieces of research conflict, and the conflict is one which must be resolved. Roe reports that eminent research workers in physical science strongly resemble the converger; MacKinnon that creative men and women in all fields are more divergent than their non-creative colleagues. These two conclusions can only be reconciled by assuming that the openness and uninhibitedness to which MacKinnon refers exist within a relatively narrow range. On this argument, all scientists are inhibited, the creative ones less so, the non-creative more. One can only make sense of this evidence, in other words, by assuming an intellectual spectrum in which each occupation (littérateur, historian, psychologist, biologist, physicist, and so on) attracts individuals of a particular personal type. The convergers are naturally attracted towards one end of the spectrum and the divergers to the other. Each field has its own waveband of emotional openness; only within the range of openness which each waveband affords are certain degrees of openness or restriction more conducive to good work than others.

The platitudes which ache to be released from this complex literature are the ones about the original scientist being the scientist who possesses some of the divergent qualities of the artist; and the successful artist being the one who enjoys some of the rigour and dedicated single-mindedness of the scientist. This notion accords neatly with Kuhn's analysis of scientific invention – that it depends

[1] Roe (1951a, 1951b, 1951c, 1953). MacKinnon (1962a, 1962b).

upon a tension between the forces of tradition and revolution.[1] His analysis is one which, I am convinced, is applicable to most of the arts as well. It is compatible with both MacKinnon's findings and Roe's; and also with the evidence set out in Chapters 2, 3 and 4 of the present text.

(5) CONVERGERS ARE NEUROTIC, DIVERGERS NOT. Psycho-analysts frequently assume that we are psychologically healthy in so far as we have access to our own unconscious impulses. And the psychologists interested in 'creativity' also assume that because the diverger appears more emotionally open than the converger, he is automatically the healthier of the two. I have argued in Chapter 5 that the diverger's openness may be deceptive: that, in many cases, he merely defends himself against his feelings by a different (and perhaps less effective) means. There is no doubt, though, whatever the merits or demerits of the diverger's internal policies, that he does entertain emotions, whereas the converger frequently turns his back on them. This denial of the personal aspects of life seems – to many, at least – self-evidently neurotic. I am not at all sure that this is so. The conventional view has been expressed pithily by Freud. Asked what was the proper end of man, he is said to have replied: '*Lieben und arbeiten*', to love and to work.[2] This is a noble ideal, and one which expresses every psychoanalyst's ambition, both for his clients and for himself. On the other hand it is a goal which not many achieve. Freud's own life illustrates the difficulty well. It is widely acknowledged that Freud advanced our theoretical knowledge of sex to a greater extent than anyone else, before or since. He was also a devoted husband and parent. Yet, according to his biographer, he enjoyed only somewhat cursory sexual relations with his wife, and experienced no sexual interest in any other woman.[3] His life, in other words, is a refutation of his own ideals. One might argue that his choice of subject-matter and his zeal in pursuing it were both a product of his personal deficiency. Or, conversely, that his personal deficiency was the price that he paid for his intellectual trepidation.

[1] Kuhn (1962, 1963).

[2] Quoted by Erikson (1963), p. 264. Erikson emphasises that Freud here refers specifically to genital sexuality, not merely to a more diffuse uxoriousness.

[3] Jones (1961), p. 359.

Either way, though, the paradox exists: and such things, as Freud himself would have remarked, are not accidents.[1]

It is arguable that physical scientists do evade personal issues; and possibly, too, that the novelist's urge to write stems from a failure to accept everyday reality for what it is. Both could be seen as 'immature'. But the standards against which such comparisons are made are exceedingly exalted – and the psychologist's position in such bandying of value judgments is itself exposed. Of the physical scientist, the very worst that one can say is that he is a robot: he turns his back on a wide range of human experience more or less completely. Of the novelist, that he is an emotional prostitute, a man retailing the events of his own private life to please his public, or for money. The psychologist, on the other hand, does something considerably more odd: he tries to make sense of human behaviour by reifying it. People are described as though they were mechanisms; their experiences are reduced to numbers. He may even make a virtue of discussing human beings as though they were rats. The physical scientist denies his emotions; the novelist exploits them; the psychologist dismantles them. Whatever the moral, it is not that some occupational groups are more neurotic than others. Although convergers and divergers use different tactics in dealing with the pressures of work and emotional experience, one tactic is not necessarily better or worse than the other. Each has its characteristic strengths and weaknesses; and the neurotic is not the man who adopts a particular intellectual and personal style, but the one who, having adopted a style, suffers its weaknesses without enjoying its strengths.

Indeed, the present maxim may be an instance of psychological doctrine accumulating by a process of projection. As Roe points out:

... it is likely that the kind of person who has gone into social science may have had a biasing effect on the theories produced by social scientists, particularly with regard to the desirable or the mature personality. Practically all current psycho-

---

[1] To reject the *lieben und arbeiten* view as impracticable is not to embrace its opposite, the view that productive thought is necessarily a product of neurosis: 'Great wits are sure to madness near alli'd. And thin partitions do their bonds divide.' (John Dryden). This popular belief has been blamed on Seneca: 'nullum magnum ingenium sine mixtura dementiae fuit.' In fact, though, he seems to have referred to the Platonic notion of divine inspiration, not insanity; and has ever since been misinterpreted. The belief that 'everything great in the world comes from neurotics' has been described by Lionel Trilling as one of the characteristic notions of our culture; but such evidence as we possess suggests that it is untrue.

logical theory of development stresses strongly the central importance in any life of the richness of personal relations as a basis for 'adjustment'. But the data of this study demonstrate, and it seems to me quite conclusively, that a more than adequate personal and social adjustment in the larger sense of an adjustment which permits a socially extremely useful life and one which is personally deeply satisfying, is not only possible, but probably quite common, with little of the sort of personal relations which psychologists consider essential. Many of the biological and physical scientists are very little concerned with personal relations, and this is not only entirely satisfactory to them, but it cannot be shown always to be a compensatory mechanism (nor are compensatory mechanisms necessarily undesirable). It can also apparently be satisfactory to others who are closely associated with them. That divorces are so much commoner among the social scientists is of interest in this connection.[1]

I shall suggest in the next chapter that the crux of a psychologist's life lies in a conflict of a particular kind between the intellectual aspects of life and the emotional. If this is so, what more natural than that he should see the struggle to reconcile these elements as a proper activity, and project its successful solution as the goal for Everyman?

(6) CONVENTIONAL EDUCATION IS HOSTILE TO CREATIVITY. PROGRESSIVE EDUCATION IS NOT. It is arguable that current educational practice in England and America stunts children's creative impulses. This conclusion is backed, or seems to be backed, by a number of important facts. MacKinnon finds that his creative individuals were often undistinguished academically.[2] This is supported by my own evidence about the degree classes gained at Oxford and Cambridge by groups of distinguished Englishmen: Fellows of the Royal Society, Doctors of Science at Oxford and Cambridge, High Court Judges, Cabinet Ministers. In each of these groups, poor degree classes were quite frequent. At Cambridge, for example, there was no relation between a research student's degree class and his chances, later on, of becoming an F.R.S. or a D.Sc. Fully a third of the future F.R.S.'s at Cambridge had gained a second or worse at some time during their Univeristy careers; and the proportion amongst future D.Sc's was over a half. In their final degrees at Oxford or Cambridge, some 54 per cent of future High Court Judges gained seconds, thirds of fourths; and the equivalent figure for future

[1] Roe (1953), p. 50.
[2] MacKinnon (1962b).

Cabinet Ministers was 66 per cent.[1] MacKinnon also reports that the creative members of his sample were frequently disliked by their teachers; and that they were frequently unhappy. Getzels and Jackson report similar reactions of teachers to their 'High Creatives'.[2] Teachers dislike 'High Creatives', even when they are academically successful, and prefer teaching the more docile 'High IQ's'.

That conventional education is uncongenial to independent spirits seems to me incontestable; also, that much of what passes for education in this country and the United States is a waste of everyone's time, pupils and teachers alike. On the other hand, such conclusions are not entailed by the evidence that we now possess. The harsh fact remains that MacKinnon's eminent men are eminent; that men like Darwin and Einstein, who were unhappy or undistinguished at school, nevertheless produced the theories of evolution and relativity, respectively. This datum is open to at least three interpretations. The one drawn by some is that Einstein and Darwin survived through luck (or genius), but that thousands of others (of equal or nearly equal potentialities) are yearly oppressed and extinguished. MacKinnon's eminent are the lucky ones that got away. The second interpretation is that the unhappiness of these great men was a causal factor in making them great. Had they not suffered at school, they would have lead comfortable, mediocre lives like the rest of us. The third interpretation is that their unhappiness was concomitant but not causal: they were unhappy because they were remarkable, but their unhappiness did not affect their creative potentialities one way or the other.

What one makes of these alternatives is largely a matter of taste. My own suspicion is that progressive schools do make most children happier than authoritarian ones; but that they withdraw from children the cutting edge that insecurity, competition, and resentment supply. Here the progressive dream comes home to roost. If we adjust children to themselves and each other, we may remove from them the springs of their intellectual and artistic productivity. Happy children simply may not be prepared to make the effort which excellence demands. Whether or not my suspicions about progressive education are justified, it is clear that we cannot use the

[1] For a more detailed account, see Hudson (1958, 1960b, 1961).
[2] Getzels and Jackson (1962).

'creativity' literature as a stick with which to beat academic education of a more leisurely kind, whether on the lines of certain English public schools or those of the American high school. These may be inept, without 'driving out creativity'. Indeed, they may provide precisely the background of mild conformity and incompetence which reinforces the potentially original child's conviction of his own worth. They provide the ideal background against which to rebel. The conscious nurture of children's creative potentialities may still be a worthwhile operation, but not because it produces more and better brainworkers. It may be worthwhile because, quite simply it makes school a more enjoyable place to be. And this, in its turn, may lead children a little nearer the 'rich emotional life' which is every progressive psychologist's wistful dream.

SOME GREAT MEN

My chief anxiety in discussing this literature is that the reader may escape with some stereotyped ideas about the productive intellectual still intact. He may yet feel that even if certain points of detail elude us, the analysis of originality is well in hand. The gulf between our simple models and the complexity of intelligent people's behaviour is so wide that we are prone to fall for over-simplification as the only alternative to despair. On the evidence, despair is certainly the more appropriate of the two. Occupationally, however, psychologists are a complacent group, so a little more undermining will probably do less harm than good. In concluding this chapter, therefore, I shall describe four great men at work, giving emphasis to their diversity.

TURNER. First, consider Turner, the greatest English painter, and arguably the best at landscapes the world has ever seen. In his maturity, he pursued his eccentric preoccupations with complete self-absorption, revolutionizing the painting of light, and dissolving the distinction between form and content 'in the visionary evocation of the cosmic forms of nature'.[1] He left behind him an enormous body of work which, a hundred years after his death, we are only just beginning to comprehend. Yet Turner made his reputation by the most conventional means imaginable; first as a brilliant topo-

---

[1] Rothenstein and Butlin (1964), p. 74.

graphical draughtsman, and then as an imitator of acknowledged masters, Claude, Poussin, Cuyp, Van der Velde, Teniers, and others besides. At twenty, he was already a young man of repute; but, as his biographer observes:

... the qualities displayed in his work are intelligence, docility, alertness, indomitable industry, patience, and great dexterity of eye and hand; we look in vain for signs of originality, for the promise of a new way of thinking or feeling, for a new vision or a new form of expression. He seems to be trying to do only what had been done before. His triumphs are the triumphs of the commonplace virtues – intelligence and industry – working upon a foundation of natural talent, rather than of what is generally understood as genius.[1]

Turner's individualistic genius (and none was more individualistic) grew from great success achieved by the most prosaic means. Anyone who assumes, as we are all prone to, that we create qualities by nurturing them, or even by opposing them, can make no sense of Turner at all. Naïve people believe that you create conformity by discipline, and originality by being permissive. Equally naïve people, it seems, believe the reverse: that beauty is born of hard times, while intellectual and material advantage produces dullards. The truth, whatever it is, is not as simple as this.

RILKE. Next, the poet Rilke, and the Duino Elegies and Sonnets to Orpheus for which he is famous. Rilke began the Elegies (in his own view his greatest work) during the winter of 1911–12.

After the publication of the Neue Gedichte, in 1907 and 1908, and of Malte Laurids Brigge in 1910, Rilke, the perpetual beginner, felt that his real task still remained undone. . . . In October Rilke visited his friend, Princess Marie von Thurn und Taxis-Hohenlohe, at Schloss Duino, near Trieste, and, from her departure in the middle of December until her return in the following April, he remained in the castle alone. One day he received a troublesome business letter which required an immediate and careful answer; to settle his thoughts, he went out into the roaring wind and paced to and fro along the bastions, the sea raging two hundred feet below. Suddenly he stopped, for it seemed that from the midst of the storm a voice had called to him: Wer, wenn ich schriee, hörte mich denn aus der Engel Ordnungen? Who, if I cried, would hear me among the angelic orders? Taking out the note-book he always carried with him, he wrote down these words, together with a few verses which seemed to follow of their own accord. He knew that the god had spoken at last. Quietly returning to his room, he dispatched the troublesome letter; and by the evening of that day the First Elegy had been written.

[1] Finberg (1961), p. 26.

He sent a copy of it to Princess Marie on January 21st, and the Second was written shortly afterwards.[1]

Making allowance for Teutonic melodrama, it would seem that a poetic idea struck Rilke unawares, and that he rapidly set down the poem which it generated. This done, he lost momentum. The greater part of the Sixth and a few lines of the Ninth Elegies were written during a visit to Spain (1912–13); The Third, begun at Duino, was finished in Paris during 1913, and in 1914 a little progress was made with the Sixth and Tenth. At this point, Rilke was interrupted by the First World War.

Although he took no part in it, the war stultified him. One Elegy (the bitter Fourth) was written in Munich late in 1915, but it was not until the war was over that he could begin to pick up the trends of 1912. In August 1921, he set himself up in solitude at Chateau de Muzot, near Sierre. 'Utterance and release' did not come to him until February of the next year (1922). He then experienced a burst of creative energy which has scarcely a parallel in history. Between 2nd and 20th February, 1922, he not only finished his series of ten Elegies, but also wrote the fifty-five Sonnets to Orpheus. The sequence as well as the size of this extraordinary outburst of work is interesting. First, the dimensions of it. Three Elegies were written in their entirety (5th, 7th, 8th); two more (9th and 10th) were written on the basis of fragments which already existed; and one (6th) was finished. This, in itself, constitutes some 460 lines of finished verse. In addition he wrote fifty-five sonnets (an additional 770 lines) making 1,230 lines in all. This, not of doggerel, but of some of the pithiest, most concentrated poetry ever written. Rilke sat down intending to finish his series of Elegies. Yet when he began to write, he unleashed not the Elegies, but the first twenty-six sonnets – works which he had no intention of writing whatever. He then completed his projected Elegies and wrote a further twenty-nine sonnets, and last of all, 'in a radiant after-storm', added one further Elegy.

Rilke's writing during these weeks affords as good an example as any in the arts or sciences of inspiration which succeeds. Indeed, his behaviour is almost a caricature of the inspirational genius at work: the long years of inactivity; the sudden insight, in which the whole

[1] Leishman and Spender (1952), p. 9.

poetic fabric of his poems seems revealed in a phrase; the extraordinary sense that in writing he was taking some divine variety of
dictation; the astonishing speed and lack of doubt with which he
worked; the totally unexpected eruption of the Sonnets when he had
set out to complete the Elegies. In all these respects, Rilke seems to
us to have enjoyed an unusual and exalted experience.[1]

KEPLER. Sadly, though, inspiration is often abortive. In science
especially, a man may have an insight and the absolute conviction
that it is valid – the 'Eureka' experience – only to find that the idea is a
dud. And sometimes such false insights may carry a man accidentally
to a discovery which he (or perhaps posterity) recognises as true. The
astronomer Kepler provides a case in point. Koestler describes the
astonishing intellectual muddle which led Kepler over a span of
years, from just such a false insight to the discovery of his three
Laws.[2]

Kepler achieved his initial insight, apparently, whilst drawing a
figure on the blackboard for his class:

The idea was, that the universe is built around certain symmetrical figures –
triangle, square, pentagon, etc. – which form its invisible skeleton, as it were.
Before going into detail, it will be better to explain at once that the idea itself was
completely false; yet it nevertheless led eventually to Kepler's Laws, the demolition
of the antique universe on wheels, and the birth of modern cosmology. The
pseudo-discovery which started it all is expounded in Kepler's first book, the
Mysterium Cosmographicum, which he published at the age of 25.[3]

'It is amazing!' Kepler informs his readers, 'although I had as yet no clear idea of
the order in which the perfect solids had to be arranged, I nevertheless succeeded
... in arranging them so happily, that later on, when I checked the matter over, I
had nothing to alter. Now I no longer regretted the lost time; I no longer tired of
my work; I shied from no computation, however difficult. Day and night I
spent with calculations to see whether the proposition that I had formulated tallied
with the Copernican orbits or whether my joy would be carried away by the
winds. . . . Within a few days everything fell into its place. I saw one symmetrical
solid after the other fit in so precisely between the appropriate orbits, that if a

---

[1] The 'incubatory' aspects of original thought have been the subject of some outstanding
studies: Hadamard (1945), Poincaré (1952), Patrick (1935, 1937, 1938). For the classical
Gestalt literature on problem solving, see Wertheimer (1961), especially, and Duncker (1945).
[2] Koestler (1959). Even though Koestler may over-emphasize somewhat the profundity of
Kepler's confusion, Part 4 of 'The Sleepwalkers' is an intriguing record of how subtly a
scientist's intuition may take its effect.
[3] Koestler, op. cit., p. 247.

peasant were to ask you on what kind of hook the heavens are fastened so that they don't fall down, it will be easy for thee to answer him.'[1]

Kepler retained his faith in this idea of symmetrical solids throughout his life. It seems to have had for him, as Koestler remarks, all the qualities of an *idée fixe*, even though it was false, and he himself had found it so:

The direction of my whole life, of my studies and works, has been determined by this one little book ... For nearly all books on astronomy which I have published since then were related to one or the other of the main chapters ... and are more thorough expositions or completions of it.[2]

By the time that he had completed the Notes to the second edition of the *Mysterium Cosmographicum* (from which Koestler's quotations are drawn), Kepler had demolished practically every point made in the original edition. Yet its subjective value to him remained. And, indeed, it seems to have contained within its errors the germs of his later discoveries; by-products, as it were, of his initial and mistaken inspiration. His faith in the idea of symmetrical solids may also help to explain both the way in which Kepler stumbled in his search for his Laws and his small regard for them, once they were discovered. His aim was to define the orbit of Mars, and he first reached a mathematical formula for this empirically, by gigantic labour, and on the strength of a series of errors which conveniently cancelled each other out. But, having achieved this formula, he still did not realize that it specified an ellipse. So he then abandoned it in pursuit of a rival explanation: a geometrical ellipse! Only after much more labour, and many more mistakes, did he realize that both methods, empirical and geometrical, produced the same answer:

Why should I mince my words? The truth of Nature, which I had rejected and chased away, returned by stealth through the backdoor, disguising itself to be accepted. That is to say, I laid [the original equation] aside, and fell back on ellipses, believing that this was a quite different hypothesis, whereas the two, as I shall prove in the next chapter, are one and the same ... I thought and searched, until I went nearly mad, for a reason why the planet preferred an elliptical orbit [to mine]. ... Ah, what a foolish bird I have been![3]

[1] Koestler, op. cit., p. 251.
[2] Koestler, op. cit., p. 260.
[3] Koestler, op. cit., p. 333; quoted from Kepler's *Astronomia Nova*, written in 1605. Kepler's slight regard for his First Law is revealed in his Notes to the second edition of the *Mysterium*. There, apparently, he discusses planetary orbits without mentioning his own First Law or its import: that such orbits are elliptical.

I

CHARLES DARWIN. The workings of the mind are, as Turner observed of painting, a 'rummy thing'. Anyone whose confidence is still unshaken should turn at last to the chastening contemplation of Darwin. Barely competent at school, he was taken away early by his father and sent, in his elder brother's footsteps, to Edinburgh to study medicine. He idled his time away there; and after two years, learning he was to inherit money and would never have to work for a living, stopped work altogether. His father, fearing that he was becoming an 'idle sportsman', decided on his son's behalf that he should join the ranks of the clergy. He was thus sent to Trinity College, Cambridge, to take the Ordinary degree, which, after three years, he did. Although a keen naturalist, his real passion was for butchering wild fowl:

In the latter part of my school life I became passionately fond of shooting, and I do not believe that anyone could have shown more zeal for the most holy cause than I did for shooting birds. How well I remember killing my first snipe, and my excitement was so great that I had much difficulty in reloading my gun from the trembling of my hands. This taste long continued and I became a very good shot.[1]

I should have thought myself mad to give up the first days of partridge-shooting for geology or any other science.[2]

His estimate of his own intellectual powers was modest; and, it seems, rightly so:

I have no great quickness of apprehension or wit which is so remarkable in some clever men, for instance Huxley. I am therefore a poor critic: a paper or book, when first read, generally excites my admiration, and it is only after considerable reflection that I perceive the weak points. My power to follow a long and purely abstract train of thought is very limited; I should, moreover, never have succeeded with metaphysics or mathematics. My memory is extensive yet hazy: it suffices to make me cautious by vaguely telling me that I have observed or read something opposed to the conclusion which I am drawing, or on the other hand in favour of it; and after a time I can generally recollect where to search for my authority. So poor in one sense is my memory, that I have never been able to remember for more than a few days a single date or line of poetry.[3]

As a boy he had enjoyed the clarity of geometry, but not in a way which distinguishes him from many of us. And as an undergraduate, even the help of a private tutor could not bring him to an understanding of the most elementary principles of algebra. He did a

[1] Barlow (1958), p. 44.
[2] Barlow, op. cit., p. 71.
[3] Barlow, op. cit., p. 140.

minimum of work at Cambridge, and spent most of his time beagling, shooting, or sedately carousing. At the age of 21, he was just the non-intellectual, pleasant, aimless, conforming, rather inhibited young man whom we would now view as a disastrous prospect for research. Even his opportunity to voyage on the 'Beagle', the experience which transformed his life (and the history of science), arose fortuitously. Henslow, the Professor of Botany, who knew Darwin from field-trips, wrote to him saying that Captain Fitz-Roy was willing to give up part of his own cabin to any young man who would volunteer to go with him without pay. Darwin, at a loose end, was eager to go, but his father objected, and Darwin duly declined. Fortunately, though, he went out shooting the next morning with his uncle, Josiah Wedgwood. His uncle strongly approved of the scheme, persuaded Darwin's father, and Darwin was allowed to accept.

Nothing of Darwin's previous development could possibly alert us. It simply is not the case that psychologists, even with the benefit of hindsight, can detect the signs of his dormant gifts. (If we detect anything, it is precisely the configuration of Non-Creative Man in MacKinnon's research). However we qualify and hedge, we now envisage originality as the expression of a powerful, self-confident personality. Yet even in these details, Darwin thwarts us. He lived in awe of his gargantuan, twenty-five-stone father; and, indeed, published nothing of a controversial nature until this domineering creature was dead. The nearest we come to a psychological explanation of Darwin's creative energies is through consideration of his adolescent bloodthirstiness, a quality which gradually disappeared as his life's work began. This, though, is selective hindsight with a vengeance, scarcely an explanation that one could propound for general application.[1]

Nothing, I am convinced, so roundly condemns its owner as the belief that originality is a simple affair. If we underestimate and oversimplify, we are bound to be the losers; but this is by no means all. However much we may complain to the contrary, psychology

[1] It does cohere neatly however with McClelland's theory mentioned in Chapter 7 and pursued in Chapter 8: aggressive impulses channelled into the analysis of natural phenomena. For a discussion of both Darwin and Einstein, see Hudson (1964b).

47643

remains a discipline with practical influence – through the beliefs of parents, teachers and administrators – over the shaping of children's lives. It follows that our over-simplifications may be translated into practical blunders. The psychologist who sets out to study original men and women does so, one imagines, because he himself is less original than he would wish: the artist or scientist *manqué*. His attitude towards his subject is bound, therefore, to include elements of both admiration and envy. If the first predominates, he will extol the uniqueness of genius; if envy, he will be tempted to belittle his subjects, showing how neurotic they are, and how simple are the laws which govern their lives. Both attitudes are clumsy. Without wishing to lapse into reverence, claiming the creative impulse as God-given and mysterious, I do think that if we wish eventually to explain the phenomena of originality, we must accord them detailed examination.

· 7 ·

A Tentative Explanation

So far, I have been concerned to present factual evidence, to interpret it psychologically, and to discuss its more practical implications. Little or nothing has been said about causes. In the last chapter but one, before discussing the question of 'creativity', I tried to show that the evidence about convergers and divergers was compatible with a reasonably simply psychodynamic model. I now wish to return to these differences between convergers and divergers, and to offer an explanation of how they might have arisen. Necessarily, any such suggestion is bound to be speculative. Convergers may differ from divergers for hereditary reasons, or because of experiences occurring at any point between birth and mid-adolescence. The crucial influences may lie within the home, at school, among their friends, or in the fastnesses of their own minds. Such causes may best be defined psychoanalytically, sociologically, psychometrically, or in terms which we do not yet possess. I shall attempt no more than to review some evidence, and then indicate a particular area of research which seems to me promising, touching (lightly, I might say, my grasp of such matters being less than vice-like) on recent developments in psychoanalysis.

Over the last decade or two, the personality of the scientist (and by contrast the arts specialist) has already been the subject of many studies, and some of these throw light on the question of causes. The best of these have concerned adult scientists, and two of them I have already mentioned: those of Roe[1] and of MacKinnon.[2] Roe's, though by no means the most massive, remains the most searching

[1] Roe (1951a, 1951b, 1951c, 1953).
[2] MacKinnon (1962a, 1962b).

study in this field. The impressive feature of her results, as other commentators have remarked, is the 'ubiquity of the contrast between a concern with people and a concern with things'.[1] The psychologists and anthropologists she studied evinced the one, the biological and physical scientists the other; and the distinction runs from top to bottom – from recollections of childhood at one extreme, to Rorschach responses at the other. She also found that biological and physical scientists showed emotional 'withdrawal' or 'estrangement', whereas psychologists and anthropologists did not. Early in life, these physical and biological scientists divorced themselves from personal relations, and in many cases experienced considerable isolation:

a general picture of shyness, lateness in developing interest in or in being able to express interest in girls, and present general disinterest in most social contacts is characteristic . . .[2]

Among the biologists, isolation seems to have been accentuated by unusually high rates of parental illness, death and divorce (factors which may have had some bearing on their choice of field); whilst physicists, especially theoretical ones, seem themselves to have suffered grave illnesses in childhood.[3] Roe also gives data about biases of intelligence. Her theoretical physicists tend to score excellently on all the mental tests and to think verbally; the applied physicists to be weak verbally and to think in terms of spatial imagery; the psychologists to score moderately well all-round; and the anthropologists to be very weak in any but tests which were verbal. She points out that these biases are probably related to the individual's choice of field, but on the question of causes – whether the bias causes the choice, or vice versa – she remains non-committal.

The work of MacKinnon and his associates includes architects and writers, as well as scientists and mathematicians, and thus permits comparisons over a wider range. He found that highly original and productive brainworkers do not differ from their fellows in terms of their intellectual abilities, but in terms of their personalities. The creative members of MacKinnon's samples differ from the non-creative by being more emotionally 'open'; less hidebound in attitude and belief; and exceptionally self-reliant. In other words, they seem

[1] Bereiter and Freedman (1962), p. 578. These authors review the large and rambling literature on differences between American college faculties.
[2] Roe (1951b), p. 67.
[3] Roe (1953), p. 48.

to differ not in their intellectual equipment, but in the use that they see fit to make of it. In this respect, MacKinnon's results agree precisely with my own, and the interpretation is supported by his finding that the creative members of his sample were frequently undistinguished at school and university. Usually, their average grade was a 'B', or less:

In work and courses which caught their interest they could turn in an A performance, but in courses that failed to strike their imagination, they were quite willing to do no work at all. In general, their attitude in college appears to have been one of profound skepticism.[1]

THE WORK OF McCLELLAND

The causal implications of this work on the scientist are pursued in a brilliant paper by McClelland.[2] I propose to draw upon this article at some length. Summarizing many other studies, he shows that the successful adult physical scientist tends characteristically:

(a) To be male – there were, for example, no women in Roe's sample, there are only a handful in 'American Men of Science',[3] and only a few who are Fellows of the Royal Society.[4]

(b) To come from 'radical protestant' (i.e. puritanical) homes, without themselves being religious.[5] One of sociology's most intriguing themes is the connection that exists historically between science and puritanism.[6] It seems that scientists, despite their origins, are among the least religious of all professional groups, turning, as it were, from their puritanical upbringings to science as an alternative way of life.

(c) To avoid personal relations. Evidence here is drawn from many

---

[1] MacKinnon (1962b), p. 494. The author refers here to architects, but this finding applies to all groups equally. See also my evidence concerning the degree classes of eminent Englishmen.

[2] McClelland (1962).

[3] Despite its title, women are not excluded from this volume as a matter of definition.

[4] The 1963 Yearbook of the Royal Society lists more than forty male Fellows for every female Fellow.

[5] Knapp and Goodrich (1952).

[6] Merton (1949). The founders of the Royal Society were explicit, too, in their vision of science as a means of avoiding civil dispute:

Sprat conceived the foundation of the Royal Society as a means of evading political and moral problems, and . . . even recommended a new English style. 'Eloquence ought to be banished out of all civil societies, as a thing fatal to peace and good manners'. Crowther (1960), p. 156.

sources, and indicates that the scientist's unsociability usually sets in as early as the age of ten.[1]

(d) To work with great single-mindedness.

(e) To avoid complex human emotions, and above all McClelland suggests open aggressiveness between people. The evidence cited is largely from projective tests like the Thematic Apperception Test, in which the individual is asked to tell a story around a picture set before him.[2] The scientists' immediate reactions to the test are fascinating:

Actually one of the most striking things about the way the eminent scientists re-acted to the TAT is their marked dislike for the task. The test requires a response to a number of dramatic human situations and the scientists reacted by trying more or less strenuously to avoid responding to them at all in the usual manner. They found it extremely difficult to empathize with the characters pictured and to tell a dramatic story as they had been instructed to do. Instead they tended to block, to analyse various portions of the picture, to consider various possibilities of action, and to be unable to decide on any one of them. The following initial reaction of one physicist to the first card (boy with violin) is typical: 'That is most objectionable. We will carry out an analysis. I have all sorts of blocks because people are so unreasonable it always makes great difficulty for me.'[3]

(f) To like music and dislike art and poetry.

(g) To be intensely masculine. On all the tests of attitude, interest and personality which distinguish men from women, the Strong Vocational Interest Blank for example, physical scientists appear unequivocally masculine (only engineers more so). Their interests early in life are characteristically those to do with things, with nature, and with outdoor sports.[4]

(h) To develop 'a strong interest in analysis, in the structure of things, early in life'. Mathematicians are often child prodigies; scientists, although not so extreme in their development, usually reveal a strong scientific bent between the ages of five and ten:

...it is the scientist's job to take apart the real world as we perceive it and to discover what lies behind it, to work out the microstructure of reality. What is required of

---

[1] Terman (1954); also McClelland (1963), Cattell and Drevdahl (1955).
[2] Roe, op. cit.
[3] McClelland (1962), p. 148. His inference, whether fair or not I am unsure, is that scientists are not numb to strong emotions, but avoid them precisely because they are so sensitive to them.
[4] Terman (1954). Their favourite interest as adults is photography.

them in their profession has been enthusiastically adopted by them in their entire attitude toward life.[1]

McClelland goes on to suggest that it is this preoccupation with analysis as much as their dislike of personal emotion which lies behind the scientists' difficulty with the TAT. They are obsessed 'with what is "really" a correct interpretation of the pictures':

They simply cannot let themselves go, in telling a tale of dramatic action, but are constantly brought up short by details which seem to require analysis and which do not fit into the story that has been started.[2]

Comments from one of Roe's scientists demonstrates these qualities as clearly as one could wish:

My wife says my most maddening trait is my unwillingness to guess. 'You want some fiction this time? I'm utterly sunk on doing anything in fiction. You have found one of the blocks in my mental processes. It's virtually impossible to associate a tale of fiction with this. That's a process I've never attempted – to tell a story about an imaginary thing.' (The examiner asked if he had ever told stories to his children.) 'They were the ones I had learned. I don't ever remember telling them stories that I created. It would have to be something associated with the acoustics of the violin rather than the boy' (referring to TAT card # I). 'The youth certainly is meditating about the violin, possibly even dreaming that some day he will be able to make a violin that will be as good as the old Stradivarius; he is in deep meditation. What is this and what are the characteristics that make the violin outstanding? By a process of trial and error he finds that it is just the breaking down of the glue in the joints that makes it better than others, and he sees that he can probably make one as good, and by checking his results he probably makes one as good.[3]

McClelland then goes on, in the remainder of his article, to consider the rival merits of two psychological explanations of the scientist's development, one in orthodox Freudian terms, the other hinging on the notions of aggression and fear of parental authority. On the evidence already in hand, there is an excellent case for believing that the origins of the future scientist's bent for analysis lies within the family. Some feature of his relations with his parents must discourage an interest in people, and encourage one in objects. The question is: what feature? McClelland eventually decides in favour of his second explanation on the grounds that it accounts better for the results of a metaphor test. Scientists and non-scientists differ significantly in their reactions to descriptions of nature. Compared

[1] McClelland, op. cit., p. 151. Roe, op. cit., Terman (1954).
[2] McClelland, op. cit., p. 152.
[3] McClelland, op. cit., p. 151.

with non-scientists, scientists show a marked preference for metaphors of nature which are anthropomorphic – with certain significant
exceptions. They *reject* anthropomorphic metaphors if these suggest
nature as threatening or anarchic. McClelland's scientists liked:

A pillar of strength and virility.
A perfect woman nobly planned.
The nurse, the guide, the guardian of my heart and soul.
A grand and inspiring father.
Lady of silences.
A banquet of delights.
A stern and loveless master.
Glens of brightness.
A vineyard to be reaped for pleasure.
Something certain and infinite.
Fairest among women.

They disliked:

The desolations of many generations.
A tyrant despite her lovely face.
A great cave that encompasses us and swallows us up like atoms.
A spring whose waters will not do our bidding.
A Titan waiting terribly to break forth.
An arrogant master who likes to rule and dominate.[1]

There is, of course, no call to accept McClelland's inferences from
this result in detail; it is arguable, for instance, that the evidence
supports the orthodox Freudian view of sexual conflict, rather than
undermining it. Sufficient to remark: (a) that scientists tend, from
an early age, to withdraw from people; (b) that the work they choose
is the analysis, and hence control, of natural, impersonal phenomena;
and (c) that, apparently paradoxically, they tend to think of natural
phenomena in quasi-personal terms. Either the scientist relates directly when a young child to objects rather than people; or natural
emotional difficulties arise between him and his parents, which he
chooses not to resolve.[2] Instead, he retreats from people into the world
of inanimate objects. In either case, he invests objects with some of

[1] McClelland, op. cit., p. 160.
[2] Roe notes instances of the former, especially in the histories of eminent experimental
physicists (1953), p. 50. Biologists, it seems, represent something of a half-way house in this
process of withdrawal. Instead of removing themselves entirely to an inanimate sphere, they
compromise, studying nature which is animate but inhuman. It lives, as it were, but does not
hit back.

the emotional significance with which other children invest people.

In summary, therefore, the adult scientist emerges from research as a figure strongly resembling our most stereotyped preconceptions of him. This is a most damaging admission, for there is the liveliest danger that as psychologists we will have interpreted our evidence about scientists, not 'objectively', but in the light of what seems to us reasonable. That is, of our preconceptions. There is an even more insidious danger that the scientists themselves will have taken on the mantle which our culture offers them, and described themselves to us not as they are but as we would expect to find them. Either way (or both), the psychologist merely succeeds in fortifying his own prejudices rather than discovering what other people are really like. We are prone, in other words, to use our evidence as Andrew Lang's drunkards used their lamp-posts – for support rather than illumination. This danger is illustrated by Beardslee and O'Dowd, who investigated the American college student's image of – among others – the typical scientist. Their results offer us little comfort. The agreement between their image and the version of reality which emerges from others' research is disconcertingly close:

First, the scientist is characterized by high intelligence dissociated from artistic concerns and sensitivities. . . . Second, there is a clear lack of interest in people . . . self-sufficient, rational, perservering, and emotionally stable. . . . The personal life of the scientist is thought to be quite shallow, his wife is not pretty, and his home life is not very happy. He is rewarded by great personal satisfaction . . . He enjoys moderate wealth and social status. . . . He is competent in organizing the world of things, but disdainful of the world of people . . . a masculine figure in a desexualized way.[1]

THE ARTS SPECIALIST

Even if we suspect that much of our information about the mature scientist is less objective than it seems, at least there is a lot of it. By comparison, the mature arts man has been neglected. If we do learn about other professions than science, engineering and medicine, they

[1] Beardslee and O'Dowd (1962), p. 615. It would be a fascinating study, at the first level of analysis, to discover whether scientists' wives were in fact any less pretty than those of men in other academic specialities (historians, for example). And, if this were true, to discover to what extent scientists choose wives who are less than beautiful because this is what our particular society expects of them. Do Russian scientists marry plain wives? – or French, or Italian, or Japanese? Perhaps, if English and American scientists do so, it is because their puritanism forbids any conspicuous sign of sexual pleasure. (And, conversely, if our arts men marry beautiful women, perhaps they do so from a concern with the conspicuous signs of pleasure rather than with pleasure itself.)

are usually the ones to attract not the diverger but the converger: law, for example, or accountancy. However, common observation and such research as we have combine to suggest a very different pattern.

In their summary of research, Bereiter and Freedman record the familiar pattern for the arts specialist: concern with people; sociability; greater sensitivity to their own emotions, and hence the impression, if not the reality, of greater emotional instability; liberality of attitude; and so on.[1] A little thought leads us to doubt, however, whether these labels are quite what they seem. In discussing divergers in Chapter 5, I emphasized the extent to which some boys display feelings as a mask for, rather than a reflection of, their true experience. These boys are in a sense 'hollow'. Another such complexity arises when we consider what, in fact, the arts man's concern with people usually amounts to. To some extent, the surface impression is the correct one; people, their habits and their institutions, are the arts man's natural fodder. On the other hand, people figure in the lives of most arts specialists, not as the other end of an intimate relationship, but precisely as fodder, as pawns in an intellectual game of order or control. We see this clearly in the case of the novelist, in a way, the arts person whose interest in other people is most acute. He views other people as 'material', and, indeed, he probably draws his impulse to write from a sense of the gulf which separates his wishes about people from the experience of them in the cold light of day. Doris Lessing expresses this well in *The Golden Notebook*:

I came upstairs from the scene between Tommy and Molly and instantly began to turn it into a short story. It struck me that my doing this – turning everything into fiction – must be an evasion. Why not write down, simply, what happened between Molly and her son today? Why do I never write down, simply, what happens? Why don't I keep a diary? Obviously, my changing everything into fiction is simply a means of concealing something from myself. Today it was so clear: sitting listening to Molly and Tommy at war, very disturbed by it; then coming straight upstairs and beginning to write a story without even planning to do it . . .[2]

Moravia, the Italian writer, has something very similar to say:

But I want it quite clearly understood: my works are not autobiographical in the usual meaning of the word. Perhaps I can put it this way: whatever is autobiographical is so in only a very indirect manner, in a very general way. I am related

[1] Bereiter and Freedman (1962).
[2] Lessing (1964), p. 225.

to Girolamo, but I am not Girolamo. I do not take, and have never taken, either action or characters directly from life. Events may suggest events to be used in a work later; similarly, persons may suggest future characters; but *suggest* is the word to remember. One writes about what one knows. For instance, I can't say I know America, though I've visited there. I couldn't write about it. Yes, one uses what one knows, but autobiography means something else. I should never be able to write a real autobiography; I always end by falsifying and fictionalizing – I'm a liar, in fact. That means I'm a novelist, after all. I write about what I know.[1]

A rather similar sense of the complexity of the arts man's involvement with people strikes us wherever we look: politics, law, history, administration, even religion. In all these spheres, there is involvement with people, but at one remove. In each one finds a relatively impersonal, intellectual, social or moral system: the law, the parliamentary machine, the organization, the church, and so on. The number of brainworkers in our society who are directly concerned with personal relations for their own sake is minute; (and – we do well to remember – the person most directly engaged with people, the psycho-analyst, is usually a product, not of the arts at all, but of medicine). It is true that the arts man lives in terms of people, whilst the scientist lives in terms of things. There is, however, an ambiguity about both relationships which it is vitally important to express. We can capture it, perhaps, by glib antithesis: the scientist searches for control over things which he treats as though they were people; the arts man searches for control over people which he treats as though they were things.

Without pursuing such generalities further, I think we may say that a spectrum of intellectual differences exists in the adult world, roughly corresponding to the convergent/divergent distinction that I have established among schoolboys. There is a prima facie case, in other words, for believing that the convergent/divergent distinction is not a passing adolescent phase: that it has bearing on the whole range of our intellectual development, from childhood to maturity. Granted this, where might we look for an explanation? If the literature that I have reviewed at length has any message, it is that we may legitimately look at the early years of convergers' and divergers' lives at home. Psychologists, it is true, have a habit of homing upon the 'first five years' as the explanation of every move an adult makes. In this case, though, the motive is not solely doctrin-

[1] Moravia (1958), p. 190.

aire. The factual evidence indicates that the early years of his life (although not necessarily the first five) are relevant to the young scinetist's development, and, in the light of this, it would seem perverse to look elsewhere.[1]

A POSSIBLE EXPLANATION

Despite the energy and persuasiveness of the argument in McClelland's article, it demonstrates certain of the difficulties in the traditional psychoanalytic approach. Notions like infantile sexuality and aggression, though meaningful enough, prove awkward to handle in practice. They are motives, rather than behaviour pure and simple; thus we can reach them only by a process of interpretation. For this reason, I am attracted to a type of explanation more directly tied to the actual verbal transactions which take place between parent and child. One possibility is not far to seek. We know, from McClelland for example, that the future scientist's (and hence future converger's) parents tend to be emotionally withdrawn and remote. And we know from Getzels and Jackson (a) that the 'High IQ's' (or converger's) parents spend more time in the home, (b) that they are more critical of their children, and (c) that they emphasise 'external' virtues for children rather than 'internal' ones – good manners, for instance, rather than sincerity.[2] So we guess as follows: the future converger's parents (themselves convergers) express their love for him not directly, or physically, but through the warmth of their approval when he masters impersonal, practical skills. Conversely, the future diverger's parents (themselves divergers) hold their son close, distrusting his mastery of practical skills. On this argument, the converger grows up *expecting* one pattern, the diverger another.

THE 'DOUBLE BIND'

However, the argument of the last paragraph accounts neither for the converger's apparent fear of emotional relations; nor for the

---

[1] Bloom has concluded, on the basis of purely statistical evidence, that the first few years of a child's life are of proportionately greater relevance to the formation of his personality than later ones:

> By an average age of about 2, it seems evident that at least a one-third of the variance at adolescence on intellectual interest, dependency, and aggression is predictable. By about age 5, as much as one-half of the variance at adolescence is predictable for these characteristics. Bloom (1964), p. 177.

[2] Getzels and Jackson (1962), pp. 61–76.

diverger's characteristic ambivalence, his preoccupation with human affairs which he does not enter into fully at first hand. Happily, recent psychoanalytic work on families brings more serviceable notions to hand.[1] Some parents (the 'good' ones, in psychoanalytical terms) bring up their children against a background of love and security which never wavers. The children take these qualities 'inside' themselves, and live happy, fruitful lives. Other parents, 'bad' ones, reject their children out of hand. They give neither love nor security, and their children grow up empty and stunted. These are the extremes. In the middle, and in the vast majority of cases, something more confusing happens. In most families, it seems, feelings are mixed. Parents both take pride in their children's growing independence and resent it. They both confirm their children in their maturing abilities and undermine them. Conversely, children wish both to outgrow their parents and cling to them. Granting such ambivalence, paradoxical behaviour is only to be expected; and this is epitomized in the 'double-bind'. The 'double-binding' parent is the one who exerts conflicting pressures on the child at one and the same time: the mother who invites her child to kiss her, whilst expressing not love but rejection. In mild forms, such ambivalence seems to be present in the daily life of most ordinary families. In extremity, it is claimed, it drives the child mad. The conflict of pressures renders ordinary life untenable. This quotation shows how such 'double binding' might work:

A mother visits her son, who has just been recovering from a mental breakdown. As he goes towards her

(a) she opens her arms for him to embrace her, and/or
(b) to embrace him.
(c) As he gets nearer she freezes and stiffens.
(d) He stops irresolutely.
(e) She says, 'Don't you want to kiss your mummy?' – and as he still stands irresolutely
(f) she says, 'But, dear, you mustn't be afraid of your feelings.'

Thus, he is responding to her invitation to kiss her, but her posture, freezing, tension, simultaneously tell him not to do so. However, the fact that she is either frightened of a close relationship with him, or for some other reason does not want him actually to do what she is pretending she wants him to do, cannot be openly admitted by the mother, and remains unsaid by both her and the son. However, the son responds to 'the unsaid situation' created by the unspoken

[1] Bateson et al. (1956), Searles (1959), Laing (1960, 1961), Laing and Esterson (1964).

message, 'Although I am holding my arms out for you to come and kiss me I am really frightened of you doing so, but can't admit this to myself or to you, so I hope you will be too "ill" to do so.' However, when he does not do so, she pretends that she is quite simply wanting him to kiss her, and in fact implies that the reason why he is not kissing her is not because he is perceiving her anxiety lest he do so, or her command not to, but because he does not love her. When he does not answer, she implies further that the reason why he is not kissing her is because he is afraid of either his sexual or aggressive feelings towards her. The mother conveys, therefore, in effect, 'Do not embrace me, or I will punish you' *and* 'If you do not do so, I will punish you'. Moreover, the 'punishment' will itself be secret.[1]

Here, I sense, is a language which could help us; and events which might possibly bear on the convergent/divergent distinction. The convergent parent, as I have said, is probably the one who shies away from all expression of strong feeling, affectionate or otherwise. If the child demands affection, the parents do their best to provide it, but fail. In this case, either of two things may happen. The parents may guide their child into less embarrassing spheres by offering approval whenever he masters some safe, impersonal skill. Or, as a reaction to the embarrassment the child has caused them (out of shame or irritation or both) they become critical. Either way, the child realizes that security lies both in choosing an impersonal field within which to work, and in being right.[2] Furthermore, the child latches on both to his parents' distaste for 'gush', and to their relief when the mood is once more safe. He learns which subjects cause his parents alarm and avoids them, their distress being a signal that the bedrock of parental security is threatened. Indeed, there is no reason why he should not go on to ascribe to his parents feelings like his own: an unintelligible brew of affection and resentment, love and fear. In every sense, therefore, impersonal work and interests become a haven: from embarrassment, from criticism, and from emotions which are disruptive and inexplicable.

The diverger's mother, on the other hand, is the one who binds her child to her by disregarding his practical, logical accomplishments (or even by ridiculing them) and by holding out a promise of love

[1] Laing (1961), p. 139.
[2] It may be that the convergent parent guides his child more negatively: by disapproving or punishing failures in the practical sphere. If this were so, convergence would be much more readily identified as the product of puritanism – and with the sadistic qualities with which puritanism is historically and psychoanalytically associated.

which she may or may not be able to fulfil. The child grows up addicted to people: he sees them as the source of his security, and fears impersonal logic as a guillotine which could sever him from them. He tries interminably to mine comfort from the discussion of personal relations, although unable perhaps to relax into them at first-hand.[1]

A 'HYBRID'

Besides these parents and their disparate products, one can easily envisage a 'hybrid'. There may, of course, be parents who success-fully channel their children into close logical reasoning without cutting them off from their concern with people. There may, in other words, be 'well adjusted' all-rounders, paragons of psycho-logical health, who flourish irrespective: young men and women who score A's on intelligence and open-ended tests alike, turn their hands with equal skill to arts or science, and do so without personal estrangement or display. Revealingly, psychology has little to say about such monsters of psychic efficiency.[2] The psychologist's affinity, one suspects, is with the all-rounder whose development is altogether a more tortuous affair. The 'hybrid' (and future psycholo-gist perhaps) is the child who, like the future novelist, is double-bound in the true sense: chronically fascinated by personal relations and emotions, yet partially debarred from them. Yet he accepts (unlike the novelist, and albeit sketchily) the scientist's ideology of

---

[1] We should not see the divergent parent as the 'good' parent and the convergent as 'bad'; or vice versa. Some convergent parents will doubtless make more use of punishment than others. Conversely, some divergent parents will have more genuine and profound feelings for their children, others less. Even at this level, judgments of value still seem to me premature. In terms of its end-product, an upbringing based on punishment is not necessarily worse than one based on encouragement; nor, by the same criterion, is an upbringing based on the show of affection worse than one based on the reality. It may well be that, within limits, each has its characteristic advantages and disadvantages.

A promising theme which I have not mentioned in this chapter is that of the child's parental identification. There is considerable evidence that scientists are exceptionally masculine in their attitudes (see, e.g. McClelland 1962); and also that original men in all spheres are less masculine than the unoriginal (see MacKinnon, 1962). It may well be, therefore, that amongst schoolboys the convergers identify with their fathers and the divergers with their mothers. What the patterns of identification amongst schoolgirls would be, on this argument, it is not easy to see.

[2] Maslow (1959) is, to my knowledge, the only psychologist to have studied such people. In practice, Mental Health and Adjustment are virtues akin to the religious notion of Grace: ideals interesting not primarily for their own sake but for all the aberrations that surround them.

K

detached rationality, of objective right and wrong. He thus combines elements from each of the two extremes.

The progenitors of such a pattern are not difficult to imagine. These are the parents who establish close emotional ties with their children, and yet who are intensely physically puritanical. The young 'hybrid', like the young physicist, grows up with the uneasy feeling that underneath the fabric of emotional expression which he can countenance, there is a tumult which he cannot. But because of his parents' hold on him, he is tied to human subject-matter; and instead of removing himself from this sphere altogether, he tries, by the application of his detached rationality, to reduce the threatening emotional charge to measurable proportions. He turns on the world of feeling and reduces it to rule.[1] One finds support for this view among Roe's eminent psychologists and anthropologists:

The biologists and physicists show a considerable present independence of parental relations, and without guilt for the most part. This has also been noted in business executives. The social scientists, on the other hand, are much less free of parental ties, in the sense that a number of them still harbour resentment and rebellion, even though they have achieved an outward independence.[2]

Her psychologists and anthropologists show greater concern for their private lives; but, at the same time, have higher divorce rates. One would predict, too, that they experience far greater emotional difficulties in their work. Many physical scientists work with a rapt absorption which, one imagines, the social scientist or novelist is usually denied.

If one accepts this view of the psychologist as a 'hybrid' all-rounder, one would also predict that the growth of his intellectual interests would be fraught with uncertainty and indecision. And this is precisely what one finds. Oldfield shows that famous psychologists do have just such a confusion in their student years, turning from one subject to another with apparent lack of purpose. William James is the paradigm. At the age of 26 he wrote:

I have not got started properly on any line of work yet, but am hovering and dipping about the portals of psychology. The fact is that I am about as little

---

[1] This may explain the psychologist's characteristic taste for grand theory, and disregard for exceptions to his rules. What matters to us, perhaps, is not subjugating data, but finding a recipe which will quell the uneasiness inside us.
[2] Roe (1953), p. 48.

fitted by nature to be a worker in science of any sort as anyone can be, and yet my only ideal of life is a scientific life. . . . Thus do I lash my tail and start myself up again.[1]

Oldfield also points out that the bulk of the famous psychologists come into the subject from a more orthodox form of science: medicine, biology, chemistry and even physics, although rarely, it seems, mathematics. At the age of 35 Freud was still an undistinguished neurologist with research behind him on histology and (disastrously) on the effects of cocaine. He turned only slowly to psychopathology, led by Charcot's work on hypnotism.[2] Psychologists seem, in other words, to split off from emotional preoccupations during adolescence and early adulthood, to consolidate their empirical skills. Only when these are sufficiently sharpened, do they return to their true vocation, the study of people.[3]

It would be nonsense to suggest that the 'double-bind' could account for all the qualities that adolescent convergers, divergers and all-rounders possess: still more that it could be used to predict all the subtleties of vocational choice. On the other hand, it might explain why convergers and divergers adopt different defensive systems initially; and also – through the notion of a 'hybrid' – why some children end up as all-rounders.

---

[1] Quoted by Oldfield (1939).
[2] Jones (1961).
[3] In caricature: we are the sons who leave home, to return only when convinced that we have our father's measure.

· 8 ·

Some Speculations On Original Thought

Having touched on possible causes of convergence and divergence, I now wish to approach an even more hazardous topic: the causes of originality. I have already expressed my view of the American literature on 'creativity'. The diverger, it seems to me, has too readily been adopted as the paradigm of Creative Man. My own belief is that original work will come from convergers and divergers alike; and that the convergence and divergence of an individual will determine not whether he is original but, if he is original, the field and the style in which his originality will manifest itself. The roots of his originality lie, I shall suggest, not in his convergence or divergence, but in other aspects of his personality.

All the suggestions that I make are psychologists' suggestions, taking little or no account of the social and intellectual framework within which original thought occurs. This, of course, is a gross omission. We have ample evidence that acts of originality are not unique, isolated expressions of an individual's will. In science, especially, one discovery lays the way open to the next – to such an extent, in fact, that the same insight is often achieved simultaneously by scientists who are not in mutual contact.[1] The pressure of events is such that a discovery, unimaginable in one generation, becomes unavoidable in the next. Most scientific break-throughs occur not because a giant strides into a world of pygmies, but because the time is ripe.

The arts are less corporate, and the social pressures less overwhelming. His predecessors certainly provide for the artist the

---

[1] Newton and Leibniz provide one classical example of simultaneous discovery, Darwin and Wallace another. For a discussion of this phenomenon, see Merton (1961).

conventions within which he works. But only a sociologist would suggest, I think, that *Lolita* would still have been written had Nabokov died young; that someone would doubtless have stepped into Dostoievsky's literary shoes had the Czar's firing-squad been in earnest. The arts, in other words, offer more elbow-room for individuality; the sciences less. Is the moral, then, that only the arts lie within the psychologist's domain? Surely not. Can we not ask, even of the sciences, what qualities lead a man to ride the wave of new ideas, and what causes others to linger behind?

Psychological explanations of originality are not the only pertinent ones, but they do have their place. In offering some, I shall try, none the less, to avoid the excessively reductive variety; the kind of explanation which explains the adult's creative energies in terms of the infant's effort's to fill and empty his alimentary canal. One *is* obliged to consider certain of the impulses which manifest themselves most clearly in childhood; but not to show that adult and child are one and the same. Especially, I shall hope to avoid any value judgments about 'maturity' and 'adjustment'. If we may take up this language for a second – only to drop it again at once – it seems that there is a continuum among men from the extremely mature and well-adjusted to the extremely infantile and mal-adjusted, from the exclusively bland to the totally ineffectual. In this chapter we shall be concerned with neither; rather the fortunate ones in the middle range who are *driven* to use their imaginations, who harness their daemons to work for their own productive ends.[1]

PERSISTENCE

Perhaps the most obvious characteristic of the original thinker is his dedication to work. Roe notes that her scientists frequently work so hard that all other aspects of their lives are bound to suffer:

> Although a few of them have cut down somewhat on their hours of work as they have grown older, it is still the common pattern for them to work nights, Sundays, holidays, as they always have. Most of them are happiest when they are working – some only when they are working. In all these instances, other aspects – economic returns, social and professional status – are of secondary importance.[2]

How do we account for such single-mindedness? Not, I think, by

---

[1] 'Shorn of all our immaturities we would be equally shorn of most of our motivations.' Comfort (1964), p. 16.
[2] Roe (1953), p. 49.

invoking any quality of a purely cerebral nature: 'curiosity', say, or 'inquisitiveness'. Some explanation of a more personal nature seems indispensable. In Chapter 5, I have already suggested (in the context of 'morbidity') that such intellectual persistence may be a by-product of the individual's need to keep irrational impulses in check. It is a means of dissipating tension or anxiety. This is of course in no way a novel idea; most psychodynamic explanations of neurotic behaviour have this notion at their root.[1] And it shares the weakness inherent in all dynamic explanations: that it is difficult to substantiate empirically. On the other hand, it does suggest a potent motive force, without which any explanation of intellectual persistence seems artificial. However, the real drawback of my suggestion is its generality. What leads one able man to become a research scientist, say, or to write novels, while his neighbour, equally able, becomes an administrator or a teacher? And what leads him, if he does go into research or novel writing, to do it really well?

SELF-CONFIDENCE

The quality which one seems to find most often in the successful scientist, and the original thinker more generally, is his adventurousness. In his work at least, he is a swashbuckler. Freud states this explicitly:

You often estimate me too highly. For I am not really a man of science, not an observer, not an experimenter, and not a thinker. I am nothing but by temperament a *conquistador* – an adventurer, if you want to translate the word – with the curiosity, the boldness, and the tenacity that belong to that type of being.[2]

This buccaneering has a number of components, of which I shall discuss three: self-confidence, aggressiveness, and a taste for risks.

Almost everything that has ever been written about original thinkers emphasizes their assurance. They are self-reliant as adults, and usually seem to have been so from an early age. There are

---

[1] Obsessional habits, for example, are seen as devices for reducing an anxiety or tension which would otherwise be intolerable. On this argument, neurotics suffer such anxiety (or its attendant defensive devices) under normal conditions of environmental stress. The greater this stress, the greater the probability of ordinary men and women producing neurotic symptoms: trench warfare has substantially the same effect on the normal man as family life has on the neurotic.

[2] Jones (1961), p. 227.

exceptions of course, of which Darwin is one; but, by and large, the generalization holds true. McClelland tells a pertinent anecdote:

What brought this matter to my attention originally was a discussion I once had with a graduate student who had read all the literature on a certain subject. He knew practically every research result that had ever been reported on this particular topic, and after he had finished summarizing in a seminar the present state of knowledge in this area, I somewhat unthinkingly asked him what he thought ought to be done next. It was obvious that the question took him by surprise, and he finally stated that he was in no position to judge, since authorities had differed on what the crucial variables were and much of the evidence was conflicting. I pressed him further. I pointed out that he must by now know as much about this field as anyone else and that he ought to be willing to make a decision as to what the most promising line of inquiry was. He still showed some unwillingness to do this and ended by suggesting that perhaps a massive research attack on all fronts at once would pay dividends. I pointed out that the research design he had in mind, in which one entertained all hypotheses at once and varied all possible variables simultaneously, was really quite impracticable and that it would take several lifetimes to carry out.[1]

This young man is a familiar figure. Every laboratory has one. Indeed, he lurks inside most of us. He is critical and passive; reviewing the literature with brilliance perhaps, but contributing little. Above all, he is scared of being proved wrong. But why? Why should one grown-up possess self-confidence and another lack it? Some facts are relevant here. First, as McClelland remarks, the successful research scientist is nearly always a man. Second, he is more likely than not to be a first son.[2] Freud (himself first born) noted this:

A man who has been the indisputable favorite of his mother keeps for life the feeling of a conqueror, that confidence of success that often induces real success.[3]

Success in most walks of life seems, in fact, to come most easily to first sons. Third, and perhaps most revealing, the productive thinker in all spheres will, it seems, have had parents who supported rather than criticized him. MacKinnon remarks this about highly original architects, but its application seems general:

What appears most often to have characterized the parents of these future creative architects was an extraordinary respect for the child and confidence in his ability

---

[1] McClelland (1963), p. 184.
[2] Cattell and Brimhall (1921), Roe (1953).
[3] Jones (1961), p. 6.

to do what was appropriate. . . . [This] appears to have contributed immensely to the latter's sense of personal autonomy which was to develop to such a marked degree.[1]

The circumstances which give a boy self-confidence also allow him a certain independence from external standards of value. Instead of turning 'outside' himself for criteria, he turns 'in'. Instead of aligning himself with expectations of friends and teachers, he feels for himself what is right and what is not. He is thus in a better position than most to withstand the pressure of social conformity, and to avoid both the benefits of criticism and its erosion. In a sense, therefore, the self-reliant child's freedom from criticism is freedom to entertain grand, even messianic, fantasies about his own gifts.[2] MacKinnon's evidence confirms this, and so does Roe's. MacKinnon found that creative and non-creative differed in their 'self-image'. The former describe themselves as 'inventive, determined, independent, individualistic, enthusiastic and industrious'; the latter as 'responsible, sincere, reliable, dependable, clear thinking, tolerant and understanding.'[3] And, as we have already seen, Roe found her gifted scientists characterized from an early age by a sense of apartness or estrangement.[4]

This first train of thought, emphasizing the importance of self-confidence, can be given one last, flighty twist. It is a commonplace of University life (although not one that I have seen quantified) that scientists, as well as being absorbed in their work, are driven, too, by a desire for fame. In England, they wish to be Fellows of the Royal Society; and their eagerness for this formal honour is frequently pressing. Although somewhat similar honours exist for non-scientists

[1] MacKinnon (1962b), p. 491.
[2] Especially marked perhaps in the first born, who grow up in a world of adults, and identify themselves more readily with them.
[3] MacKinnon (1962), p. 487.
[4] In half Roe's psychologists and almost all her anthropologists, this sense of apartness was wedded to 'consciously felt superiority':

Certainly psychology to some extent, particularly social psychology, and anthropology to a large extent, particularly cultural anthropology, offer an ideal vocation to the person whose conviction of personal superiority is not accompanied by asocial characteristics; they permit a somewhat Jovian survey of their own society as well as others, and maintain the social scientist in a state of superiority just because he is able to make the survey. (This accounts nicely for the observation that some rather paranoid indications in the test material are not accompanied by forms of paranoid behaviour, except perhaps as regards their own colleagues.) Roe 1953, p. 50.

(Fellowship of the British Academy and the Order of Merit) they seem to exert less appeal; and non-scientists often view such 'pot-hunting' as childish. Yet the scientist's desire for formal status may not be as simple as it seems. The scientist searches, as many do, for some achievement which will realize for him the grandiose illusions that he entertained as a child. On this argument the aim of every intellectual is ultimately the same: not to be respected by his colleagues, (nor by his bank manager), but 'to go down in history', to make a contribution which carries him from a prosaic world to a transcendental one. In this sense, the scientist's ambition is not a naïve scramble for status, but a literal-minded, conventional expression of the desire to be immortal.[1]

The reader may judge this far-fetched, although I do not believe that it is. The practical difficulty is that one cannot easily conceive of an experiment which would put such suggestions to the test. Even so, certain things are clear. The upbringing which creates self-confidence in a child also insulates him from criticism, and may free him, too, to enjoy unrealistic ideas of his own power. Granted that the discoveries of one generation are the unrealistic hunches of the previous one, the recipe for invention seems complete. Great men show absorbed self-confidence, often unrelated to objective difficulties; and they frequently pursue unpopular hunches for long periods of time and with a minimum of support. On reflection, however, this argument carries us only a little way. Self-confidence is necessary for originality, but is not in itself sufficient. Hundreds of thousands of men have unbounded self-confidence without being intellectually or artistically successful: cranks, eccentrics, and others besides.

PREDATORINESS

Again, why? One is tempted to answer 'luck'; and there is probably something in this. It is an argument, in any case, which appeals strongly to the unlucky. Yet it sounds feeble. In science (and every other line of work) there are, we know, a tiny minority who seem to strike lucky quite unexpectedly often: time and again, their experiments work. Rutherford is a good example of this.

---

[1] I suggest that this form of ambition stems from the child's messianic ideas of his own worth. It may be – although this does not account so well for the evidence – that it derives more prosaically from the fear of dying.

Rutherford was a moderate mathematician, and Townsend and he were the two first 'research students' at the Cavendish under J. J. when that status was first officially established. Townsend . . . was a good mathematician and people used to say that though of course both were very good Townsend would go farther because of this. . . . Rutherford's genius lay in his uncanny physical insight, combined with a flair for designing very simple experiments which worked. In both these he showed what is fundamentally the same quality, namely the ability to see the essential and discard all the rest.[1]

This quality of Rutherford's, the gift of being right, suggests a second train of thought, or, rather, an elaboration of the first.

One finds this propensity for being right in many fields: money-making for example, and sport. Money seems to produce in us a curious mixture of desire and inhibition, one which only a few 'robber-barons' avoid. Similarly, some of the most talented footballers are known as 'goal-shy'. Others, a small minority, score goal after goal without necessarily having the greatest skill or finesse. My suggestion is that the parallels between money-making, sport, and research are closer than we might imagine. All three display an abundance of clever midfield players, but a relative scarcity of good finishers. In sport these good finishers are sometimes said to have the 'killer instinct' – a turn of phrase which I find illuminating.

Why should a few have this 'killer instinct' while the rest of us lack it? At the level of psychological platitude, the answer is that we are too inhibited. McClelland's results with his metaphor test show in more detail how such an explanation might work. Already summarized in the previous chapter, these suggest that scientists viewed nature anthropomorphically; and that the root of their energy is a 'strong aggressive drive which is normally kept carefully in check and directed into taking nature apart'. If McClelland is right about this, his interpretation accounts not only for scientists' energy, but their inhibitions too. Few people can express aggression fluently, even on a harmless substitute. It is not surprising, therefore, that most scientists feel inhibited when what they are subjugating is not nature, but nature vested with human (and presumably parental) significance. The minority who have the 'killer instinct' are the few who enjoy an aggressive fluency that the rest lack. They pin down the

[1] Thomson (1961), p. 55. 'J. J.' is the author's father, the discoverer of the electron – both are Nobel Prizemen.

data with the ease of a farmer wringing a chicken's neck.[1] Mac-Kinnon's evidence suggests that the good intellectual explorer is emotionally open. This may now mean one of two things. He may be open in the sense that he copes well with a mixture of strong and conflicting feelings – aggression and guilt, for instance.[2] Or his openness may depend on a lack of guilt. In this second case, he would be able to entertain the feeling of straightforward aggression which most of us find shocking. The second interpretation seems to me the more likely; and if so then the successful intellectual may be seen as a predator, not of flesh but of new ideas.

Of course, McClelland may be wrong in his inference that aggression and fear of authority are crucial in a scientist's working life. Or even if he is right, these emotions may well prove irrelevant to other lines of work. There is a case, for example, despite McClelland's evidence, for believing that the emotions which some scientists transpose are those connected with sex or love.[3] My own results, unfortunately, are of little help here. Convergers seem to repress all forms of emotional expression alike; and the fact that they are more likely than divergers to express extreme violence does not show that aggression is more or less important than sex in the formation of their attitudes to their work. My results offer no comparable data on responses referring to sex; and even if they did, I do not see how they could be used to decide such an issue as this. On the other hand such uncertainty is not as damaging as it sounds. The core of the present idea is that some basic emotions get translated into work, and that these inhibit discovery in the majority and facilitate it in a few. There is no reason, in fact, why the intellectual's emotional investment should not cover the whole range of normal human emotions,

[1] It is tempting here to lapse into shorthand and talk of scientific analysis as an attempt to dismantle not Mother Earth, but Threatening Dad. And what is dismantling Father if not castrating him? However, such flights of the interpretative imagination are optional.

[2] The notion of ambivalence, of having mixed feelings, is one to make the scientific nape bristle; and not without reason. To admit talk of 'unconscious ambivalence' is usually to admit conceptual anarchy. But if we are to consider attitudes at all, we must surely allow them sometimes to be confused; and to deny that they may be confused for any but superficial reasons is surely arbitrary. If the phenomenon of mixed feelings exists, it is our job to discuss it – and guard against the conceptual difficulties as best we can.

[3] Einstein once said, ostensibly about Planck, but evidently about himself too, that his devotion to work sprang not from discipline but from an 'immediately felt need'. He likened it to the behaviour of a deeply religious man, or a man in love. Quoted by Vallentin (1954.)

each profession encouraging its own emotional brew. Sexuality, aggressiveness and fear of authority are in any case inextricably mixed in most people, and it may well be that the attempt to distinguish between them is at this stage academic.[1]

CRISIS-SEEKING

One of Scott Fitzgerald's characters observed that:

Exploration was for those with a measure of peasant blood, those with big thighs and thick ankles who could take punishment . . .[2]

His intuition here seems correct, or partially so. Exploration in all fields does seem to involve a certain peasant toughness, and even perhaps a streak of brutality. Like rock climbers, explorers must harden themselves to risk. Yet they seem not merely numb to danger, but positively to court it. The successful research scientist is the man who chooses to work within tight intellectual systems, yet enjoys throwing them partially or wholly into doubt. Like Gagarin or Columbus he sets off into the void, without guarantee of landfall.[3] Stepping away from a firmly rooted intellectual scaffolding demands strong nerves, even if it is only done in order to replace one system of scaffolding with another. But why, granted that everyone needs a degree of order, do a few seem positively intrigued by its absence? Why do they find uncertainty exciting?

REBELLION AND SEXUALITY

There are two simple answers to this, and a third which is more elaborate. The first is that a taste for disorder is part of a more general assault on established knowledge. The *enfant terrible*, the natural rebel, attacks the older generation and their theories much as he would like (in psychoanalytic caricature, once again) to have attacked his father. Rebelliousness is certainly found as a concomitant of innovation in some fields. MacKinnon notes it among creative people in general, and Roe finds it particularly among social scientists.

---

[1] The tendency of psychoanalytic thinking over the last three or four decades has been, in fact, to emphasize just such subtle inter-relations between sexual and aggressive motives.
[2] Scott Fitzgerald (1955), p. 205.
[3] This point about crisis-seeking is in fact a commonplace of intelligent journalism: 'A real work of art is grown in the dark, by one man, around a core of risk.' Gilliatt. P., *The Observer*, 4th October, 1964.

On the other hand, the idea of the perpetual rebel seems rather a weak explanation of risk-taking *for its own sake*, and it is this which is the defining characteristic of the intellectual's work.

The second explanation is the one which, I think, would spring to the mind of the orthodox Freudian psycho-analyst. He would argue that the artist's or scientist's fascination with intellectual crises springs from doubt as to his own sexual potency. And his satisfaction in discovery and achievement is the satisfaction (and relief) of discovering that he is potent after all. The readiness with which this explanation trips from the tongue is of course no guarantee that it is correct. All the same, it is an analogy which sits quite neatly upon the data.[1] Sadly, though, this begs the question. Even if we may grant, for the sake of argument, that the man who is profoundly satisfied with his private life will not worry much about his social status, or his powers of intellectual discovery, it does not follow that social self-esteem and intellectual discovery are *substitutes* for private contentment (and that the sexual interpretation is therefore correct). A lepidopterist loves his moths and may not care two hoots for football; but it does not follow that love of moths is a potential substitute for a love of football, or vice versa. It does not follow that if we magically removed his love of moths, a love of football would automatically spring up in its place. We have, in other words, not merely to show that the sexual explanation of intellectual discovery might be true, but to find evidence proving that it is so. And this is not easy.

The sexual interpretation has, moreover, an awkward weakness. A simple prediction from it is that original thinkers have poverty-stricken sex lives. Now the evidence does suggest that the attitudes to sex of various types of intellectual may differ; but there is no evidence that, as a whole, they are sexually deficient. (Popular mythology about artists indicates quite the reverse, in fact.) One's guess about this is that scientists who dissociate their private lives from their intellectual ones, enjoy 'normal' sex lives which do not greatly involve them; whereas the novelists and artists who mingle the two, care deeply about their sex lives and experience considerable unhappiness

---

[1] The terminology of discovery seems if anything to support this Freudian view: 'breakthrough' for example is a term with an obvious sexual connotation. Potency, too, can be interpreted liberally. The tennis-club hero revving his Jaguar asserts his virility; but not in terms which necessarily concern his genitalia.

and muddle. As a basis for an explanation of the exploratory urge, physical sex seems, in other words, both too specific and too simple.[1]

AN EXISTENTIAL EXPLANATION

The explanation of risk-seeking which I myself prefer derives from work of Laing and, indirectly, of Sartre.[2] Neither is easy going, so I shall attempt a potted account of Laing's work, already touched on in Chapter 7, before drawing a few cautious inferences from it.

Sense, it seems, can be made of many otherwise incomprehensible clinical symptoms by considering the confusion which exists in the minds of the insane about the boundaries between themselves and other people. Some patients make mistakes about the power which others' thoughts may have over their own. Some see other people not as sentient (as equivalent to themselves, in fact) but as things. In other words, such patients' ideas about themselves overflow the conventional, appropriate boundaries; and this happens, as far as one can tell, either because they want to 'immerse' themselves in other people, or out of fear that others will 'swamp' them. In old-fashioned terms, they are extremely dependent, or extremely fearful of dependence. Doubtless few of us are free from such inclinations. In the majority, though, the urge to open ourselves to others, and the fear of being swamped achieve a reasonably satisfactory balance. Normal people, like the mad, feel insufficient in themselves; but unlike the mad, their need for support is less frenzied, and hence their search for it more controlled. We differ from the insane in that we can harness our impulse to depend on other people, whereas in them it runs amuck. These are Laing's tenets; or those, at least, which I am able to comprehend clearly enough to translate. Henceforth, the deductions are my own.

[1] Most psychoanalytic contributions to the literature of creativity have paid less attention to sexual motives than to the idea of regression (see Kris, 1953). Original thoughts are seen as arising when the individual gives rise to his libidinous, irrational impulses. Although a useful idea, 'regression in the service of the ego' seems to me to represent only a small part of the contribution which psychoanalysts could make to the topic of original thought. The sexual explanation, as I have expressed it, is an over-simplification. In more refined form, it is by no means incompatible with the existential explanation which follows. Indeed, this could be seen to rest on sexual feelings existing within the family.

[2] Laing (1960, 1961).

NYMPHOLEPTS

All who search (whether for insight, fame, the perfect woman, gold, or what have you) do so, I would argue, from a sense of personal incompleteness similar to that described by Laing. They look for some ideal outside themselves. In a word, they are nympholepts.[1] One notes, too, that nympholepts' goals, or ideals, occupy a continuum, from the personal to the impersonal. At the 'human' end, there are those who search for a state of complete openness with some other person. Openness here may take several forms. A man may search for his ideal wife or mistress either directly, or in fantasy, in literature, sculpture, or painting. At the other end of the scale, the scientist searches, not for a relation with another person, but for an insight or theory which is, in itself, completely impersonal. There are, in addition, any number of half-way houses between these two extremes.[2] My assumption is that all these ideal objects stem from the same source: the child's fear of independence. And I assume, too, that they differ only in the extent to which they have been abstracted. This fear of independence (or isolation), however abstracted, remains a powerful motivating force:

> The fact that we are I don't know how many millions of people, yet communication, complete communication, is completely impossible between two of those people, is to me one of the biggest tragic themes in the world. When I was a young boy I was afraid of it. I would almost scream because of it. It gave me such a sensation of solitude, of loneliness. This is a theme I have taken I don't know how many times. But I know it will come again. Certainly it will come again.[3]

I think that we can now put Laing's ideas to work: to explain both the fascination of intellectual discovery and also the sense that it is dangerous. Earlier, I treated this matter of risk as though it arose entirely from the danger of being proved wrong. But there is more to it than this. If we open ourselves to someone else, we feel imperilled, as though we have placed ourselves in their power. And the same feelings may obtrude if the openness, the ideal relationship,

---

[1] '*Nympholepsy*, a species of ecstasy or frenzy said to have seized those who had seen a nymph: a yearning for the unattainable; *nympholept*, a person so affected.' Chambers's *Twentieth Century Dictionary*.

[2] Religious aspirations are one obvious example; and, in literature, the Holy Grail and Golden Fleece. Social reformers, too, frequently have ideological aspirations which are only tangentially concerned with human beings.

[3] Georges Simenon, the novelist; (1958), p. 138.

is only with an idea. We hover tremulous on the brink of insight because (or so the hypothesis goes) we see this objective in quasi-personal terms. This anthropomorphism is readily explicable. All children wish when they are very young indeed, to depend on, and to identify themselves completely with, their parents – their mothers especially. But when they are older, and less than helpless, the case is different. Their urge to depend is bound to carry with it uneasiness and distrust, the sense that if they lower all their defences, they might never again be able to assert their self-control. The child's desire for the comfort and security of total dependence carries with it, then, in inexorable perversity, the fear that the other person might engulf him.[1]

In searching for crises, therefore, the intellectual plays a solitary game in which, in a sense, the integrity of his personality is at stake. He abandons himself, and finds, once the crisis has passed, that he has survived intact. This is not thrill-seeking for its own sake, but thrill-seeking of a kind which enables a man to stir the embers of a primitive desire: the longing to be engulfed totally by someone else. His difficulties (and our apprehension) arise both from the fear of abandoning his autonomy, and from the more specific horror that this impulse was originally incestuous. It was directed towards his mother.

Some readers will doubtless find this train of thought preposterous. To my mind, nevertheless, it encompasses neatly our intuition that intellectual discovery is dangerous; the fascination that it exerts over a small minority; the inhibitions which they may experience; and the much greater inhibitions which the prospect of discovery evokes in the rest of us.

There are, of course, any number of rational objections to speculation of this nature, and it will earn the contempt of philosophers and experimentalists alike. The tight-lipped will express incredulity that one should make fast-and-loose with concepts as slippery as those of identity and sub-conscious experience. And the methodologically minded will ridicule the use of concepts without operational defini-

---

[1] An alternative, and in some ways simpler, interpretation rests on the idea of the security which we feel in corporate beliefs. We are secure because we believe what everyone else believes. A new idea is threatening because it threatens to cut us off from everyone else. On this interpretation, the vital relation is not with personified ideas, but with other people *via* ideas.

tion. Scientists will find the discussion of their private lives cranky; yet psychoanalysts will view it as platitudinous. Pedants will object to the lack of detailed reference to enormous and problematic literatures; plain men will see much fuss about not a great deal. Everyone will point out, too, that this discussion ignores the gulf between searching and finding, between the intention and the accomplished fact. Every brainworker has had insights, luminous at the time, which turn out to be mistaken. The validity of an insight depends, in other words, on factors connected not with psychology but with logic. It is true, too, that any number of important discoveries are made by accident – or simply by riding sufficiently close to the crest of intellectual and technical innovation. Consequently, a sad dissociation exists between effort and reward.

All these criticisms are justified; yet what I have said still seems worth saying. Intellectual discovery *is* a personal business, not a purely intellectual one. As Roe says:

Once it was fully understood that *personal* research was possible, once some research had actually been accomplished, there was never any question. This was it. . . . From then on, absorption in the vocation was so complete as seriously to limit all other activity.[1]

To make sense of such dedication, one must be prepared to talk about the individual's personal life; and if one is to deal with personal matters, one must be prepared for the ill-defined and seemingly irrational. Further, reference to childhood is virtually inevitable, with the scientist especially, precisely because his emotional life as an adult is frequently so restricted. The criticism, I find, which cuts closest is not this, nor any of the other more logical objections, but that of the analyst. 'We know all this in general terms,' he says, 'now work it out in detail.' The point which I feel most tempted to expound is the solitary nature of the intellectual's crisis-seeking; the sense that his search is curiously narcissistic. However, I am inhibited from doing so by the fear both of alienating non-analytic readers, and of lapsing into jargon.[2]

[1] Roe (1953), p. 49.
[2] The sexual implications of the nympholept's relationship with his ideal object seem to me inescapable. And the solitary nature of his desire offers close parallels with the fantasies of masturbation. Both Sartre and Laing touch on this topic in their discussions of Jean Genet (see Laing (1961), Ch. 4). However, this is precisely the topic to clench growing scepticism into disgust, so it is perhaps best held over.

Further speculation would also be an indulgence. Virtue amongst psychologists consists in a steady concentration upon observation and measurement – and thither we must return. However soothing to the speculator speculations may be, they do not advance our knowledge as they ought. We have to justify our fancies empirically, puritanically – to show that we speculate the better to measure. I would claim, therefore, that I have aired my ideas not for their own sake, nor as a prelude to a more rigorous theoretical statement about the causes of convergence, divergence, or originality (I have already argued at length that this would be a waste of time). My hope, rather, is that the last two chapters will suggest directions in which fresh experimental sorties might be made.

Statistical Tables

TABLE 1 Test 'Profiles' for the various Sixth Form Subjects (n = 562)

	IQ	Bias of IQ	Accuracy	Spatial Ability	Vocabulary	General Knowledge	Interests	
History	Low	Verbal	Low	Low	Average	Sometimes Very High	Cultural and Political; Often Strong	112
Modern Languages	Average	Verbal	Average	Average	Low	Variable	Diverse and usually weak	95
Classics	Above Average	Slightly Verbal	Sometimes Very High	High	Very High	Variable	Diverse	43
Physical Science	High	Non-Verbal	High	Very High	Average	Variable	Practical and Outdoor Often Strong	247
Biology	Average	Slightly Non-Verbal	Average	Average	Low	Occasionally Very High	Practical and Outdoor	65

Notes on Table 1.

1. This is the kind of table of which one normally disapproves. It reports averages, not distributions; and it does not indicate which of the differences are statistically significant. For this information (on a smaller sample), see Hudson (1962). In practice, the best individual discriminators are 'Bias of IQ, and 'Interests'.

2. Not all of the sub-samples in Table 1 are as large as the row totals make them seem. Only 113 boys sat the spatial ability test (Hudson 1961); only 479 gave answers for vocabulary and general knowledge.

55

TABLE 2 Intelligence Test Scores of Future Open Scholars
and Exhibitioners at Oxford and Cambridge Compared
with Those of Their Less Successful Form-mates

| | *(Age when tested, 15–17; n = 375)* | | | | | |
| | Intelligence Test Scores | | | | | |
	E	D	C	B	A	n
Scholars and Exhibitioners at Oxford and Cambridge	3	12	20	18	9	62
Commoners at Oxford and Cambridge	5	21	38	20	7	91
Other Universities	14	20	45	26	15	120
No University	13	28	39	18	4	102

Notes on Table 2.

1. This Table presents follow-up data on boys tested at the age of 15–17.

2. Implicit in the four categories is a scale of academic accomplishment. Scholarships and exhibitions at Oxford and Cambridge are customarily regarded as the highest academic achievement for a Sixth Former leaving school. Furthermore, at the schools at which I test, there is unquestionably a difference in prestige separating Oxford and Cambridge from all other Universities. Although this prejudice is gradually changing, the very large majority of able boys would go to Oxford or Cambridge if they could.

3. Future scholars and exhibitioners do not differ significantly in their IQ scores from the rest of the sample. Indeed, the only group distinguishable from the rest are those who do not go to University at all. (The difference between their scores and the rest of the sample just attains statistical significance: $P < 0.05$.) This finding suggests that IQ has lost much of its predictive value by the time a boy has entered the Sixth Form; and that this dwindles to insignificance once he has reached University. This seems at first sight incompatible with results of other studies reporting correlations between IQ and degree class at University. However, such correlations are invariably rather low. Heim (1956) reports correlations between A.H.5 and Tripos of 0.43 and 0.40 – these were based, however, on a sample of only sixty-one. In my earlier research, see Hudson (1961), I found such correlations on much larger samples to range between zero and 0.4, depending on the subject. Such correlations yield, at best, a predictive improvement of only 20 per cent over chance. If scholarships and exhibitions had been awarded to members of my present sample on the basis of their IQ's alone, 15 or 16 would have been given to boys who actually won scholarships and exhibitions, 14 or 15 would have been given to Oxford and Cambridge commoners, 21 or 22 to boys who went to other Universities, and 10 or 11 to boys who went to no University at all. In other words, we would have given scholarships to only a quarter of those who received them in fact: only a handful more than one would have expected by chance.

4. The scores plotted are, of course, those on A.H.5. All the other indices used in the early stages of my research have also been examined: verbal, numerical, and diagrammatic intelligence (the components of A.H.5); worse and range accuracy; spatial ability; general knowledge; and vocabulary. Only the last of these discriminated significantly between scholars and exhibitioners and the rest; $(P < 0.001)$. However, easily the best predictors were indices of boys' interests outside the curriculum (self-assessment; form-mates' ratings; general knowledge); and form-mates' ratings of each other's industriousness. This last is doubtless contaminated by the future scholars' academic prowess: their form-mates may well have mistaken their ability for sheer diligence. On the other hand, some future scholars in arts and science alike were clearly considered very idle. The correlation with indices of interest may also be a little misleading; there may be a tendency among scholarship examiners to pick from a group of very able boys those with wide interests.

5. It might be objected that this evidence is useless because University scholarship examinations are themselves invalid. The evidence is against this view: scholars tend to get good degrees. In a study of Tripos results conducted at King's College, Cambridge, it transpired that in the academic years 1960–62, 62 per cent of the boys awarded major scholarships, minor scholarships and exhibitions took firsts or good seconds in Tripos examinations; only 29 per cent of boys without such awards did so. Less than 10 per cent of the scholars and exhibitioners gained thirds or failed in Tripos; whereas 30 per cent of the remainder did so. The first class in Tripos, moreover, was dominated by scholars, both proportionately and in absolute numbers: seventy-three scholars and exhibitioners gained firsts, as compared with only eighteen non-scholars. (I am indebted to Dr D. A. Parry for these figures.) Critics may counter that the mere act of winning a scholarship enhances a boy's self-confidence; and that it may also ensure him better teaching. In other words, there may exist a vicious circle – and this possibility certainly cannot be denied.

Clearly, then, Table 2 is not easy to interpret. The general tendency of the results, however, cannot be avoided: academic ability at this level does not reflect itself to any great extent in psychological test scores. It is worth noting, too, that the only significant difference in Table 2 separates those who do go to University from those who do not. This accords with MacKinnon's suggestion (discussed in Chapter 6) that the relevance of IQ to intellectual accomplishment begins to peter out somewhere in the region of IQ 110–15.

6. Although only a few members of my sample have as yet taken their degrees, there is every indication that the result shown in Table 2 will be duplicated when IQ's are compared with degree classes. Eight have so far taken first-class degrees at Oxford or Cambridge (in one case with the highest distinction). The IQ grades of these boys comprise one 'A', 'one 'B', three 'C's' and three 'D's'.

TABLE 3 The Sixth Form Subjects Chosen By Convergers and Divergers
(n = 267)

	Extreme Divergers	Mild Divergers	All-Rounders	Mild Convergers	Extreme Convergers
History	7	15	17	3	2
Modern Languages	3	18	26	7	
Mixed Courses	4	1	14	4	
Classics	1	2	3	7	3
Physical Science	3	12	33	37	19
Biology	1	4	14	4	3

Notes on Table 3.

1. The distribution of convergence and divergence scores is skewed, because, over all, I have tested more science specialists than arts ones.

2. The numbers are rather small in some of the groups, classicists and biologists especially.

3. The sample is drawn from four schools: three boarding, one day, (three public, one grammar). The inter-school differences are negligible; much less, apparently, than those in one school from one year to·the next.

4 The relation of the convergence/divergence distinction to that between the arts and sciences is probably greater than this table suggests. The two extreme convergers studying history, for example, both wish to become solicitors. Similarly, most of the mild convergers in modern languages appear to be weak students studying this subject as a prelude to business, or boys with aspirations for the diplomatic service. Conversely, two of the three extreme divergers studying physical science are budding architects, and the third wished to become an archaeologist. This interpretation of the data will be easier to check when the sample reaches University. Results on Bias of IQ (Hudson 1960a), show that differentiations at University are sharper than those at school.

TABLE 4 A Summary of Differences between Convergers and Divergers

TESTS AND INDICES	CON	DI	Relative frequencies	Statistical sig. $p <$	n
Uses of Objects					
Fluency	Low	High	1:5.5	0.001	285
Unusual responses (10%–1%)	Low	High	1:1.8	0.005	285
Rare responses (1% or less)	Low	High	1:2.7	0.001	285
Humour	Low	High	1:2.3	0.001	285
Messy responses	Low	High	1:2.3	0.001	285
Sex	Low	High	1:4.9	non sig.	285
Mild violence	Low	High	1:2.0	0.001	285
Extreme violence	High	Low	3.0:1	see note 6	285
Specific uses (v. General physical properties)	High	Low	1:4.1	0.005	285
Drawing					
Rare themes (1% or less)	Low	High	1:3.2	0.005	249
Violence	Low	High	1:2.7	0.05	249
No people	High	Low	1:3.1	0.01	249
Empty streets, diagrams	High	Low	3.3:1	0.05	249
Zebras crossing roads	High	Low	2.4:1	0.05	249
Controversial Statements					
Vehemence	Low	High	1:3.2	0.001	119
Minority attitudes	Low	High	1:1.8	0.005	119

Authoritarian attitudes	High	Low	1·5:1	0·001	119
'Happy at School'	High	Low	2·8:1	0·01	119
Detailed criticism (No. 11)	High	Low	2·3:1	0·05	119
Personal Qualities Questionnaire					
Rigidity	High	Low	1·5:1	0·001	138
Authoritarianism	High	Low	1·3:1	0·005	138
Social conformity	High	Low	1·3:1	0·01	138
Strongly expressed	Low	High	1:1·2	0·05	138
'Highly imaginative'	Low	High	1:3·9	0·001	138
Intelligence Test					
Verbal	High	Low	3·6:1	0·001	285
Numerical	High	Low	4·0:1	0·001	285
Diagrammatic	High	Low	8·9:1	0·001	285
Total Score (IQ)	High	Low	14·3:1	0·001	285
Accuracy (Worse)	High	Low	3·0:1	0·001	285
Interests					
Cultural/Technical	Technical	Cultural	1:4·0	0·001	138
Broad/Narrow	Narrow	Broad	1:3·4	0·001	138
Sixth Form					
Arts/Science	Physical Science and Classics	History and Mod. Lang.	1:3·6	0·001	267

Notes on Table 4.

1. The column headed 'Relative Frequencies' expresses the size of each differentiation between convergers and divergers in terms of a proportion. In the first row the figures quoted show that divergers were five and a half times more likely to have high scores for fluency than convergers. It will be noted that such proportions are not always in keeping with the statistical significances quoted in the next column. In some cases, the proportional difference is marked, but the statistical significance weak. This arises when (as in the case of references to sex) the number of boys producing a particular response is low. Conversely, the statistical significance sometimes gives the impression that discrimination is more marked than it really is: P may be reported as < 0·001 when the differentiation is slight but the sample large. Generally, we seem to have fallen into the way of accepting reports of statistical significance as though these automatically reflected the *magnitude* of a given discrimination, when in fact they reflect the adequacy of the experimenter's sampling.

2. The figure quoted in the last column refers not to the number of boys producing a particular response, but to the overall sample from which such responses are drawn.

3. All estimates of statistical significance are based on the X^2 Test.

4. Some of the samples, it will be seen, are rather small, especially those for *Controversial Statements* and the *Personal Qualities Questionnaire*. Nevertheless, all the results quoted have been replicated, in the sense that the statistics have been calculated for at least two sub-samples separately. Only those differentiations which hold for each of the sub-samples have been reported. In one or two cases, differentiations which were marked on the first sub-sample, failed on the second or third. The outstanding instance of such failure is that of Verbal/Non-Verbal bias in I Q. This was initially reported (Hudson 1962), at a high level of significance (P < 0·005), but subsequently dwindled (P > 0·05). This illustrates clearly the dangers of reporting a finding on a small sample without first taking the precaution of replicating it. It follows that some of the findings reported in Table 4 inspire more confidence than others. Those concerning *Controversial Statements*, the *Personal Qualities Questionnaire*, and *Interests* are based on a sample drawn from three separate testing sessions (involving only two schools). Those for *A.H.5* and *Uses of Objects* are drawn from seven separate testing sessions (at four schools).

5. Some of the differences reported in Table 4 are not independent measurements, but merely the logical consequence of the ways in which convergence and divergence are defined. Divergers are more fluent than convergers on *Uses of Objects* (and also on *Meanings of Words*, of course) because the diverger is defined as the boy who scores more highly (who, in other words, is more fluent) on open-ended tests than he does on the intelligence test. Similarly, the fact that convergers have higher I Q's than divergers follows automatically from their definition.

6. The statistical treatment of extremely violent or 'morbid' responses to *Uses of Objects* presents great difficulty. One aim of such statistical analysis would be to show that convergers were more likely to produce such responses than divergers, considering such responses in isolation from all others. The sample here is too small to use the X^2 Test with any confidence; and in any case, this test does not give the data their due. Their really interesting feature is that, for violent responses as a whole, the distribution is 'U' or 'pot-hook' shaped. Convergers usually show no violence. Relatively few offer mildly violent responses – on the other hand, they dominate the category of extremely violent ones. On psychological (as opposed to statistical) grounds, what we would expect to find is exactly the opposite of what one finds in practice. We would expect to find that most of the extremely violent responses come from divergers. What we might do, although this still does not fit the case properly, is to compare mildly violent responses with extremely violent ones. If we take a sample of twenty as the minimum number of extremely violent responses which enables us to use the X^2 Test, we find only three divergers giving such responses (as opposed to eight all-rounders and nine convergers). On the other hand, forty divergers give mildly violent responses (as opposed to thirty-nine all-

rounders and only twenty convergers). We can then do a 3 × 2 X^2 Test and find that P nearly reaches the 0.025 level of significance. This, however, gives only a poor reflection of the data. It takes no account (a) of our expectation that divergers should dominate the 'extreme violence' category to a greater extent than they dominate the 'mild violence' one; nor (b) of the rank order effect – in the list of extremely violent responses given in Chapter 4, divergers occur (with one exception) only low in the list. However, there seems to be no means of bringing out these features of the evidence in a statistically respectable way.

APPENDIX B
The Tests

I illustrate here the open-ended tests, and the *Personal Qualities Questionnaire*, to which I refer in the preceding text. Of the other tests, A.H.5, the intelligence test, may be obtained from the National Foundation for Educational Research in England and Wales. A variety of Vocabulary and General Knowledge tests were used, all of them conventional; see, Hudson, (1961). In addition, I reproduce the questionnaire which I circulated to adults concerning 'morbidity'.

(1) USES OF OBJECTS

Below are five everyday objects. Think of as many different uses as you can for each.

A barrel
A paper clip
A tin of boot polish
A brick
A blanket

Notes

1. I copied this test from Getzels and Jackson (1962), although the objects are in three cases different.

2. This test, perhaps the most convenient and versatile of open-ended tests, was administered without a time limit. The majority, however, had finished writing within fifteen minutes. It is a good scheme to arrange (a) that there is not unlimited space, so that the less fluent are not upset by how little they produce, and (b) that there is another task which they can move on to when they are finished. The *Drawing* serves as a useful 'buffer' in this respect. In presenting the test to groups, I was at pains to emphasize that they could write down anything they liked.

3. The scoring seems to present few intractable difficulties see Chapter 3.

4. Scores tend to be heavily skewed. A typical distribution clusters about a mean of 16–17 (for all five objects), but with a tail of A grades which may stretch up into the 50's – or in one case, the 140's.

5. It is important to note that boys' responses vary with the conditions under which this (or, one imagines, any other) open-ended test is given. Where *Uses of Objects* has been used as a component in competitive examinations, the responses have been noticeably less violent and less witty, although not noticeably more numerous.

(2) MEANINGS OF WORDS

Each of the ten words below has more than one meaning. Write down as many meanings for each word as you can.

Bit	Pink
Bolt	Pitch
Duck	Port
Fair	Sack
Fast	Tender

Notes

1. An almost identical format was used by Getzels and Jackson (1962), and, before them, Guilford, from which mine is copied. They call it, misleadingly I feel, Word Association.

2. This test is even easier than *Uses of Objects* to mark, but produces much less interesting material. I administered it under conditions similar to *Uses of Objects*, and found that, similarly, fifteen minutes usually sufficed. Slang was welcomed, and boys were discouraged from precise grammatical definition.

3. Scores are roughly normally distributed, because, of course, the task is not truly open-ended. The mean score was usually in the region of 28–29; the range from 17 or 18 at one end to 35 or 36 at the other. Sometimes a boy reaches the 40's but this is unusual.

4. Correlations with a conventional vocabulary test are remarkably low, being of the order of 0·3–0·4. Correlations, likewise, with *Uses of Objects* are usually low.

(3) DRAWING

Draw a picture in the space below to illustrate the title – 'ZEBRA CROSSING'. You can draw whatever you like as long as it seems appropriate.

Notes

1. This, once again, is lifted directly from Getzels and Jackson. Only the title is different. They used 'Playing Tag in the School Yard'. I administered it without a time limit.

2. Scoring here is much more a matter of judgement than in the previous two tests. The test is also viewed more light-heartedly by the boys themselves. Some drawings are hard to categorize; at the extremes, nevertheless, differences are unmistakable.

3. In as much as Getzels and Jackson's and my *Drawings* were comparable, my findings seemed to replicate theirs fairly well.

(4) CONTROVERSIAL STATEMENTS

On this and the following pages you will find twenty-four statements. These come from many sources and cover a wide range of topics. Most of them are controversial. Go through, pick out the ones that interest you, and comment on them. You are free to choose as many or as few statements as you like, and to comment on them in any way which seems appropriate.

1. 'A man ought to read just as inclination leads him; for what he reads as a task will do him little good.'
2. 'Science fact will soon be stranger than Science Fiction.'
3. 'Genuinely creative people don't need to wear strange clothes.'
4. '"Raising the standards of television" means taking away what people do enjoy and substituting what they don't.'
5. 'Human nature being what it is, you can't run a boys' school without corporal punishment.'
6. 'The English country gentleman galloping after a fox – the unspeakable in full pursuit of the uneatable.'
7. 'Money is indeed the most important thing in the world; and all sound and successful personal and national morality should have this fact for its basis.'
8. 'The United Nations' intervention in the Congo was a fiasco.'
9. 'Coeducation after the age of 11 is one of the breeding spots for contempt between the sexes. It encourages familiarity, and contempt automatically follows.'
10. 'The Boy Scout movement is the ideal means of learning to enjoy an outdoor life.'
11. 'No horse has two tails;
    Every horse has one more tail than no horse;
    Therefore, every horse has three tails.'
12. 'With the single exception of Homer, there is no eminent writer, not even Sir Walter Scott, whom I can despise so entirely as I despise Shakespeare. . . .'

13. 'Increasingly, experts favour duodecimal rather than decimal systems of measurement.'
14. 'Truth, in matters of religion, is simply the opinion that has survived.'
15. 'Aeroplanes and sports cars – not paintings and music – are the twentieth-century's works of art.'
16. 'It would be most unfair to exclude South Africa from the next Olympics. Its internal politics are none of our business.'
17. 'The Public Schools should be public – not private.'
18. 'Modern Americans like Hemingway and Faulkner make English novelists of the nineteenth century seem tedious.'
19. 'Is it reasonable to think in terms of a 3-minute mile?'
20. 'If Combined Cadet Forces were voluntary, the boys who have most to gain from them would not join.'
21. 'Their Royal Family costs the British taxpayers some £2,000,000 per annum.'
22. 'Happy the man with an interest to pursue in his spare time.'
23. 'The most dangerous person in the world is the instructed pagan.'
24. 'The happiest years of your life are spent at school.'

Notes

1. This test involves judgment to an even greater degree than the *Drawing*. The material, on the other hand, is frequently absorbing. Some of the questions, particularly the religious ones, are altogether too difficult for 15-year-olds. Others are too topical for re-use.

2. No time limit. Thirty minutes usually sufficed, the space provided being restricted. Five statements were placed on a foolscap page.

3. The following questions were used to form a scale of Liberal/Authoritarian Values: Nos. 1, 3, 5, 6, 8, 9, 10, 14, 16, 20, 21, 24,

(5) AUTOBIOGRAPHY

Use this page to write a brief autobiography. There is no special form which this ought to take – just describe those aspects of your life which seem to you interesting or important.

Note

1. I used this test on a sample of only ninety-five, but did do an exhaustive analysis of results. Over thirty indices were calculated, but not a single quantifiable difference between convergers and divergers could be found. Getzels and Jackson, by contrast, seemed to find their autobiographical material highly discriminative, although they do not express this statistically. Why I failed to replicate their results I cannot see.

(6) PERSONAL QUALITIES QUESTIONNAIRE

Schooling is supposed to train the character as well as the mind. Unfortunately, there is little agreement – even among experts – about which qualities are desirable and which are not. Say whether you personally approve or disapprove of the qualities listed below.

M

	Strongly Approve	Mildly Approve	?	Mildly Disapprove	Strongly Disapprove
1. Physically tough					
2. Fond of animals					
3. Mixing well, socially					
4. Personally neat and tidy					
5. 'Highly strung'					
6. Obedient					
7. Sense of responsibility					
8. Low opinion of yourself					
9. Highly imaginative					
10. Respect for adults					
11. Independent of parents					
12. Affectionate					
13. Mildly eccentric					
14. Very enthusiastic					
15. Having set opinions					
16. Consideration for others					
17. Slightly effeminate					
18. 'Stiff upper lip'					
19. Gentleness					
20. Accepting expert advice					
21. Courage					
22. 'Arty' clothes					
23. Trying to be original					
24. Self-control					
25. Using bad language					
26. Very well mannered					
27. Good team member					
28. Artistic sensitivity					
29. Hide strong feelings					
30. Manliness					

Notes

1. This Questionnaire was compiled with five scales in mind.

(a) *Authoritarianism*; comprising Obedient, Low Opinion of Yourself, Respect for Adults, independent of Parents, Sense of Responsibility, Consideration for Others.

(b) *Rigidity*; comprising Highly Imaginative, Mildly Eccentric, Having Set Opinions. Accepting Expert Advice, Trying to be Original, Artistic Sensitivity.

(c) *Social Conformity*; comprising Mixing Well Socially, Personally Neat and Tidy, 'Arty' Clothes, Using Bad Language, Very Well Mannered, Good Team Member.

(d) *Defensiveness*; comprising Physically Tough, 'Highly Strung', Slightly Effeminate, Gentleness, Courage, Manliness.

(e) *Freedom of Emotional Expression*; comprising Fond of Animals, Affectionate, Very Enthusiastic, 'Stiff Upper Lip', Self-Control, Hide Strong Feelings.

Only the first three of these scales discriminated significantly between convergers and divergers; and even in these, two individual qualities had to be omitted. Sense of Responsibility and Consideration for Others were qualities which nearly every boy approved of strongly – consequently the inclusion of such items in the scale swamped the discrimination achieved with the other four.

2. As a whole, the Questionnaire seems to present few difficulties to schoolboys. They nearly all do it rapidly and without fuss.

QUESTIONNAIRE ON 'MORBIDITY'

In the course of some recent experiments on different types of intelligence, school-boys were given a test in which they were asked to suggest a variety of uses for everyday objects: a barrel, a paper clip, a tin of boot polish, a brick, a blanket. A few boys made suggestions which appear to me unpleasant or even morbid. It would be most valuable to discover whether morbidity is entirely a matter of personal judgement, or whether there is some general agreement about what is morbid and what is not. I should be most grateful, therefore, if you would be kind enough to select from the suggestions listed, the dozen or so which strike you as the most gruesome, cruel or warped. Please place ticks in the appropriate squares.

Barrel

To put a cat in when half full .... ——

For stuffing dead, headless bodies in, see A. Hitchcock .... ——

To use (full of nails) to torture people .... ——

Fill with stones and roll it down a hill on to somebody to squash him.. ——

Close the lid on someone and roll him over cliff or something .... ——

To tar and feather in .... ——

Bury someone in.. ——

To put spikes round the inside and put someone in and roll the barrel along the ground .... ——

Nailing up one's study-mate inside .... ——

For primitive Carthaginian torture .... ——

For hiding a corpse in .... ——

Drowning someone in (i.e. Duke of Clarence)...................... ——

Tin of Boot Polish

Suffocating insects .... ——

To make people sick with by putting small quantities in their food .... ——

To daub on unpopular persons in embarrassing places................ ____
To slap in someone's face .... ____

Paper Clip
As a thumbscrew .... ____
Jab an enemy with it .... ____
Suicide .... ____
Pinching skin .... ____
Unrefined torture .... ____
Hurting someone's finger .... ____

Brick
Making 'brick' traps for sparrows .... ____
Smash sister's head in .... ____
As a weight to remove a pistol after committing suicide.............. ____
Hitting and killing people.. ____
Attaching to unwanted cats .... ____
Dropping on someone's toes...................................... ____
To tie to cats and drown them in ponds............................ ____

Blanket
Suffocating a person to death .... ____
Murder by smothering .... ____
To wrap a corpse in .... ____
Wrapping up dead wife so as blood does not stain car seats .... ____
Suffocating an animal... ____
Covering such things as dead bodies .... ____
Smother my sister .... ____
Strangle somebody.. ____
To remove from baby sister's bed in mid-winter while asleep .... ____
Setting fire to, to raze school house to the ground .... ____
For suffocating someone .... ____

Notes

1. This Questionnaire was *not* distributed to my schoolboy sample. Rather, it was used to provide a criterion for the 'morbid' responses discussed in Chapters 4 and 5.

2. One item was omitted from the analysis. It was pointed out that 'suffocating insects' might well refer, quite harmlessly, to a skill of the natural historian.

3. The Questionnaire has, in fact, potentialities which I have not yet explored. It would be interesting, for example, to compare individuals who produce idiosyncratic answers with those who produce conventional ones.

References

Some of the books and articles cited in the preceding text are of a highly specialized and technical nature. I have taken the liberty, therefore, of marking with one asterisk those works which seem most likely to interest the general reader; and those of exceptional interest with two.

*ABERCROMBIE, M. L. J. (1960). *Anatomy of Judgment*. London: Hutchinson.

ANASTASI, A. (1961). *Psychological Testing*. 2nd edition. New York: MacMillan.

ARGYLE, M. (1957). *The Scientific Study of Social Behaviour*. London: Methuen.

**BARLOW, N. (ed.) (1958). *The Autobiography of Charles Darwin*. London: Collins.

BARRON, F. (1958). 'The Psychology of the Imagination'. *Scientific American*, 199, 50, p. 151.

BATESON, G., JACKSON, D. D., HALEY, J. and WEAKLAND, J. (1956). 'Toward a Theory of Schizophrenia'. *Behavioral Science*, 1, p. 251.

BEARDSLEE, D. C. and O'DOWD, D. D. (1962). Students and the Occupational World, in *The American College*, ed. Sanford, N. London: Wiley.

BEREITER, C. and FREEDMAN, M. B. (1962). Fields of Study and the People in Them, in *The American College*, ed. Sanford, N. London: Wiley.

BLOOM, B. S. (1964). *Stability and Change in Human Characteristics*. New York: Wiley.

BROWN, J. A. C. (1964). *Freud and the Post Freudians*. London: Penguin.

BUGELSKI, B. R. (1956). *The Psychology of Learning*. New York: Holt.

BURT, C. (1962). Critical Notice: 'Creativity and Intelligence', by Getzels, J. W. and Jackson, P. W. *Brit. J. Educ. Psychol.*, 32, p. 292.

CATTELL, J. M. and BRIMHALL, D. R. (1921). *American Men of Science*. New York: Science Press.

CATTELL, R. B. and DREVDAHL, J. E. (1955). 'A Comparison of the Personality Profile (16 P.F.) of Eminent Researchers with that of Eminent Teachers and Administrators and of the General Population'. *Brit. J. Psychol.*, 46, p. 248.

COMFORT, A. (1964). *Sex in Society*. London: Penguin.

COX, C. M. (1926). *Genetic Studies of Genius. Vol. II. The Early Mental Traits Of Three Hundred Geniuses*. Stanford: University Press.

CRAWFORD, A. B. and BURNHAM, P. S. (1946). *Forecasting College Achievement*. Yale: University Press.

CROWTHER, J. G. (1960). *Founders of British Science*. London: Cresset.

*CRUTCHFIELD, R. S. (1962). 'Conformity and Creative Thinking'. In *Contemporary Approaches to Creative Thinking*, ed. Gruber, H. E., *et al.* New York: Atherton.

DALE, R. R. (1954). *From School to University*. London: Routledge and Kegan Paul.

DUNCKER, K. (1945). 'On Problem Solving'. *Psychol. Monogr.*, 58, No. 270.

ERIKSON, E. H. (1963). *Childhood and Society*, 2nd edition. New York: Norton.

EYSENCK, H. J. (1952). *The Scientific Study of Personality*. London: Routledge and Kegan Paul.

FINBERG, A. J. (1961). *The Life of J. M. W. Turner, R.A.*, 2nd edition. Oxford: University Press.

FITZGERALD, F. SCOTT. (1955). *Tender is the Night*. London: Penguin.

**GETZELS, J. W. and JACKSON, P. W. (1962). *Creativity and Intelligence*. New York: Wiley.

GOLDMAN, R. J. (1964). 'The Minnesota Tests of Creative Thinking'. *Educational Research*, 7, No. 1. p. 3.

GORDON, R. (1962), 'Stereotypy of Imagery and Belief as an Ego Defence'. *Brit. J. Psychol., Monogr. Suppl.*, 34.

GREGORY, R. L. (1960). A review of 'Psychology: A Study of a Science', ed. Koch, S. *Brit. J. Psychol.*, 51, p. 88.

GUILFORD, J. P. (1950). 'Creativity'. *Amer. Psychol.*, 5, p. 444.

GUILFORD, J. P. (1956). 'The Structure of Intellect'. *Psychol. Bull.*, 53, p. 267.

GUILFORD, J. P. (1964). 'Progress in the Discovery of Intellectual Factors', in *Widening Horizons in Creativity*, ed. Taylor, C. W. New York: Wiley.

GUNTRIP, H. (1961). *Personality Structure and Human Interaction*. London: Hogarth.

*HADAMARD, J. (1945). *The Psychology of Invention in the Mathematical Field*. Princeton: University Press.

HARMON, L. R. (1958). 'A follow-up study of A. E. C. Fellowship Candidates'. *Tech. Report No. 13, Office of Scientific Personnel, National Research Council, Washington, D.C.*

HARMON, L. R. (1959). 'Validation of Fellowship Selection Instruments against a Provisional Criterion of Scientific Accomplishment'. *Tech. Report No. 15, Office of Scientific Personnel, National Research Council, Washington, D.C.*

*HARTOG, P. and RHODES, E. C. (1936). *The Marks of Examiners*. London: Macmillan.

HEIM, A. W. (1956). *Manual for the Group Test of High Grade Intelligence A.H.5*. London: National Foundation for Educational Research.

HILGARD, E. R. (1956). *Theories of Learning*, 2nd edition. New York: Appleton-Century-Crofts.

HIMMELWEIT, H. T. (1950). 'Student Selection: an Experimental Investigation'. *Brit. J. Sociol.*, 1, p. 328.

HIMMELWEIT, H. T., and SUMMERFIELD, A. (1951a). 'Student Selection: an Experimental Investigation'. *Brit. J. Sociol.*, 2, p. 59.

HIMMELWEIT, H. T. and SUMMERFIELD, A. (1951b). 'Student Selection: an Experimental Investigation'. *Brit. J. Sociol.*, 2, p. 340.

HORST, P. (1954). 'A Technique for the Development of a Differential Prediction Battery'. *Psychol. Monogr.*, 68, No. 380.

HUDSON, L. (1958). 'Undergraduate Academic Record of Fellows of the Royal Society'. *Nature*, 182, p. 1326.

HUDSON, L. (1960a). 'A Differential Test of Arts/Science Aptitude'. *Nature*, 186, p. 413.

HUDSON, L. (1960b). 'Degree Class and Attainment in Scientific Research'. *Brit. J. Psychol.*, 51, p. 67.

HUDSON, L. (1961). *Arts/Science Specialisation*. Ph.D. dissertation. University of Cambridge.

HUDSON, L. (1962). 'Intelligence, Divergence and Potential Originality'. *Nature*, 196, p. 601.

HUDSON, L. (1963a). 'Personality and Scientific Aptitude'. *Nature*, 198, p. 913.

HUDSON, L. (1963b). 'The Relation of Psychological Test Scores to Academic Bias'. *Brit. J. Educ. Psychol.*, 33, p. 120.

HUDSON, L. (1964a). 'Future Open Scholars'. *Nature*, 202, p. 834.

HUDSON, L. (1964b). 'Academic Sheep and Research Goats'. *New Society*, 108, p. 9.

HUDSON, L. (1965). 'Intelligence: Convergent and Divergent', in *Penguin Science Survey B.* 1965, ed Barnett S. A. and McLaren, A. London: Penguin.

HULL, C. L. (1943). *Principles of Behavior*. New York: Appleton-Century-Crofts.

JAMES, W. (1890). *Principles of Psychology. Vol. I.* New York: Holt.

*JONES, E. (1961). *The Life and Work of Sigmund Freud*, ed. Trilling, L. and Marcus, S. London: Hogarth.

KELLY, E. L. and FISKE, D. W. (1950). 'The Prediction of Success in the V.A. Training Programme in Clinical Psychology'. *Amer. Psychol.*, 5, p. 395.

KNAPP, R. H. and GOODRICH, H. B. (1952). *Origins of American Scientists*. Chicago: University Press.

*KOESTLER, A. (1959). *The Sleepwalkers*. London: Hutchinson.

KRIS, E (1953). 'Psychoanalysis and the Study of Creative Imagination'. *Bulletin of the New York Academy of Medicine*, 29. p. 334.

**KUHN, T. S. (1962). *The Structure of Scientific Revolutions*. Chicago: University Press.

**KUHN, T. S. (1963). 'The Essential Tension: Tradition and Innovation in Scientific Research'. In *Scientific Creativity: Its Recognition and Development*, ed. Taylor, C. W. and Barron, F. New York: Wiley.

**LAING, R. D. (1960). *The Divided Self*. London: Tavistock.

**LAING, R. D. (1961). *The Self and Others*. London: Tavistock.

**LAING, R. D. and ESTERSON, A. (1964). *Sanity, Madness and the Family*. London: Tavistock.

LEISHMAN, J. B. and SPENDER, S. (1952). Introduction to *'Duino Elegies' by Rainer Maria Rilke*. London: Hogarth.

*LESSING, D. (1964). *The Golden Notebook*. London: Penguin.

**MCCLELLAND, D. C. (1962). 'On the Psychodynamics of Creative Physical Scientists', in *Contemporary Approaches to Creative Thinking*, ed. Gruber, H. E. et al. New York: Atherton.

*MCCLELLAND, D. C. (1963). 'The Calculated Risk: An Aspect of Scientific Performance', in *Scientific Creativity: Its Recognition and Development*, ed. Taylor, C. W. and Barron, F. New York: Wiley.

*MACKINNON, D. W. (1962a). 'The Personality Correlates of Creativity: A Study of American Architects'. *Proceedings of the XIVth International Congress of Applied Psychology*. Copenhagen: Munksgaard.

**MACKINNON, D. W. (1962b). 'The Nature and Nurture of Creative Talent', *Amer. Psychol.*, 17, p. 484.

MASLOW, A. H. (1959). 'Creativity in Self-actualizing People', in *Creativity and its Cultivation*, ed. Anderson, H. H. New York: Harper and Row.

MEDAWAR, P. B. (1964), 'Is The Scientific Paper a Fraud?', in *Experiment*, ed. Edge, D. London: British Broadcasting Corporation.

MERTON, R. K. (1949). *Social Theory and Social Structure*. Illinois: Free Press of Glencoe.

MERTON, R. K. (1961). 'The Role of Genius in Scientific Advance'. *New Scientist*, 259, p. 304.

*MILLER, G. A. (1964). 'Review of "The Act of Creation" by Koestler, A.', in *Scientific American*, 211, 5, p. 145.

*MORAVIA, A. (1958). In *Writers at Work*, ed. Cowley, M. London: Secker & Warburg.

*OLDFIELD, R. C. (1939). 'Some Factors in the Genesis of Interest in Psychology'. *Brit. J. Psychol.* 30, p. 109.

OSGOOD, C. E. (1953). *Method and Theory in Experimental Psychology*. Oxford: University Press.

PARNES, S. J. and MEADOW, A. (1963). 'Development of Individual Creative Talent', in *Scientific Creativity: Its Recognition and Development*, ed. Taylor C. W. and Barron, F. New York: Wiley.

PATRICK, C. (1935). 'Creative Thought in Poets'. *Archives of Psychol.* 26, p. 73.

PATRICK, C. (1937). 'Creative Thought in Artists'. *J. Psychol.*, 4, p. 35.

PATRICK, C. (1938). 'Scientific Thought'. *J. Psychol.*, 5, p. 55.

PERELMAN, S. J. (1959). *The Most of S. J. Perelman*. London: Heinemann.

*POINCARÉ, H. (1952). *Science and Method*. (Trans. F. Maitland). New York: Dover.

POPPER, K. R. (1963). *Conjectures and Refutations*. London: Routledge and Kegan Paul.

*ROE, A. (1951a). 'A Psychological Study of Eminent Physical Scientists'. *Genet. Psychol. Monogr.*, 43, p. 121.

*ROE, A. (1951b). 'A Psychological Study of Eminent Biologists'. *Psychol. Monogr.*, 64, No. 331.

*ROE, A. (1951c). 'A Study of Imagery in Research Scientists'. *J. Pers.*, 19, p. 459.

**ROE, A. (1953). 'A Psychological Study of Eminent Psychologists and Anthro-

pologists and a Comparison with Biological and Physical Scientists'. *Psychol. Monogr.*, 67, No. 352.

ROGERS, C. R. (1959). 'Toward a Theory of Creativity', in *Creativity and its Cultivation*, ed. Anderson, H. H. New York: Harper and Row.

ROTHENSTEIN, J. and BUTLIN, M. (1964). *Turner*. London: Heinemann.

SCHWAB, J. J. and BRANDWEIN, P. F. (1962). *The Teaching of Science*. Harvard: University Press.

SEARLES, H. F. (1959). 'The Effort to Drive the Other Person Crazy – an Element in the Etiology and Psychotherapy of Schizophrenia'. *Brit. J. Med. Psychol.*, 32, p. 1.

SEARS, R. R. (1943). 'Survey of Objective Studies of Psychoanalytic Concepts'. *S.S.R.C. Bull.* 51.

SEGAL, H. (1964). *Introduction to the Work of Melanie Klein*. London: Heinemann.

*SIMENON, G. (1958). In *Writers at Work*, ed. Cowley, M. London: Secker & Warburg.

*SIMON, H. A., NEWELL, A. and SHAW, J. C. (1962). 'The Processes of Creative Thinking', in *Contemporary Approaches to Creative Thinking*, ed. Gruber, H. E. et al. New York: Atherton.

*SKINNER, B. F. (1959). *Cumulative Record*. London: Methuen.

STOKES, A. (1963). *Painting and the Inner World*. London: Tavistock.

TAFT, R. (1955). 'The Ability to Judge People'. *Psychol. Bull.*, 32, p. 1.

*TERMAN, L. M. (1954). 'Scientists and non-Scientists in a Group of 800 Gifted Men'. *Psychol. Monogr.*, 68, No. 378.

*THOMSON, G. (1961). *The Inspiration of Science*. Oxford: University Press.

TORRANCE, E. P. (1962). *Guiding Creative Talent*. New Jersey: Prentice-Hall.

VALLENTIN, A. (1954). *Einstein*. London: Weidenfeld and Nicolson.

VERNON, P. E. and PARRY, J. P. (1949). *Personnel Selection in the British Forces*. London: University Press.

VERNON, P. E. (1956). *The Measurement of Abilities*, 2nd edition. London, University Press.

VERNON, P. E. (Ed.) (1957). *Secondary School Selection*. London: Methuen.

VERNON, P. E. (1961). *The Structure of Human Abilities*. 2nd edition. London: Methuen.

VERNON, P. E. (1964). Creativity and Intelligence. *Educational Research*, 6, No. 3, p. 163.

*WERTHEIMER, M. (1961). *Productive Thinking*. London: Tavistock.

Index

Abercrombie, M. L. J., 95

Accuracy
  arts and science, 22–28; convergers and divergers, 69; emotional instability, 27–28; violence, 57

Aggression
  adult scientists, 126–8; convergers and divergers, 57–67, 89 ff.; development of, 126 ff.; humour, 62; 'killer instinct', 144–6; 'messy' responses, 63–64; morbidity, 58–61, 89–90; predatoriness, 143–6; rebellion, 136, 146–8; violent responses, 57–61

All-rounders
  definition, 38–42; hybrids, 135–7; intellectual promiscuity, 49–50; neglect of, 98; originality, 109–11; psychologists, 135–7; and morbidity, 58–61, 89–90

Anthropomorphism
  in original thought, 149–50; among scientists, 127–9, 131

Anastasi, A., 19, 37

Argyle, M., 6, 15

Arts
  arts/science differences, 19 ff., 42 ff., 53 ff., 84 ff., 123 ff.; attitudes, 129 ff.; convergers and divergers, 42 ff., 53 ff., 84 ff.; education, 94–95; intelligence, 19 ff., 35 ff., 68–69, 90 ff., 103–9; interests, 22 ff., 43–44, 55–57, 90 ff., 130 ff.; lawyers, 28, 42, 129; low IQ/high general knowledge, 31–32; novelists, 129–31; originality, 130–31,

138 ff.; personality, 108–15, 129 ff., 138 ff.; practicality, 43–44, 55–57

Attitudes
  and originality, 124 ff., 138 ff.; convergers and divergers, 64–68, 84 ff.; liberal/authoritarian, 66–67, 127–9, 145; masculinity, 126, 135; minority, 64–66; of scientists, 123–9; self-image and originality, 142; stereotyped, 64–66; strongly expressed, 67–68

Authoritarianism
  and originality, 124 ff.; convergers and divergers, 66–67; among scientists, 127–9, 145

Barlow, N., 13, 120

Bateson, G., 133

Beardslee, D. C., 129

Bereiter, C., 124, 130

Binet, A., 3–4

Bloom, B. S., 132

Brandwein, P. F., 45

Brimhall, D. R., 141

Brown, J. A. C., 9

Bugelski, B. R., 6

Burt, C., 40, 107

Butlin, M., 115

Cattell, R. B., 126, 141

Charcot, J. M., 137

Claude (Lorraine), 116

Collusion, 32; and the 'double bind', 132 ff.